SECRETS OF *A*

G000150840

The Influence of Espionage & Secret Agreements

Johnson Parker

University Press of America,® Inc.
Dallas · Lanham · Boulder · New York · Oxford

Copyright © 2004 by
University Press of America,® Inc.
4501 Forbes Boulevard
Suite 200
Lanham, Maryland 20706
UPA Acquisitions Department (301) 459-3366

PO Box 317
Oxford
OX2 9RU, UK

Library of Congress Control Number: 2004100977
ISBN 0-7618-2795-1 (paperback : alk. ppr.)

Contents

Acknowledgments

Following are the names of those who contributed to the conception and writing of this book: Winifred E. Parker, Ph.D. and James M. Hall, Ph.D., both of Livermore, California; Stephen S. Parker, M.S. and Maureen O. Parker, B.S., both of Burlington, Massachusetts; also Henner Kätelhön of Westphalia, Germany for supplying information on World Wars I and II. Further, we wish to thank the librarians of the Bethany, Woodbridge, and Yale University libraries in Connecticut for their assistance.

Chapter 1

Secret Alliances And The First World War

Friedrich Wilhelm Viktor Albert, better known as Wilhelm, King of Prussia and Emperor of Germany, rose early that autumn morning in 1905 at his retreat castle "Sans Souci" just outside Berlin. He asked his orderly to prepare one of his more impressive uniforms, explaining that he was to meet that day with Admiral Alfred von Tirpitz of the Imperial Navy. Although Wilhelm's first love was his army, he announced back in 1875 a drive for greater German sea power. But the Reichstag (Parliament) had resisted this policy. Nevertheless, he told his brother that he would not rest "until my navy is brought to the same height as my army." Thinking of the problems of the Far East, he claimed that "each new battleship is one more guarantee of peace on earth." As for Africa, he knew that one could travel from C to C (Cairo to Capetown) without leaving British territory, although Germany had its own colonies there at the time. Protecting those colonies was of great importance to Germany's economy (Herzfeld 1973, 529).

Tirpitz soon arrived and after the usual saluting and other formalities, they retreated to a room where they could talk confidentially. Tirpitz was a tall, imposing, and highly motivated man, distinguished by a long, grey, forked beard. Exactly what happened was not divulged, but later the Kaiser made a statement claiming that they had agreed that Germany's future lay upon the water. He is supposed to have said that Germany must demand a place in the sun. This last bit referred to the new colonies overseas contested by other nations. The British were worried by these statements while the Germans had their own suspicions of the aims of France and Britain. In fact an Anglo-French convention was held during which France was promised diplomatic support by the British. Yet the British press claimed Germany was trying to break up the Anglo-French "entente" (understanding) which actually did not exist. More importantly, a Franco-Russian entente was formed about this time. It later became a Military Convention and was supplemented by a very secret naval and military arrangement. The French also sought an alliance with the British through Britain's Foreign Office, but the British pointed out that parliament would have to vote on England's course in case of a general war (Fay 1930,224, Kohn 1973, 682).

Also in 1905, France's leader Delcassé (before he was overthrown) was said to have been promised by the British that if Germany attacked France, the British fleet would mobilize and seize Germany's Kiel Canal, then land 100,000 troops in Schleswig-Holstein, North Germany. This plan probably came from the British Admiralty's Sir John Fisher and became known to the Germans. But the British called the rumored Anglo-French alliance fictitious. Nevertheless, Britain's Sir Edward Grey showed his strong sympathy to France, continuing conversations with the French military up to 1914 when the war began. But the British cabinet knew nothing of these conversations until 1912 and the British public knew nothing about them until 1914. The Russians, meanwhile, found out Britain's connections with France and expected the British would fight on France's side.

In all this sparring for position among European nations, the Italians in 1900 joined the Franco-Russians, but then dropped out because of certain disagreements. At the same time, the French were worrying about the possibility of an Anglo-German agreement in the event of a general European war. This fear was fostered by the German Kaiser's remarks about the need for friendship with the British. Prince Lichnowsky, the German representative in London, having understood how the British public felt in their dislike of the Kaiser and his apparently expansive ideas in various parts of the world, warned Wilhelm that the "Anglo-Saxons" (a term the Kaiser liked to use since it suggested that the Germans were cousins of the English) would not stay neutral in a possible war. Lichnowsky hinted, moreover, that he suspected that Britain would join the French in a general European war.

These various secret negotiations left Germany, Austria-Hungary, and Turkey against the French, Russians, and British, a situation that persisted until the outbreak of war in 1914. Most all these agreements were theoretically kept secret, although there were always leaks and rumors. But even by 1907, the British were concerned with Germany's growing power on the world's seas. Japan, having won a naval war with the Russians, could be a problem in the Far East with the British, Germans, Dutch, French, and Portuguese vying with one another for various plums to be picked in the Far East as well as in the Middle East and Africa (Wells 1931, 1058).

Most likely, Admiral Tirpitz had encouraged the Kaiser's ambitions on the world's seas, although the British had "ruled the waves" more or less since the defeat of the Spanish Armada in the late 16th century. With the Germans embarking on a big shipbuilding program, the British decided on constructing a number of "Dreadnaughts," huge battleships each weighing some 17,000 tons fitted with ten 12-inch guns. Although the British public complained loudly about the expense, they hoped to outclass and out-gun the Germans.

* * * * * * * * * * * *

In the years just before 1914, the French General Staff proposed a succession of plans for a possible war with Germany. In the darkest of secrecy, a plan was made (but not carried out) to create a-number of fortresses along the Franco-German border. If the Germans began an offensive into France, gaps between the fortresses were intended to "canalize" the invaders so that where-ever they came through, the French would attack their flanks and destroy them. In moving large masses of men, there was always the danger that in advancing, their flanks would become vulnerable to an enemy counterattack.

As time went on, the French General Staff felt that an offensive into Germany would be more effective and more likely to achieve victory than taking a defensive stance. After a series of plans were accepted and then discarded, Plan XVII (17) was developed and finally approved. The French staff believed, on the basis of dubious analyses of the situation, that the main German drive might come through the southeast corner of Belgium, then make a scythe-like drive to the southeast to trap the central French armies in one coup. But considering the limited numbers of troops that were thought available to the Germans, the French staff felt that the German sweep would have to be a narrow one. The French command thus believed that the Germans would not come through all of Belgium to make one giant sweep for lack of manpower. Unknown to the

French, the Schlieffen plan envisaged just such a sweep (Keegan 1999, 36-38).

According to Plan XVII, the main attack against Germany would be carried out by the First and Second armies advancing into German-held Alsace-Lorraine on the southeastern extent of the Franco-German border. The Third Army would attack into the Ardennes in the center of the French line. This would then be facing the German border near the fortress of Verdun with the Fourth army supporting it in the original plan. The Fifth, further northwest, was to advance into southeastern Belgium. The French Ninth would be initially drawn up between the Fourth and Fifth. Still further northwest, the French Sixth, together with the British Expeditionary Force (BEF) would be ready to advance into Belgium, this advance to be delayed so the French could claim it was Germany's plan to trample on Belgian soil first and thus break Belgian neutrality.

The French command estimated that the Germans could field at most some 68 divisions and of these only about half were considered "active troops." As it turned out later, this was a gross underestimation. The French staff agreed that it should be an offensive "à outrance" (to the utmost), one they thought fitting to the French character, charging forward with rifles and fixed bayonets after the French 75s had laid down an artillery barrage.

Actually, the Germans in great secrecy, could assemble some 83 and a half divisions, including the Landwehr (generally overage men) and the Ersatz (untrained men). But amid all this worry, a worry that also plagued von Schlieffen, the inventor of the plan, was the festering question among all the members of the German General Staff: would even this many men be enough and could they move fast enough to make the grand sweep through Belgium and outflank the French central armies? The key to this German sweep through Belgium was the advancing phalanx of the First, Second, and Third German armies (Keegan 1999,34).

Would the Belgians resist? Would the BEF be a big factor in teaming up with the French in Belgium? Even the French had their doubts and suspicions about the BEF and after fighting began and the BEF arrived in France from Britain, the French had to consider the possibility that the BEF would, having made a secret plan with the Germans, turn against the French. After all, the British connection with the French was largely a secret and flimsy at best.

The original Schlieffen plan called for the First German army to pass south of Paris to attack it in the rear while another part of the First would also pass south of Paris but cut in behind the French armies as it approached Auxere. The Third German army, further south from the First and Second at the start, would cross the French border at Givet then head south into France to cross the Aisne river, then the Marne, all the while maintaining its position with the First and Second armies so they would advance together, hopefully leaving no wide gap between any two of them. The Fourth German army would pass through northern Luxembourg and swing southward through the Ardennes into France, while the Fifth would go through southern Luxembourg and approach the vicinity of the Verdun fortress in France, planning to pass on either side of it. At the same time the Sixth and Seventh would carry out a holding action in the region of Alsace-Lorraine on the southeastern frontier where France and Germany bordered on each other near Switzerland. The secret plans of both sides were made. No one knew when the beginning of a general conflagration would come.

* * * * * * * * * * * *

It was a warm, uncertain sort of day in June of 1914 when the match was lit that began World War I. Bosnia, lying to the southwest of Austria-Hungary and loosely a part of it, had a long history of turmoil. With a large Serbian population, the Serbs hoped fervently for their freedom, feeling they were not represented in the Bosnian government and were now oppressed by the Austro-Hungarians. Serbia itself, situated southeast of Bosnia and abutting on Austria-Hungary to its east, harbored only ill-will for the Austro-Hungarians, creating a secret organization known as the "Black Hand." With the Duke and Duchess of Austria-Hungary coming to Sarajevo in Bosnia, it planned to assassinate them. It was intended, on June 28th, for seven assassins to be distributed along the route the Royal couple was supposed to take on the way to Sarajevo's town hall (Hayes 1972,2-3).

At first, the parade of cars went by one of the revolutionaries who found no chance to attack the royal couple. But the second one further on tossed a bomb into the Duke's open car as it went by. The Duke saw it coming and deflected it with his arm. The bomb exploded, wounded some in the car but spared the royal couple. The Duke then ordered the driver to speed up and proceed to the hospital, passing three more of the conspirators. Even the sixth conspirator failed to act because of the milling crowd. On proceeding from the hospital, they lost their way and stopped to back up and change the route. The seventh assassin, Gavrillo Princip, saw his chance, stepped forward, and fired two shots, one striking the Arch Duke, the other his wife Sophie.

Military police quickly seized the assassin while local photographers took pictures of the mêlée, these pictures soon shown worldwide. But Sophie lay dying and the Duke, trying to comfort her, evidently could do nothing for her. Then the Duke too soon passed away.

The effect of this was electrifying to the civilized world, mostly in astonishment that such a thing could happen. What would it mean to peace in Central Europe? How would Austria-Hungary react? These were questions asked without satisfactory answers. Some guessed that it would be war between Austria Hungary and Serbia, although the German ambassador to Austria-Hungary stated publicly that he had warned the Austro-Hungarian government in Vienna not to take any hasty or drastic steps. But reports from Berlin stated that the Kaiser was outraged at the event and urged Austria-Hungary to do something to clear up the Serbian problem. Then on July 5th, Wilhelm met with Austro Hungarian representatives in Potsdam, Germany, assuring them that Germany would support Austria-Hungary in any action against Serbia.

Considering the innumerable political secrets that existed in Europe at this time as to when and where a war might start, things were in a turmoil behind the scenes. Some historians have claimed that the German government was misled by three things. One was that they did not know for certain what the agreements between Russia and France really meant. Another was the German suspicion that France and Britain were at odds because of a quarrel in East Africa. Also, the British and Russians seemed in sharp disagreement on the development of East Asia. All this led the German government to think that Britain might not aid France or Russia in an extensive conflict. In any case, the Kaiser tried as best he could to stop the trend towards a general war.

Early in July of 1914, the Austro-Hungarian government sent an ultimatum to the Serbian government making various demands, then severed diplomatic relations with the Serbs. By July 28th the Kaiser realized things were fast getting out of hand and stated that he would not have ordered mobilization as Austria-Hungary had done. He then stated that Vienna should be told that this was not justification for war. Unfortunately, Franz Josef, Emperor of Austria Hungary, had already been persuaded by his foreign minister to make a declaration of war against Serbia (Kohn 1973, 689).

The next day, the Austro-Hungarian military began to shell Belgrade with its artillery, this city just over the border into Serbia (Pavlowitch 1973,237). For many years the Russians, who were associated with the Serbs by culture and history, even in the use of Cyrillic writing (also found in Bulgaria), ordered a partial mobilization against Austria-Hungary. This, in turn, alerted the German military command that had already decided that in case of war, it would try to bring about the defeat of France, then attack Russia which would be slow to mobilize.

July 29-30: Following the declaration of war by Austria-Hungary on Serbia, the Russians began a partial mobilization of their military forces, claiming that they feared the Germans might mobilize first.

July 31: Although the Kaiser still hoped to localize the Serbian problem, he soon received the news from Intelligence that a general Russian mobilization was beginning.

August 1: The Germans therefore delivered a declaration of war to Russia's Sazanov at Saint Petersberg, Russia. The British, meanwhile, still hesitated to go along with the French while the latter was linked as above-described to secret agreements with the Russians. The German war proclamation was announced in Munich one day before the Russians in Saint Petersberg declared full mobilization. About this time a German-Turkish treaty was signed.

August 2: The Russian cabinet debated the declaration of war and agreed to mobilize. The French, bound by their agreement with the Russians, decided also to mobilize, although they wanted to wait until the Germans did so to avoid being accused of starting the war. Germany next gave its last ultimatum to the French and Russians to stop mobilization. At this extremely crucial point in time, the Kaiser thought that Britain might be kept out of the war if Germany did not attack France. He therefore approached Moltke with the idea of holding up the great Schlieffen plan of invasion of Belgium. Moltke was horrified, stating that years of preparation would be lost and it would take a year just to undo the intricate plan. Still, the British were debating what they should do and considered that talks might be arranged and an agreement obtained.

August 2-3: Germany delivered another request to Belgium to allow German troops to cross Belgian soil. Belgium refused. Germany then regarded Belgium as an enemy and declared war on France.

August 4: Britain demanded that the Germans stop their Belgian invasion. Receiving no reply, Britain, along with France and Russia, declared war on Germany.

* * * * * * * * * * * * *

The highly secret German plan was to knock out the French with one great blow. Put forth by Field Marshall Alfred von Schlieffen, the German forces were to crash through the fortified Belgian border and head west then southwest on their way to France where many of the French forces would be outflanked and forced to surrender (Pitt 1973,693). The Germans knew the Belgians had built a number of forts of steel and concrete, a stumbling block that would have to be removed in certain sectors. To this end the German armies had been secretly provided with a number of heavy howitzers to blast the forts into rubble. The Austrians had built two 305 mm howitzers which were available for the initial drive into Belgium that August of 1914. The larger Krupp guns were to be used whenever ready. Called Big Bertha after Krupp's wife, each gun could fire a shell upwards at a steep angle and descend to blast the heavily-fortified blockhouses. A full-scale model of one of these guns was exhibited after the war in Soest, Westphalia in 1937, although made of wood. Also secret at the time were smaller 210 mm howitzers that could be brought up via roadways, while the heavier guns had to be brought in on railroad tracks and jimmied into place by the gun crew (Keegan 1999, 78).

German troops were brought to the Belgian border by trains, great numbers of trains being seen crossing the Rhine river on their way toward concentration areas. When mustered into battalions they were soon on their way on foot across Belgium, carrying knapsacks and rifles. Food and ammunition were largely brought along in horse-drawn carts. The troops were animated by the thought of a swift victory, having been told they would be "home before the leaves fall" in early autumn. With France defeated, Russia could be dealt with later, although German units on the Eastern front were already in action by early August.

The French, as before mentioned, had their own secret aggressive plans. According to Plan XVII, the French offensive began near the eastern end of the Franco-German border in Alsace-Lorraine, known to the Germans as Elsass-Lothringen, striking toward the town of Morhange and Sarrebourg, at the time in Germany. Although the French offensive went well, all the news reports, echoed in Britain and the United States, were about the "rape" of Belgium. All sorts of wild stories were told of German "atrocities" and embellished with various gory details based on flimsy and even nonexistent evidence. There were cartoons in many newspapers showing German soldiers marching around with babies skewered like shishkabobs on their bayonets and of the Great god Thor bashing Belgian towns with his mighty hammer.

On August 6th, it was reported in the US that the Belgians had defeated the Germans at Liège in Belgium and that the Russians had "driven out" the Germans in Prussia. The truth was just the opposite. One big Belgian fortress was taken without a fight, others were pulverized by the big howitzers, and the long grey columns of German infantry complete with their spiked helmets, rifles, and knapsacks marched onwards. By the 10th, the French were said to be advancing toward Saarebourg, unknowingly acceding to the Schlieffen plan for the Germans to fall back in an orderly manner. Although the French newspapers claimed the French left wing was winning (de Mirjian 1976, 14), by August 13 the opposite occurred. On the 30th, the big secret next emerging was that the Germans were swinging wide in their offensive, apparently across most of Belgium. "Great losses" of the Germans were reported in French newspapers and promptly echoed in the US press. Although the Allies claimed the Germans were stopped at Amiens in northwest France —which was only a delay —they correctly stated that German troops were being withdrawn from Belgium to be sent to aid the Germans against Russia on the Prussian border. Generally unknown, this was on Moltke's order. In a few more days the French admitted that their left wing had been "turned" in Belgium by the German advance. Parisians were beginning to worry that their capital city, Paris, would soon be under siege. Meanwhile, the persistence of Belgian troops in northern Belgium forced Moltke to withdraw some of his troops from the big drive to hold the Belgians in check on his western flank.

While the French left wing, together with the BEF, fell back after lost battles at Mons in Belgium and Le Cateau in France, the German First, Second, and Third armies marched onward. By the 21st, it was reported from Paris that a German cavalry detachment had taken Brussels in central Belgium.

As August came to an end, it had become all too apparent to the Allies (France, Britain, and Belgium omitting Russia in this case) that the Germans, now called "Huns" by the Allied propaganda consortium, were swinging wide through Belgium and not through southern Belgium as the French had thought probable. Allied news writers found it hard to face the truth: nothing was stopping the Kaiser's troops.

On September 4th, the German First, Second, Third, and Fourth armies had crossed the Aisne river in France, the First headed toward Paris, in fact only 40 miles away from it. The citizens of that ancient city were preparing for a long siege, even demolishing buildings in the city's outskirts to make it easier to fight off the approaching enemy.

At the southeastern end of the German-French frontier, the French had advanced according to plan XVII to the vicinity of Sarrebourg. Although the German plan had been to allow the French to advance a few miles into what was then German territory, the German command in that sector took it on its own and ordered an attack on the advancing French. This action was a surprise to the French and drove them back to their fortifications near Épinal where they finally stopped the Germans. The resulting stalemate allowed the French command to move troops from the Épinal region and send them west by rail to support the defense of the western end of their lines, a sector where the Germans were still advancing. Moltke and his staff, however, seeing his left wing advancing toward Épinal, ordered troops from the Belgian drive to be moved to his left wing and achieve a possible breakthrough in Lorraine. Once again this weakened the Schlieffen plan. Worse, the breakthrough failed.

With a gap forming between the First and Second German armies, Moltke agreed that the First should move east of Paris and support the Second in its continuing drive. At this point French strategists began to realize that it was not the aim of the Germans to surround Paris, but to cut in behind the French Fifth and Ninth to achieve the basic idea of a classic encirclement. But now the right flank of Kluck's First was exposed to a French counter-attack.

By early September the gap between the German First and Second armies was some 40 miles wide. Although the gap was filled by a cavalry force, it was an open invitation to the French-British forces to march in and attack the flank of one or the other of the German armies (Keegan 1999, 114). At an earlier time, this had been solved by Kluck's First moving towards von Bülow's Second. But now a German airplane had spotted four columns of men marching north into the gap. These were the BEF troops reluctantly sent by Marshal French who had been persuaded by the pleas of Joffre whose French forces could only supply a few troops.

The German command on the Western Front faced a serious dilemma. Not only was the gap getting wider, but the Second and Third armies were up against a broad marshland around which they would have to pass. All this called for a desperate consultation. A certain Lieutenant-Colonel Hentsch, head of the Intelligence Section of the Great General Staff, claimed that the First, Second, and Third armies were now in a dangerously exposed position (Keegan 1999,114). Von Bülow of the Second had already concluded that he was too far advanced and ordered soon after his consultation with Hentsch, to withdraw to a defensive line north of the Marne. Although von Hausen's Saxons of the Third had advanced against the French under Foch, the withdrawal of the First and Second German armies required that he had also to withdraw to the north. All this brought to an end the mighty drive planned mainly by Schlieffen and carried out largely by Moltke and his staff.

* * * * * * * * * * * * *

From the beginning of the war, the British launched a propaganda campaign to sway Americans into coming to Britain's aid. That there was a propaganda organization set up for the purpose remained largely a secret for many years. On May 7, 1915, the British passenger ship Lusitania was torpedoed by a German submarine off the coast of Ireland (de Mirjian 1976, 14). A great many Americans were aboard. While the British trumpeted about the "wanton brutality" of the Germans, all this echoed in the US press, there were a number of secrets kept by the British pertaining to the event. One was that the British admiralty, as revealed after the war, knew there was a submarine in the vicinity of the Irish Sea, yet failed to order a battleship that was then in Queenstown, Ireland, to escort the Lusitania as she came into Saint George's channel between Ireland and England. Also Churchill, then of the Admiralty, had managed to leave England for Paris for reasons that were never quite clear. This left the Admiralty in London somewhat adrift, the man in charge later suspected of complicity in the events. As a result, the Lusitania was not warned of her danger. The British government later denied there was any ammunition on board, but many years later toward the end of the century divers found ammunition in the rotting hulk in the form of fuses for shells to be sent to the on-going war on the continent.

There were other inventions by the propagandists. One of these was that poison gas was included in the German torpedoes. Also they claimed that a second torpedo was sent at her to be sure she sank quickly. But the reputed second torpedo could have been an explosion caused by cold ocean water pouring in on the boilers which then exploded. Another thing touted by the British was that the ship was purely a passenger ship. Yet she was listed as an armed merchantman and had emplacements on the decks for guns, although at the time of the event the guns were strangely absent during the ship's last voyage.

Returning to the war on the Western Front, the Schlieffen plan had literally gone to ground. This front, extending from the coast southeastward to the Swiss Border, became fundamentally a line, or complex, of trench and dugout emplacements. Following the withdrawal of the German First, Second, Third, and Fourth armies to that line, came the "Race to the Sea." This developed into a fierce battle around Ypres, labelled "Wipers" by the British, a town about 20 miles from the seacoast on the Franco-Belgian border. Finally, things became stabilized there and along most of the Western Front, although various fierce battles were fought in the next few years. One of these was the German attack on the Verdun fortress in France. Attempting two simultaneous attacks, one on each side of the central stronghold, thousands of infantrymen on both sides died in the mud and blood and ruin with nothing really accomplished. It was said by the Germans that the roar of the battle could be heard some 50 miles away like a frightful extended thunderstorm. And this was only one of many other such battles.

* * * * * * * * * * * * *

Spying in this war had become more sophisticated than in previous wars as telephone and telegraph came more into use. But radio was still in its infancy, although much used at sea and sometimes by the armies of both sides. The Germans used stationary bicycles to generate the power to send dot-dash code between command posts and units at the front. Yet radio was at best unreliable and transmissions could be obliterated by "jamming" rival transmitters. One of these was set up in the Eifel tower in Paris where a spark-gap emitted a broad band of noise that blotted out some of the German signals. As a result of this and the cutting of telegraph lines by the Belgians, orders were often sent by staff cars over the nearly impossible roads.

One of the simplest ways to spy on one's enemy was to send a person across the enemy's border, discover secrets, and return to tell of army positions, numbers of men, and anything pertinent to the enemy's aims. Such a person was said to have been Mata Hari.

Born August 7, 1876 in Leeuwarden, Netherlands, she was the daughter of a hat merchant. While still in her teens she married a Dutch Colonial Army officer, Captain Campbell MacLeod, and moved to Java. She proceeded to have two children, but with Campbell becoming a drinker, their marriage fell apart. Her son was evidently poisoned as a result of an internal family problem concerning a feminine friend of Campbell. But Mata, meanwhile, had learned the Javanese way of dancing and on travelling to Paris, she began a stage career dancing the "Dance of the Veils" (Castaing 1973, 1050). So it was that in 1905 she was billed as a Javanese princess, doing her scantily-dressed gyrations in front of ever-larger audiences. At this time she used the name "Mata Hari" meaning "Eye of the Dawn" in the Malay language. All this enhanced a certain mystery about her that lasted long after her death.

When the earth-shattering events of World War I broke on Europe in 1914, she had developed a great attachment to a Captain Vadim Maslov of the Russian Navy who later flew an airplane for the French in the war on the Western Front. When wounded in battle and hospitalized, she asked permission to visit him in the hospital in Germany. The Deuxième Bureau, an espionage organization connected with the French Army, gave her the chance to go on condition that she would spy on the Germans. As a reward for this they would pay her a million francs - although some said 10,000 francs.

To carry this out, she travelled to Spain, then to the neutral Netherlands with the aim of visiting her old friend the German Crown Prince. But en route, she stopped off at Falmouth, England where the British were wary enough not to be charmed by her beguiling manner. After a thorough interrogation about her goals, they sent her back to Spain. There she fell in with a German official: Major Kalle. It was evidently he who sent a coded message to Berlin mentioning that "H-21" was a valuable spy. Whether this was a code name for Mata Hari was not clear, but she was arrested soon afterwards in France in February of 1917 and imprisoned.

On examining her apartment, it was claimed by the Bureau that they found "spy paraphernalia" such as the means to make secret writing. She protested that these were for her makeup and never had spied for the Germans. The evidence against her was at best flimsy, but in a seemingly unFrench manner, was condemned to death by firing squad. She was said to have refused the usual blindfold and smiled when the soldiers pulled their triggers to send her out of this world but to assure her fame for the rest of the century and even into the next one (Schinmann 2001, 8A). Some critics have claimed that the French needed an excuse for losing so many battles and thought it would boost French morale when it had fallen so low.

* * * * * * * * * * * *

In January of 1915, the British became aware of German plans to make a sortie with a portion of their navy into the North Sea. These plans became known to the British since they had captured three German cipher books from various ships damaged at sea. One of these, discovered by Australian naval forces, included the zeppelin and U-boat cipher used in their radio traffic. As a result, the British held the keys, as it were, to some of the cipher systems used by the German admiralty. Yet the Germans, thinking their ciphers safe, refused to believe they had been compromised (Keegan 1989, 115).

On January 24, von Hipper of the German Imperial Navy led a number of warships out into the North Sea, including three battle cruisers, one heavy cruiser, four light cruisers, and 18 torpedo boats (Keegan 1989,116). The British ships were capable of nearly 25 knots (Warner 1973, 192-203) and soon caught up with Hipper's ships to begin the action. The Germans, probably because of superior optical equipment for judging distances, hit and badly damaged the British ship Lion. But the German Seydlitz was hit by a 13.5 inch shell and although damaged, managed to escape further action. The German ship Blücher, the slowest of the squadron, took repeated shellfire hits from the pursuing British and was gradually demolished. Although the British got the better of it, victory eluded them in this, the Battle of the Dogger Bank.

In the spring of 1916 the staff of the German Imperial Navy worked out a plan to lure out a portion of the British fleet with a small German fleet, then attack the British with a larger German fleet coming up from over the horizon. Part of the German plan was to send a few ships to bombard Lowestoft and Yarmouth on England's east coast. This would theoretically bring out part of the British fleet to be attacked by a large German fleet. Anticipating that the British would come east, Vice Admiral Reinhold Scheer planned to intercept the British first of all with a fleet of 14 submarines stationed just off the northern British coast as far south as the Humber to report by radio any enemy activity. One other submarine would be posted near the Dogger Bank, roughly half way between Britain and the Danish coast. Scheer planned to appear with his force off the southern Norwegian coast.

In late May the German navy began sending radio signals from Wilhelmshaven by dot-dash code, a German variety of the widely-used Continental code. These transmissions included the call-sign of Scheer's battleship: "DK." This was done to try and convince the British that the German fleet was still in port (Bodiansky 2000,50). At first the British code-breakers were in much disagreement about the growing signs of German naval activity. Their top Intelligence man in "Room 40" at the British Admiralty offices, was convinced the Germans were still in Jade Bay despite the anguished objections of the rest of his staff. In any case, the British command was impressed by the large amount of radio traffic and decided to come out in force, not only from Firth of Forth near England's Scottish border, but further north from the Orkney Islands and Moray Firth, the first one under Admiral David Beatty and the last two under Admiral John Jellicoe. Beatty and Jellicoe planned to meet at the entry to the Skagerrak, that body of water between Denmark and Norway, Beatty with battle cruisers and other ships, Jellicoe with the Grand Fleet including the dreadnaughts. At the same time, the Germans sent five zeppelins up the Danish coast, radioing their observations to Jade Bay on the German mainland. Mine sweepers cleared a path for the German warships near the Danish and German coasts. The plan was for the leading German ships to serve as bait to lure the British into the range of a larger German force astern (Hayes 1972, 2-3).

At 10:00 A.M. on May 31st, the British order to "Prepare for Sea" went out to all hands concerned. This force included 28 dreadnaughts (battleships), 9 battle cruisers, 9 cruisers, 22 light cruisers, and 82 destroyers. Such a sight had never before been seen on the oceans' seas and would never again be repeated, at least with battleships, cruisers, destroyers, and smaller craft.

Also on the 31st, Vice Admiral Hipper, commanding the German advanced force, left Jade Bay at 2:00 A.M. His orders were to proceed to a position approaching the Skagerrak. Then Scheer's powerful fleet came out to sea shortly after Hipper.

Phase I: 2:15 P.M. May 31, 1916

By 2:30 P.M. Beatty's ships had headed north-northeast and were 44 miles west of Hipper's force, Beatty unable to locate the enemy. At this time Hipper was 57 miles north of Scheer with his main German force. By then, Jellicoe's formidable fleet was 65 miles north-northwest of Beatty, too far north to be of any immediate help to Beatty. Scheer was then roughly 30 miles northwest of Horn's Reef off the Danish coast and to the south of Hipper.

At about this time, Hipper's light cruiser Elbing sighted smoke on the horizon, but this turned out to be only a Danish freighter. The British too, had seen the smoke and came towards it. Beatty then discovered Hipper's force and thought he might cut it off from the Danish coast. But Hipper kept moving north and eluded the British attempt.

3:24 P.M.: Hipper's battle cruisers, having been observed by the British, still moved northward, the two sides separated by about 14 miles. (Anon. 1922, 660)

4:24: The German ship Lützow opened fire at about 7 miles distance. Both sides were then in single file moving northerly, firing rapidly at each other. The British Lion took a hit in a gun turret, but she did not explode and Von der Tann's guns hit the British Indefatigable which soon sank stern-first.

4:26: Derfflinger managed to land a salvo directly on Queen Mary, causing a serious explosion and she began to go down bow first, stern high, followed by a tremendous explosion and an immense cloud of black smoke visible for miles.

4:30: A sharp exchange between destroyers of both sides occurred. A few minutes later the Southhampton sighted Scheer's powerful fleet to the south, headed northerly. Beatty then turned north to lead Scheer's ships toward Jellicoe's. In the resulting confusion the British found themselves under fire from Scheer's ships. Barham, Warspite, and Malaya in the 5th British Battle Squadron were hit by German fire. But the German Lützow caught fire and was left behind by Hipper's group. The Germans then attacked Beatty's forces with torpedoes from gunboats, but the main result was that two of the gunboats were sunk.

By now the main German battle fleet was arriving from the south and succeeded in sinking two smaller British ships. The arriving German fleet then went into echelon positions and accosted Beatty's squadron at 20,000 yards (roughly meters, about 11 miles) distance. Jellicoe's ships were still far to the north over the horizon, but received a radio message that told of Scheer's ships arriving, although such reports were difficult to copy and were often confusing.

4:48: Hipper was leading Scheer's forces northward. Scheer was then 10 miles from Beatty while Hipper's ships were off to the east. Jellicoe, coming south, again heard of the enemy's advance toward him, partly by radio and partly from hearing the boom of gunfire to the south.

5:37: Hood and his British squadron, including Invincible, were plowing southward at full steam, 12 miles to the east of Hipper's ships, putting the Germans in a box between Beatty and Hood. Scheer, meanwhile, was arriving from the south in single line.

Phase II 5:40-9:00 P.M.

6:00 P.M.: Beatty and Hipper were blasting away at each other while Hipper's optical range-finders were handicapped by having to look into the sun, now low on the horizon. As a result, they took much shellfire from Beatty. But now Hood's cruisers to the east of Beatty were sighted by Boedicker and his German cruisers. Among the latter was Wiesbaden which was gradually destroyed. Then a number of engagements followed in which the British ship Shark was sunk and the German ship Seydlitz was hit by a torpedo, but did not sink.

6:12: Jellicoe was by this time coming southeast in divisions with ships abeam (side by side, widely separated). Visibility was then poor with the gathering mists of afternoon. Despite this, Beatty's forces were seen by Scheer heading northward to lead the Germans into Jellicoe's dreadnaughts, but then turned eastward leaving Scheer moving northeast, distanced about 7 miles from Jellicoe (Anon. 1922,661).

6:15: Scheer and Hipper were moving northeast, ships in single file. Scheer then realizing his danger in running into the dreadnaughts, facing the classical "crossing of the T", ordered a "Gefechtswendung" (battle turning) in which each ship in line, one by one, turned 180 degrees to reverse course. Orders for turning were sent by means of signal flags. Hipper made the same maneuver with his force. Scheer then retired toward the southwest. About this time the British ship Defense was hit by shellfire from two German ships and exploded. Scheer next decided to return to the fray on a northeast course.

6:40: The Germans were by now having difficulty seeing through the fog while under fire from Jellicoe's Iron Duke. But as Invincible approached the Germans, the mists cleared enough for the latter to send a salvo that hit the British warship amidships. She then blew up and partially sank, leaving her bow protruding from the water like a monument in the wide grey sea.

6:55: Jellicoe's ships were now moving south in pursuit of the smaller German fleet. Despite the power of the British, Scheer decided to face them. The reason for this he explained later: it was partly to surprise the enemy and partly to spoil the British plans for the rest of the fast-fading day. Scheer felt that he could escape in the darkness. It was a desperate and dangerous move.

7:15: British and German forces were then side by side at barely 6 miles distance. Derfflinger and Seydlitz came under heavy British fire, Derfflinger taking hits from huge shells in the after-turret, but managed to hit the British Colossus twice. Both Derfflinger and Colossus survived, however.

7:17: Scheer turned again, this time to the west under a smoke screen and a torpedo attack against Jellicoe's battle line.

7:22: The British ships, led by the Iron Duke, turned away, following the German torpedo attack. A few minutes later the British were moving southwest while Scheer went off westward about 7:35.

Phase III: 9:00 P.M.-2.45 A.M. June 1

9:00 P.M.: Jellicoe's fleet was moving southward while Scheer's ships to the west came south-southeastward to cut across the wake of the British in the dark. Jellicoe was evidently not aware of what had happened.

12:00 Midnight: the Germans, using searchlights, were able to hit the Black Prince which then blew up in a tremendous fireball. But the British later hit the German battleship Pommern which by 2:00 A.M. sank (Anon. 1922,667).

2:45: Jellicoe turned back north while the Germans proceeded into Horn's minefields, although the Ostfriesland ran into a British mine to badly damage her near the island of Sylt on the German coast.

The British had lost 3 battle-cruisers, 3 cruisers, and 5 torpedo boats. The Germans had lost one battleship, 1 battle crusier, 4 light cruisers, and 5 torpedo boats. As for the naval personnel, the British lost as drowned or killed about twice as many as did the Germans, a few of these taken prisoner. There was little opportunity for either side to stop and pick up prisoners from the sea since stopping one of the various ships caused confusion in battlelines.

German historians described the British Grand Fleet as having 37 "Grosskampfschiffen" (big fighting ships) or what the British called "battle cruisers" for the most part. The German High Seas fleet had 21 "Grosskampfschiffen." According to German estimates, the British lost about twice the German tonnage. Listed by the Germans as lost: Lützow a battle cruiser, Pommern another battle crusier in the British terminology or "Schlachtschiff" in German, plus light cruisers: Wiesbaden, Elbing, Rostock, and Frauenlob besides 5 torpedo vessels (Ploetz 1956, 955). British losses included Indefatigable, Queen Mary, and Invincible all sunk by gunfire, plus three cruisers: Defense, Warrior, and Black Prince, the last two abandoned and the first sunk. The German ships, according to the British as sunk, were the same ships listed above.

Most of these details were secret for many years and it only came out later just before WW II that the Germans had redesigned their main turrets on many of the battle cruisers to prevent what happened to the Queen Mary and used more compartmentalization of the hulls than did the British to prevent flooding the whole ship. Some of the German ships were down to their gunwales when they returned to Jade Bay, water nearly filling some of the compartments. Also, German deck armor was more resistant to incoming shells than that of the British. One of the reasons for the loss of the Invincible was probably because she had light armor to enhance her speed.

The Battle of Jutland (de Mirjian and Nelson 1976,63) or the

"Seeschlacht vor dem Skagarrak" as the Germans called it, was not the only naval engagement of the war but was certainly the largest. Scheer came out again, contrary to some accounts, but with few results. German historians concluded of Jutland that "it did not go to a decision."

* * * * * * * * * * * * *

Turning now to the more secretive doings of the war, one odd story of espionage and code-breaking was that involving the German Foreign Minister Arthur Zimmermann. Contrary to some reports, he was much interested in finding ways to keep the US out of the war in Europe. When the German government decided on unrestricted submarine warfare against British shipping, this was bound to raise the hackles of Americans wanting to trade with Britain. In any case, Zimmermann sent a cable to the German ambassador in the United States. But the message was intercepted since the underwater cable laid down across the Atlantic came close enough to Britain and in shallow enough water that it could be tapped by British navy sleuths and the message recorded. The only difficulty was that the message was in code: appearing as a series of numbers in 4-numbered groups. The British had been lucky to obtain from the Russians a code book retrieved from the sinking ship Magdeburg of German registry. After much work, the code-breakers were able to decipher most of the message at Room 40 at the Admiralty headquarters in Britain (Norman 1973, 166). It told of the decision by the German government to undertake unrestricted submarine warfare beginning February 1, 1917. When this was released to the US press, it did not raise much excitement; it was only later sinkings that began to irritate the Americans plus another note said to be from Zimmermann. The British claimed they had intercepted this second telegram, since (they claimed) they had sent an agent to break into the German embassy in Mexico City to lift a copy of this second Zimmermann telegram. The British then claimed they had decoded it and found that the Mexicans, under the German plan, would attack the United States and as a reward, retrieve the states of Texas, Arizona, and New Mexico. Room 40, having claimed to have decoded the message, sent it to President Wilson who was dutifully horrified and sent it to the newspapers, causing an enormous rise in the war-fever against Germany. Whether this was a case of genuine code-breaking or of code-invention remains uncertain to this day.

* * * * * * * * * * * * *

When World War I began, the Russians, Serbians, and Romanians, along with their allies: the French and British, were standing up against the Germans, Austro-Hungarians, Bulgarians, and Turks. Germany, wanting to be sure of Russia's defeat, despite their successes against the Russian armies, planned the destruction of the Russian Czarist government, all this in the greatest of secrecy. The German military made a deal with the exiled revolutionary Vladimir I.U. Lenin, then living in Switzerland, to allow him to travel across Germany, then to pass through Sweden and Finland to Russia. Lenin agreed to the plan and, together with many of his Communist associates, was transported in a sealed train across Germany, thence to Moscow.

On September 17, 1918, Austria-Hungary made an appeal to end the war. Then, on September 29th, an armistice between the Allies and Bulgarians was signed. The Germans were next. In October of 1918, Generals Hindenburg and Ludendorff secured permission from the Kaiser to make a peace plan. Negotiations were to begin October 3 to 4, based on Wilson's Fourteen Points. But these points practically took on the status of a secret for all the attention they got from Britain, France, and the United States.

Finally, on November 11, 1918, an armistice was signed by the Germans and Allies, this taking place in a railroad car at Compiègne Forest near Paris. Its terms, humiliating to the Germans, were remembered by them long after the war until a new war saw the conquest of France, this time with the Germans insisting on making their armistice with the Allies in the same railroad car.

In spite of all that, President Wilson was manifestly frustrated in reaching lasting agreements on armaments in hopes of avoiding another World War. An international Commission was therefore created in 1921-1922, the major participants being the US, Britain, and Japan with France and Italy as less important and four other nations still less so: Belgium, Holland, Portugal, and China. Battleships of a certain size were banned and in early 1922 a 5:5:3 ratio was to be the limits for the US, Britain, and Japan. Less well-known was that all German warships were sunk or used for target practice by the Allies. Only the smallest fleet was allowed the Germans, no motorized air force (only gliders), and merely a token military land force. Russia, at the same time was struggling to revive itself from the ruin of the old monarchy and its antique secret services.

At the time, the American public was more interested in enjoying the "Roaring Twenties" what with fast cars, fast airplanes, fast deals on Wall Street, and fast living despite "prohibition" of alcoholic drinks. Yet the government tried to form international agreements that would deny the arrival of another World War. These were the League of Nations, the Kellogg-Briand Peace Pact, the Nine-Power Treaties, and the Open Door policy, all of which were supposed to "check aggression" and bring "lasting peace" (Hamm, Bourne, and Benton 1935,818).

However, the Soviet Union, born like a large and misshapen baby from an equally large war-worn mother, spread the veil of secrecy over the ruined and impoverished country. One of the earliest intelligence organizations formed just after the end of World War I, was the GRU, a branch of the Soviet military, created in October of 1918. A leading revolutionist Communist, Leon Trotsky, urged the new leader Lenin to create it in the interest of stability in a notoriously unstable nation. Its purpose was to observe and coordinate military affairs and develop an espionage organization to inform on the activities of the top military staff. Also undertaken, was spying on various foreign nations all over the world. At the time, little or nothing of this was known outside Russia and inside it as well. But collection of foreign intelligence was considered by the top Communist leaders as of paramount importance. While the "Cheka" had been the organization devoted almost entirely to internal affairs and brutally controlling them, the GRU was not. Also, there was the dictator's Secret Police: the NKVD, which actually overlapped to some extent the workings of the GRU, a problem that seems to have been ignored. In fact the GRU itself was purged in 1920, implying that many of its leaders were murdered on Lenin's order, all this concerned with the mistreatment of Poland during the war.

In 1926 the GRU became a "bureau," a French word that has become international, then part of the Red Army, gathering information from the unsuspecting German, British, and American governments. When Stalin became dictator, a number of purges took place, especially in 1929 and 1930. Then in 1935 the GRU itself took part in purges of the NKVD, these being merciless beyond the standards of western nations. With the GRU doing the dirty work, top officials of the NKVD were disposed of, usually in one of Moscow's prisons with a bullet in the head. Another such purge occurred in 1937 initiated by Stalin. This included hundreds of Soviet Army officers, the dirty work being carried out by NKVD squads (Polmar and Allen 1997, 245). And the purges went on into 1938 just before the German invasions. Although the GRU had given warning of that invasion, Stalin ignored the information.

Americans, meanwhile, may have thought there were no such secret services in the US even though of much milder character. This was not exactly true. In fact J. Edgar Hoover was becoming known in some circles as the head "G-man" (Government man), a name given him by gangsters that he chased to their lairs. Hoover's saga began in 1917, progressing into the 1920s when he rose from a lowly clerk in the U.S. Department of Justice, an organization that soon fostered the birth of the Bureau of Investigation (BOI). This mainly concerned itself with the spread of the Communist revolution from Russia, now the USSR, into America. Hoover, tending to be a strongly conservative anti-Communist, climbed up through the ranks, his diligence and accumulative instincts producing files on as many as 200,000 people. By 1920, Hoover was leading raids on suspected radicals whose names numbered in the thousands. Many of these were deported. In 1924, Hoover's abilities led him to become Director of the BOI with some 400 or so "Special Agents" under his wing with the power to make arrests (Polmar and Allen 1997,266).

After Franklin Delano Roosevelt climbed from the position of Governor of New York state to become President of the US, defeating the conservative Republican Herbert Hoover in 1932, Roosevelt became much interested in preventing "subversives" —not necessarily Soviet agents —but German agents and saboteurs who were finding their way into US politics and various other paths of life. Roosevelt even allowed the British espionage agency MI6 to set up shop as an intelligence organization in the US. Except for a small inner circle, few knew of this and even fewer ever heard of MI6.

As the 1930s progressed and witnessed the rapid revival of Germany from the depths of disaster and poverty after WW I, Roosevelt appointed a Canadian, William Stephenson, to the position of Director of British Security Coordination. Strengthening the US-British bond, Winston Churchill, then Prime Minister in 1940, appointed Stephenson as his personal representative to President Roosevelt. Stephenson, as might be expected from his record as a combatant in WW I against the Germans, was strongly opposed to the American "Isolationists" which included the famous trans-Atlantic flier Charles Lindbergh. Meetings were held where Lindbergh spoke in favor of staying out of any war in Europe, although the press down-played their activities, pointing to the low-grade kind of people that were joining the movement against war in Europe. Lindbergh visited Germany at the time and was greeted with much publicity by German Army officers, all this anathema to the pro-British faction in the US.

In May of 1940, when the war in Europe was already going on, the "British Security Coordination" apparatus was created to operate clandestinely out of New York City. One of its functions was to spread pro-British propaganda, something reminiscent of WW I. Just a few months before the Pearl Harbor event in December of 1941 when the Japanese attacked the U.S. Navy's installations, Roosevelt appointed William Donovan, a gung-ho, strongly anti-German of natural warrior tendencies to be Director of the Office of Strategic Services (OSS), supposedly working under the US Joint Chiefs of Staff.

As for J. Edgar Hoover, he found himself the leader in the effort to hunt down "subversives" as early as 1939 when the Germans and Soviets divided up Poland between them, thus beginning —in the Anglo-French point of view — World War II. It is possible, but not probable, that there might never have been a WW II if Britain and France had not declared war on Germany, the sins of the Russians conveniently ignored. Germany might then have dominated Europe, no doubt a thought that Hitler had been nurturing for some time. In fact, any mention of the Soviet invasion of Eastern Poland was largely ignored in the western media, while few knew of the cruelties perpetrated by the USSR's NKVD on the Polish army at that time.

Hoover made it clear, despite the US government's tendency to favor Britain, that British Intelligence officers should not go roaming around the US looking for subversives (Polmar and Allen 1997, 268). Later, however, Stephenson seems to have convinced Hoover to favor the British. Despite all this attempted cooperation between Hoover's FBI and Stephenson's boys, the Germans managed to steal from Canada the plans for the Norden bomb sight, used to assure accurate bombing from aircraft.

While the British had succeeded in penetrating the halls of the US government with Roosevelt's blessing, the German military secret service, the Abwehr, was also working its machinations in its own way in the US. The Abwehr, meaning literally "Defense," was organized soon after WW I in 1921. But in the late 1930s it came into sharp conflict with the SS (Schutzstaffel, or Protection Division, loyal to Hitler). Apparently, the Abwehr began on its own to try and make an agreement with the Russians and avoid a German-Soviet war. But Hitler, exasperated with the Abwehr for meddling in his plans, sent a contingent of the SS in 1937 to break into Abwehr headquarters at the Offices of the General

Staff and burn their papers. After that, the Abwehr was relegated to serve strictly under the German High Command (Oberkomando Wehrmacht). Nevertheless, by 1940, the Abwehr was deep in espionage in the US. For the American scene, this involved an agent the Abwehr trusted: Dusko Popov, a handsome, charming man, apparently from Yugoslavia. Yet Popov was actually a double agent, ostensibly run by the Abwehr for spying on the US and relaying his information to the Abwehr. But the British, not at all charmed by his beguiling manner, managed to turn him around to become a spy working for them. One of Popov's goals, as directed by the Abwehr, was to report on "conditions" at Pearl Harbor's Naval Base in the Hawaiian Islands. But Hoover, now of the FBI (Federal Bureau of Investigation formed in 1935) was able to discover Popov's aims and prevented him from traveling to Hawaii (Polmar and Allen 1997,445).

At this point the British decided to inform Hoover of Popov's role as a double agent working for both the Germans and the British. But it seemed that Hoover thought Popov was strictly a German spy, pulling the wool over the eyes of the British. In any case, the FBI soon learned that Popov was sending messages by microdot, writing so small a microscope was required to read it, apparently to the Germans. Popov was also allowed by the FBI to operate a secret radio for sending (actually sanitized) information to the Germans.

In the end, Popov, his usefulness expended, returned to Britain to work for British Intelligence until the end of the war. It would seem that the US government never entirely grasped the connection among the Abwehr, Popov, MI6, and Stephenson. But what the FBI and therefore the US government missed was the mention of Pearl Harbor and Popov's orders to report on it. The German connection to Japan was already known at this time.

While the secret workings of the US government were thus occupied, Hitler and his trusted cohorts were going inexorably on the warpath, first to take over Austria, even though there was only a minority of Austrian National Socialists. On June 24, 1937, in great secrecy, a directive was issued by the German government called "Fall Otto" (Case Otto) for a military takeover of the Austrian government in Vienna.

In November of that year, Hitler told his military and diplomatic cohorts of his plan not only to take over Austria, but Czechoslovakia as well. Although Britain's Lord Halifax told Hitler that Britain had no objection to the Austrian "Anschluss" (Joining) or to take over the German-speaking Sudeten part of Czechoslovakia, he warned Hitler not to use force in these settlements. As for the Italians, the dictator Mussolini in March of 1938 acquiesced to Hitler's ambitions, much to Hitler's great relief (De Weerd 1973, 780A).

In September 1938, Daladier and Bonnet of the French government came to London to talk with Chamberlain and Halifax about Czechoslovakia, the results kept mostly to themselves. Chamberlain then decided, as Prime Minister of Britain, to make one last attempt to reason with Hitler and perhaps obtain a written agreement not to invade all of Czechoslovakia.

Beginning on the 9th of September, 1938, the National Socialists held a gigantic rally where Hitler spoke at the Sports Arena in Nuremberg to massed ranks of the Schutzstaffel in their black uniforms while radio carried his haranguing over the air to many listening Germans, all this at night illuminated by glaring floodlights for maximum effect. However, at the same time, the top military leaders of OKW (Oberkommando Wehrmacht, or High Command of the Armed Forces) were arguing among each other over the Hitlerian plan to take over the rest of Czechoslovakia, having fully realized Germany's shortcomings in a possible war with Britain and France. Yet Generals Jodl (pronounced Yodel) and Keitel (pronounced Kitel as in kite) stood for Hitler, arguing in favor of the importance of "duty" (Warlimont 1964, 17).

On September 12th, Neville Chamberlain, Britain's P.M., planned to fly to Germany to warn Hitler about a possible war. But unknown to the German public and to most of the rest of the world, a conspiracy was being hatched by top civilian and military people in Germany to overthrow Hitler. These included Economics Minister Schacht, General Witzleben, Hans Oster of Germany's Counter Intelligence, Beck, former Chief of the General Staff, and Hoeppner, head of a Thüringen division of troops. Hitler was to be tried before a People's Court. However, they could not persuade top-ranking Army man von Brauchitsch as well as Chief of Staff Halder. The failure of these two to go along with the plot spelled its doom. Beck was later to commit suicide, his fate already sealed by the SS. Beck tried to shoot himself in the head but survived and was finished off by his orderly according to Beck's wishes.

On September 13, Chamberlain arrived at the Berghof, Hitler's mountain retreat in southern Bavaria. Hitler talked about breaking free from the Versailles Treaty and how he had made an agreement with Britain in the form of a naval treaty. But concerning Czechoslovakia, he wanted no interference. Chamberlain next asked him what use was it for him to come to Germany if force was to be used? Hitler seemed stumped by that, but then agreed not to act (Bullock 1952, 422). On the 29th they agreed to assure the peace of Europe and Hitler signed the document.

On September 28, 1938, at Chamberlain's urging, Mussolini asked for a conference of representatives from Germany, Italy, Britain, and France. On the 30th, an agreement was signed to carve up Czechoslovakia with the western part going to Germany and the eastern part going partly to Poland and Hungary. While the Czech army had collapsed almost as soon as it was mobilized, the Germans marched in to take over Prague. By March of 1939, Hitler had arrived in that city, declaring the end of that "Child of Versailles."

Unknown to most everyone in the world, the USSR's Vyachaslav Molotov and Germany's Joachim von Ribbentrop had engineered a Soviet-German nonaggression pact, the news of this only leaking out in the summer of 1939. This was soon ratified by the Soviet parliament and was, of course, a bitter disappointment to France and Britain, both having hoped, as in WW I, that Russia, now the USSR, would go to war on their side against Germany. In the German-Soviet agreement, Germany was to retrieve certain German-speaking territories in Poland, lost to Germany in the Versailles treaty, while the USSR, for its part, would take over Eastern Poland.

As 1939 progressed inexorably toward war, few in the world knew that relations between Germany and Poland were fast deteriorating, their negotiations kept largely secret. At the same time, the Munich agreements among Germany, Italy, Britain, and France were beginning to fall asunder, mostly because they were being ignored by Hitler. The Poles, seeing the handwriting on the wall, asked the British for an Anglo-Polish agreement for "mutual assistance." An agreement was in fact made in March of 1939, evidently in secrecy, stating that Britain would come to Poland's assistance if Poland's independence was threatened. This agreement was accepted by the Poles on April 6, 1939. But already on the 3rd of April Hitler had given the order to OKW for war against Poland. The war was set by Hitler to begin September 1st, 1939.

Chapter 2

World War II In The Making: A Study In Secrets

No matter what a government represents, there are always those who would thwart it and even overthrow it. Not all Germans went along blindly with Hitler's ambitions to seek revenge for the conclusions of World War I and the Versailles Treaty. From the top government leaders down to the little-known secret agents, there were those who took a dim view of Hitler and worked against his goals.

On one side of the German government in 1938 stood Hitler and his Schutz-Staffel (Protection Echelon) or SS who believed they were of "pure" ancestry and were sworn to protect the "Führer" or leader and even to die for him if necessary. Originally, the SS was under the SA (Schutz Abteilung) or Protection Division who had marched in brown uniforms in Munich's streets in the old days just after WW I. In time, the SS grew and was then divided into those who served as front line troops and those who did the dirty work behind the scenes, not unlike the Soviet NKVD (People's Commissariat for Internal Affairs).

On the other hand there were the doubters, dissenters, and outright revolutionists, not only in the military but in the espionage services, planning the overthrow of Adolf Hitler. One of these dissenters was Hans Oster of the Abwehr, the Military Intelligence Service formed in 1921 when the Reichswehr was allowed in Germany as a small defense force. The word "Abwehr" comes from the word "abwehren" to ward off, and grew in time to do much more than that. By 1939, Oster had become Chief of Staff of Abwehr under Wilhelm Canaris (Polmar and

Allen 1997, 417).

During 1939, Oster gave information to the Allies: Britain and France, concerning the intended invasion of Poland, but few knew of this double-dealing. Oster was a quiet-spoken sort of man, the kind that would relax his visitor by leaning back in his chair and blowing smoke-rings in the air while seeming not to care what was being said. From the beginning of WW II, he tried to find various ways to end the war. When the British and Germans both tried to take over Norway, he was said to have provided the British with the timing of the German invasion.

After the German invasion of Poland had begun, Oster tried to pre-vent Jews from being packed off to the then little-known concentration camps. Still others were sent to work in factories, as in Essen, Hamburg, Dresden, and Berlin. There they did things like assembling artillery shells. The huge Krupp factories as in Essen made use of foreign labor, thus to free up men for the army. Each foreign laborer, including German Jews, wore a certain colored uniform to indicate their origin. In later years during the war many workers were Russians, while Jews who lived in small German towns or in ghettos in larger cities like Munich were urged by subtle means to leave the country, many going to the Middle East, to Constantinople and Palestine, as told by Viktor Klemperer in his diary "I Will Bear Witness," originally published by Aufbau Verlag, GmbH, Berlin, 1995.

The SS long suspected Oster of being a renegade, especially after the Gestapo (a state police organization) found he had been negotiating with the Vatican to end the war. Canaris dismissed him in 1943 and he was later hung following Hitler's order.

Another famous actor on the stage of the German Aufschwung (re-vival) and high in the National Socialist hierarchy was Wilhelm Franz Canaris, formerly a well-known naval officer who had once captained a U-boat and had been high up in rank in the operation of a German battle cruiser. Back in 1905 he had enlisted in the Navy, survived the war, and by the late 1930's had risen to become Chief of Naval Intelligence. At first he went along with the Hitlerian revolution, approving of Germany's rejection of the Versailles Treaty and Hitler's anti-Commu-nism. But when he became head of the Abwehr, he found himself strongly opposed to a rival secret service, a branch of the SS (Polmar and Allen 1997, 417).

There was something odd about Canaris from the beginning. With a Greek name and his casual manner and appearance, he was hardly a con-vincing military figure. Added to his prematurely white hair, he had a habit of dressing in street clothes and sloppy ones at that, frequently slipping out of his office and back in again unnoticed by anyone. After WW II began, he became more at odds with the SS, often hiring people the SS did not approve of, such as those of Jewish extraction that grated against the SS ideas of racial background.

When the German armies failed to advance through the outskirts of Moscow in 1941, Hitler's popularity began to decline while more than one plot was conceived to assassinate him. Canaris was convinced by 1942 that Germany would lose the war. Whether he was involved in it or not, a plot was hatched out toward the end of the war to put a bomb in Hitler's airplane when he flew back from his "Wolfschanz" headquarters near the Russian front.

The bomb's fuse was made so that an acid solution would eat through a small metal barrier allowing a spring-switch to close a circuit between a battery and the bomb. But the plane had flown so high that the extreme cold froze the acid and the bomb never went off.

In early November of 1939 about two months after the German-Soviet invasion of Poland began, Walter Schellenberg of German Counter Intelligence got wind of a British plot to unseat or kill Adolf Hitler, making use of German dissidents. One idea was to offer the German government the territories Hitler claimed if the German dissidents overthrew the Führer. To gain the ends of the so-called dissidents, Stewart Menzies, Chief of British Intelligence (MI6) hatched out a plan to send two MI6 men plus a Dutch Intelligence officer across the Dutch border into Germany to team up with certain Germans including dissident General Ludwig Beck.

Schellenberg decided to set a trap to catch the two British agents: Captain S. Payne Best and Major H.R. Stevens. The result was that the two Britishers made contact with a man who was in fact a double agent working for the Sicherheitsdienst (SD) and associated with the SS. After two meetings between the Brits and the phony German representatives during which they discussed the deal, Schellenberg conceived a plot to meet at Venlo on the Dutch-German border with Best and Stevens (Polmar and Allen 1997, 595).

Britain's Prime Minister Neville Chamberlain still hoped to stop the war before it went too far and did his best to make a bargain with the German dissidents thus supporting the MI6 plan to get Best and Stevens into Germany and team up with those dissidents. But Schellenberg himself posed as a German Army dissident, planning to meet at Venlo on the Dutch-German border with Best and Stevens.

The day came and Best, Stevens, and the Dutchman waited in their car for the supposed dissidents. The tension must have been enormous. Suddenly, as if from nowhere, a black Mercedes burst through the border control station and shot the Dutch guards there. More shots were fired and the two Brits were forced at gunpoint to get into one of the German cars,then rushed back through the checkpoint. The deed was done and with it went the hopes of stopping WW II before it engulfed much of the world.

Best and Stevens were interrogated endlessly and kept in prison. Evidently they were forced to "talk" and after weeks of interrogation revealed the names of many operatives from other countries working in Germany against the Hitler government.

* * * * * * * * * * * *

When WW II began and the Soviets had taken over eastern Poland, making sure the Polish military would be crippled by murdering thousands (21,857, shot in various locations and buried in mass graves, according to Crozier), of Polish officers and others, they soon began in 1940 to attack Finland. This may have been partly because of valuable mines in northern Finland and also for strategic reasons, such as gaining the use of Finland's lengthy coast on the Gulf of Bothnia that leads into the North Sea. The Soviets could point out in their defense that the former Imperial Russia had owned Finland for many years.

While the United States still was not involved in the European war in 1940, there was much sympathy for Finland. Unknown to most everyone at the time, an interesting object was discovered on a Finnish-Russian battlefield and handed over to British Intelligence people. The object was a small pack of pages, only an inch on a side, made of celluloid that would burn readily. The pages of the pad, as it was called, had printed on them numbers in groups of four. MI6 operatives, on receiving it, realized it was a way of encoding or decoding messages sent and received in Soviet military operations by radio.

In Britain, MI6 figured out that each page was used on a particular date so the recipient would have the same page with the same numbers on that date.

But how could the numbers be turned into letters or words? The mystery remained. The British knew from radio intercepts that the Soviets were using a code consisting of numbers in groups of four, but still the riddle of decipherment went unsolved.

To explain how the code was used and why it was so difficult to decrypt it, let us suppose we wanted to send the word "MAC." Each letter of the alphabet (and the Russian alphabet had a few more letters than the English) was assigned a number: A=1, B=2, C=3 and so on to letter M=13. A number representing, say M was added as 13 to a group of four scrambled numbers, best shown in the following:

To send the word MAC:

	Letter 1	Letter 2	Letter 3
Infinitely scrambled numbers	4972	3964	9645
Added by the sender	+13 for M	+1 for A	+3 for C
Sum sent by radio	4985	3965	9648
Recipient subtracts	-4972	-3964	-9645
Results of subtraction	13	1	3
Standing for	M	A	C

Later versions of the "One Time Pad" were made more complex and for years it was essentially unbreakable. However, the Soviet military became careless and used the same page more than once, allowing the code-breakers, such as the Venona effort in the United States (Romerstein and Breindel 2000, 3), to at least figure out how the cipher was set up and with the aid of computers (then in their infancy) to discover some of the names of Soviet agents in the US and Britain.

The Germans, however, being mechanically inclined, came up with a completely different way of enciphering and deciphering messages. Through the ages there have been many ways of encrypting messages. Caesar is supposed to have used code for sending and receiving orders. But the invention of the "Enigma" machine during the 1920s had the advantage of speed of encryption and decryption as well as making the message nearly impossible to decrypt, nearly. In time there were ways to break into its cipher.

The idea of using rotors as in the Enigma machine, 3 of which were used in the early models, may have come from a much simpler machine invented by, oddly enough, Thomas Jefferson, the third president of the United States. The US President, having come through a war with the Barbary pirates of North Africa and a brush with France's Napoleon, saw the need, as in the war with Britain, for a fast way of encrypting messages and decrypting them.

Electrical metal gadgets were not available in those days around the year 1800, when the White House was a sort of oversized mansion surrounded by a cow pasture. So this machine was made of wood. It consisted of a series of flat discs, 24 in all, like wheels put on an axle, packed together. On the edges of each disc were all the letters of the alphabet in order from A to Z.

A message was encrypted by arranging the letters on the wheels or rotors to spell out the words of the message in a straight line as determined by a horizontal ruler or some such guide. Once the message was spelled out, such as: "MAC is coming Tuesday," the operator would read the scrambled message off the other side of the rotors. For the letters "MAC" he would find something like YMO, being opposite the encrypted letters. Then with a similar machine the recipient would set YMO on the one side of the machine and on the other would be MAC.

As already mentioned, the Germans had adopted a machine for military use called "Enigma," the word coming from the Greek "aenigma," meaning something mysterious. It was invented in 1923 by a German, Arthur Scherbuis and a Swede, Boris Hagelin, for use in business transactions that were to be kept secret. Looking like a typewriter, it had a nearly-standard keyboard and three discs or rotors, any one of which could be activated by pushing a key on the typewriter, thereby rotating a disc to a certain position. Each rotor had the complete alphabet on its outer rim, something like the Jefferson machine. By pushing a key on the typewriter, an electrical impulse was sent from a battery to one of the rotors to set it. In its simplest form one rotor might have been all that was needed, but by adding two more, the complexities of encryption were greatly increased.

Enciphered letters would appear on the back of the typewriter called the "lamp board" and read by another operator for transmission by radio or telegraph. When exhibited at a trade fair in Germany in the 1920s, the German Navy and the Swedish Army soon adopted it for sending secret messages to ships at sea or armies in the field. Later on it was used by the German Army and Air Force while the commercial machines could no longer be sold.

In military models, a plug board, like that of a telephone switchboard in the old days, was included in the circuits so that rotor settings could be different at different times. Later models used four rotors to greatly increase the chances that no one could theoretically decipher a certain message. Toward the end of the war eight rotors were used by the Germany Navy, and in later years the Americans used 10 rotors, producing an almost infinite complexity.

Another way of sending secret messages was RTTY or radio telephone telegraphy, a system replacing Morse code, invented by the Siemens Electric Company. RTTY, or Baudot, was used for Hitler's command traffic to and from OKW (Oberkommando Wehrmacht). Using two frequencies alternately for each letter, it made a curious warbling sound that was finally solved by the USSR and the British, with a machine called "Sägefisch" by the Germans and "Fish" by the British.

In the months just before the German and Soviet armies began to invade Poland in September of 1939, a team of Polish code breakers had been working in a bombproof cellar just outside Warsaw. They had already made a number of discoveries about the German Enigma machines and in their hatred of the Germans felt they should impart their ideas to the French and British. They had at least partly broken the Enigma ciphers by means of hooking together six Enigma machines in series to reveal the Enigma settings for a particular day (Parrish 1986, 52).

A British delegation soon arrived, consisting of Commander Alistair Denniston, Delwyn Knox an Intelligence expert, and Sir Stewart Menzies who later became Chief of British Intelligence. The French delegation also arrived, having already collaborated with the Poles in earlier months. They all assembled in the bombproof shelter. In August of 1939, only days before the German-Soviet invasion, the British and French each went home with the present of a Polish-built Enigma machine. More importantly, they carried away the plans for building the "Bomba" as the Poles called their deciphering machine. On returning home, the British began building their own Bomba, now calling it the "Bombe," adding even more Enigma-like machines to reveal the German Enigma settings at a particular time.

The British Bombe was a massive collection of rotors and wiring, all fitted into a huge box about the size of a standard upright piano. But at first, it did not work. A few months later, electronics expert Alan M. Turing succeeded in making the monster function. The Bombe was finally set up in one of several large "huts" or wooden buildings out in the country at Bletchley Park, about 45 miles NW of London. The entire operation of radio operatives, code specialists, and electronic experts was carried on in the numerous huts, all this effort going by the name of "ULTRA."

In later years after the war, Bletchley Park became a tourist attraction where the various deciphering machines, including the world's first electronic calculator, were housed.

* * * * * * * * * * * * *

As World War II progressed it also expanded into other territories. In North Africa the Italians had at first done well against the British but decided to set up a number of forts across the desert to prevent the British from progressing from Egypt. Such a system might have worked in Caesar's day, but the British soon began to penetrate it and move westward. Hitler, seeing the strategic importance of controlling North Africa, decided to support his ally and send German forces equipped with tanks and artillery.

Although the Bombe at Bletchley Park had begun to read some of the German Afrika Korps radio traffic, it seemed to do little to help the British in planning attacks on the Germans. This was because the Germans were reading the British command traffic which was regularly put on the air to inform the United States of the British moves there.

The German forces were outnumbered by the British by a ratio of 1 to 2, but the Germans had an ace in the hole. This came about because the Germans had deciphered the US "Black" code used in communicating with the British in Egypt. The code appeared at first to be undecipherable. Unfortunately for the British, however, the details of the code were kept in a safe in Italy and were stolen by Italian Secret Service men who promptly gave them to the Germans. Since the Americans kept up a frequent correspondence with the British in Cairo, Egypt, the Germans listened in on their frequency, copied the "continental" code being sent, and were able to decipher the British-American messages. All this told the exact disposition of the British troops and even gave the times when the British airforce would attack in their support (Norman 1973, 170).

The result was that along with good planning and modern weaponry, German General Erwin Rommel's forces won battle after battle and drove the British eastward hundreds of miles, even across the Egyptian border. But at this point the British figured out what was happening. While Rommel got a great deal of credit for his brilliant generalship, he probably was unaware that the British had captured a German mobile intelligence vehicle, complete with its codes and ciphers. This must have helped the British even more after they had stopped the transmissions from Cairo to the United States.

By then the Germans were approaching the gates of Cairo, but with the leak stopped and the British reading the German ciphers, British troops were winning battles and proceeded to drive the Germans back, eventually to defeat them.

* * * * * * * * * * * * *

In 1941 before the event at Pearl Harbor, the British were depending more and more on supplies sent by freighter across the Atlantic to Britain. The German Navy realized the importance of their submarines and were building them at an extraordinary rate. Admiral Doenitz of the German Kriegsmarine (Navy) laid out a plan of unified U-boat attacks in "Wolf Packs" to sink the freighters in the Atlantic. The toll began to become a serious problem to the British. But they had a lucky break that practically turned the submarine war into Britain's favor and crippled the U-boat fleets. This came about in the following way.

It was in May of 1941 when a convoy of British supply freighters, supported by destroyers and corvettes off the southeast coast of Greenland, were attacked by a German U-boat. The Germans fired a torpedo at the convoy and sank a freighter, but British warships saw where the torpedo had come from and dropped depth charges with no apparent effect. Then miraculously the U-boat appeared from the depths and to the astonishment of the British, the crew began emerging from the conning tower and many were leaping into the sea. The depth charges had so damaged the submarine to cripple it and cause it to come to the surface.

One of the destroyers prepared to sink the submarine with gunfire, but it occurred to the ship's captain that a British crew could board the U-boat before it sank and retrieve whatever they could from the hold. The destroyer's guns were told to hold their fire and a party was sent in a life boat to the submarine. Several of the British, having come alongside the submarine, went aboard and then down the conning tower. There in the radio room they found an Enigma machine completely intact together with all the essential papers on how to operate it as well as all other papers telling when and how to change the settings.

The British did their best to keep the secret of the lost submarine from the outside world, claiming simply that they had sunk the U-boat. The discovery of the Enigma machine allowed the code-breakers at Bletchley to predict where the U-boats would strike next, picking up the messages from the German command to the submarines at sea. The great loss of freighters miraculously diminished thereafter, with the British carefully keeping their secret.

The German admiralty figured that there was a spy somewhere giving the command orders to the British, but when all the stones had been turned they realized something else was wrong and changed their cipher systems, finally using Enigma machines with 8 rotors producing an almost infinite complexity of the Enigma's readouts.

This German submarine loss was apparently only one of subsequent events when other Enigma machines were discovered during the war at sea. But as for the Polish experts who did not escape to Britain and were captured by the Germans in September of 1939, they evidently did not talk. It was not until a book appeared in French about Enigma in 1973 that the secret of it came out. This was followed by F. W. Winterbotham's book "The Nazi Connection" (Winterbotham 1978, 259).

* * * * * * * * * * * *

During the US Revolutionary and Civil Wars, secret messages enciphered in very crude ways were mainly transported by messengers on horseback. Even in World War I, the US had no organization for decrypting secret messages. The British, however, were well aware of the importance of espionage, secret ciphers, and secret communications by wire or radio.

By the end of World War I, Americans interested in solving secret codes had to depend on private funds. Such an operation was set up in Geneva, Illinois at the "Riverbank Laboratories," initially to find out whether Shakespeare or Bacon had written the famous plays. To have a leading role in the project, a young man, William F. Friedman, was hired to be the leader of the group to solve this puzzle. After months of work they concluded that Shakespeare had indeed written the plays, not Francis Bacon (Polmar and Allen 1997, 222). But the controversy still goes on.

When World War I was over, The Army Signal Corps, holding forth in Washington D.C., hired Friedman in 1920. Messages were being picked up mostly off telegraph lines and required deciphering. Friedman was chosen to be the leader of the organization, then called the Signals Intelligence Service (SIS). Working with six assistants, he began to try and decipher one of the Japanese codes, some of which were military and some diplomatic.

By the early 1930s, the SIS was working on the problem of the Japanese cipher machine Type A, calling it "Red" for no other reason than red was the first color in the visible spectrum. A later development by the Japanese was the type B machine where vowels and consonants were enciphered separately (Parrish 1986, 43).

By the mid 1930s, the type B code, after the SIS realized it made use of an Enigma-like machine, was later deciphered by Naval Intelligence at OP-20-G in Washington D.C. In 1939 the Red code was superceded by the mysterious JN-25 code, version A (Bodiansky 2000, 86, 351).

Even before the invention of the baffling Japanese JN-25 code, there were other codes that used stepping switches, instead of rotors as in the Enigma machines. Such switches were used by telephone companies automatically to transfer telephone calls to and from a particular party, replacing manually-operated "plug boards." One of these codes was called "Coral" and another "Jade." The latter used the "Katakana" syllabary which had 48 symbols instead of the fewer Roman letters used in English, each symbol representing a syllable. When sent out on the air, US radio men had great difficulty copying a code with 48 symbols.

When the JN-25 type B code came into use just before Pearl Harbor's attack, US code breakers were stumped by it. But Friedman's group finally realized the Japanese were using stepping switches as in the Jade code. Friedman's group then built a Japanese enciphering machine they called "Purple." Deciphering the code then followed, the whole effort referred to as "Magic."

There was a story that Navy sleuths broke into the Japanese embassy in Washington D.C. and photographed their enciphering machine. This story was later much doubted. Actually, both Army and Navy codebreakers began to read the JN-25 code, but only the diplomatic one. This meant that they were unable to warn Washington of the impending attack on Pearl Harbor (Layton 1985, 78). However, the code breakers learned from the diplomatic code that the Japanese government had told their representatives in Washington to break off relations with the US. Washington should have known from this that an attack was coming, but where? The diplomatic code did not reveal when and where the Japanese attack would come. It was only just after the fateful day of December 7 that the US code breakers were reading the JN-25 Naval code. Even if read earlier, Washington might still not have reacted, since the top levels of the government wanted to "wake up" America to the dangers of war.

With the JN-25 naval code unbroken and the government in Washington ignoring the warnings of the British and Dutch secret services, either purposely or out of ignorance, the Japanese fleet was able to pounce on the Pearl Harbor Naval Base, hardly losing any of its aircraft, and withdraw off to sea to the west without reprisal. It all had the effect that Roosevelt had hoped for, although he claimed he thought the attack would come to the Philippine Islands. Roosevelt's fault or not, it galvanized a nation in a way that the fondest hopes of the interventionists had not dared to dream of. Considering what we know at the end of the century, the Pearl Harbor attack was all for the good of America, at least in the view of the interventionists. But the Japanese command was worried. They had seen Halsey's task force appear just as they were completing the bombing and wondered where the other US aircraft carriers, of which there were thought to be three, had gone. It proved in 1942 to be a big problem for the Japanese, since there were four in all: Enterprise, Saratoga, Lexington, and Yorktown.

* * * * * * * * * * * * *

In March of 1942 the Japanese naval code JN-25 had been broken (Bodiansky 2000, 12) or at least enough so that the Americans had a good idea as to where the Japanese were headed in the East Indies. One of the decrypts of a Japanese transmission indicated that a Japanese fleet was headed for Port Moresby on the southeast coast of New Guinea. Knowing about where the Japanese were, the carrier Yorktown launched her airplanes to attack the Japanese fleet which was evidently supporting an invasion of Tulagi in the Solomon Islands just east of New Guinea. The Yorktown's planes managed to badly damage several Japanese transports and sink a Japanese destroyer (Cooney 1965, 274).

By now a formidable collection of US ships was approaching from the south through the Coral Sea which lies to the southeast of New Guinea. These ships included Task Force 17 with 5 heavy cruisers and 5 destroyers, Task Force 44 with 2 heavy cruisers, 1 light cruiser, and 2 destroyers, then finally Task Force 11 with 2 aircraft carriers: Lexington and Yorktown together with 4 destroyers and 2 oilers. Their main purpose was to confront the Japanese fleet and prevent their troops from landing at Port Moresby, as indicated by the code-breakers that were reading the JN-25 code.

Action began when aircraft from Yorktown bombed Japanese transport ships near Tulagi in the Solomons on May 5. By the 7th, British Royal Navy forces joined the two US carriers to sink the Japanese carrier Soho while the US lost the destroyer Sims. On May 8th, US carriers launched their aircraft to damage the carrier Shokaku, but the Japanese planes set fire to the Lexington and so badly damaged her that she had to be sunk by the USS Phelps. Yorktown was also damaged. Although a little over 200 men had been lost on the Lexington, US forces had turned back the attempt to take Port Moresby and may have prevented the Japanese invasion of Australia. It was the first naval battle in history when opposing ships were not in sight of one another (Cooney 1965, 276) known as The Battle of the Coral Sea. Although the Japanese were having little trouble in taking over the Philippine Islands, the Japanese command, after much haggling, decided to send a veritable armada of warships and transports to the Midway Islands (hereafter called Midway) and take it over. A northern force would head for the Aleutian Islands to act as a diversion. The First Carrier Striking force with the main body of warships was to approach Midway on its northern side, coming from the west. A second Covering Group was to head just south of Midway where they would merge with 12 troop transports, a support group, and a mine-sweeping group (Natkiel 1986, 78-79).

But the U.S. Navy had an ace up its sleeve. This was the accomplishment of Naval Intelligence in breaking the JN-25 code, unknown to the Japanese. The Intelligence staff, headed by Commander Joseph J. Rochefort, USN, went to meet the top U.S. Navy command with Admiral Frank J. Fletcher at its head. Rochefort told the assembled brass that his staff was convinced that the Japanese were headed for Midway and that if they did not stop it, there would be a major disaster for the Americans in the Pacific. To strengthen their theory, the code-breakers Rochefort and Layton sent a cable to Midway asking it to send a short radio message "in the clear" (not encrypted) to report that Midway's water distillation plant was not working. The Japanese using the JN-25 code, dutifully reported to their command that Midway was low on water. This report was picked up by a US listening post and relayed to the Naval command which then realized the Japanese were headed for Midway. As a result, Rochefort's pleas were heeded by the US Naval Command and orders put out for the US fleet, consisting of two Task Forces, to progress to the region just northeast of Midway.

On June 4th, 1942, the Japanese northern fleet approached Midway on its north side and was detected by a PB-Y scout plane. The news was sent by radio to the overall commander Fletcher in the Yorktown carrier. The order was quickly given for US ships to launch torpedo planes, dive bombers, and fighter aircraft from the carriers. The Americans had the carrier Yorktown in Task Force 17 and the carriers Enterprise and Hornet in Task Force 16. Meanwhile, the Japanese reconnaissance aircraft had located the US ships and sent news that US carriers were nearby, northeast of Midway. But the Japanese carriers were then loading their bombers for an attack on Midway and next had to rearm 108 airplanes with armor-piercing bombs and torpedoes for use against enemy warships. This delayed their attack. When the Japanese attack came, the Yorktown was hit in her conning tower and left burning, while other Japanese aircraft bombed oil storage tanks on Sand Island, Midway, producing clouds of black smoke.

On June 5th at 0500 (5:00 a.m.) the Japanese aircraft carrier Akagi was hit by bombs from dive-bombers and later scuttled. At about 1015 Kaga and Soryu aircraft carriers were attacked by aircraft from Yorktown and Enterprise. The US dive bombers could not at first find the enemy, but then, through a break in the clouds, saw the Japanese carriers below them looking like tiny chips of wood on the broad blue sea. The torpedo planes had been the first to attack the Japanese and, with no air support from late-arriving fighter planes or dive-bombers, were shot down in droves. Only six torpedo planes survived. In squadron 8, only the famous Ensign Gay survived. But now, with the Japanese fighters at low altitude, they were unable to attack the dive bombers which were soon arriving at a high altitude in force. At 1100 the Soryu was again hit by dive bombers from Yorktown and Enterprise. Hiryu, another Japanese carrier, had proceeded northeast some 80 miles when attacked by planes from Enterprise and later on the 7th, sank. But Yorktown was repeatedly hit and later rolled over and sank. As for the Japanese, four aircraft carriers had been sunk (Cooney 1965, 276 and Natkiel 1986, 78-79).

The battle proved to be the turning point of the war for the U.S. Navy, although details were censored at the time. The US public only knew that a great battle had been fought and the Japanese had been stopped in their eastward advance.

Astonishingly, the Japanese did not suspect that their ciphers were compromised and continued to use the JN-25 code. This was a mistake that cost them dearly in the years to come.

* * * * * * * * * * * *

Turning back to the early days of the Russian Communist struggle to take over the power of the Czar, we find Vladimir I.U. Lenin a leading figure in this difficult quest. A former school teacher and later director of schools in the Simbirsk (Uljanovsk) region of the upper Volga, he took part in the abortive revolution of 1905, which only led to his momentary departure to Finland.

Lenin made it clear to his constituents that revolution was the only way to obtain Communist domination of Russia. As a member of the Bolshevik faction which advocated the overthrow of capitalism, he was confronted by the Mensheviks, who favored a gradual change to Socialism. But at a conference held in 1912, the people in Lenin's party succeeded in shutting out the Mensheviks. When WW I began in 1914, Lenin, at the "Second International" accused the Socialist parties, who wanted to join the war against Germany, of betraying the idea of International Socialism and called for a revolution against the Czarist government. When that revolution broke out in 1917 in the midst of WW I, Lenin fled to Switzerland, then a neutral country.

German Intelligence was aware of Lenin's adventures and his recent stay in Switzerland. It then conceived a plan to overthrow the Czarist government in Moscow and stop the Russian armies from fighting. This was to allow Lenin and his Bolshevist cohorts in exile to cross Germany in a sealed train in the greatest of secrecy, then to travel through Sweden and Finland to Moscow, this to take place in July of 1917. Lenin had made it clear that he wanted the war ended and acceded to the plan.

Nevertheless, when this scheme had been carried out, the war between Germany and Russia was not ended and Lenin had to go again to Finland, then on returning to Russia, to be jailed. But the revolution did finally come to pass in November, 1917. (Details of this plan are given by Crozier, ibid., p. 9.) During July, Lenin had been arrested, but escaped to a secret hiding place from which he could lead an armed revolution. This succeeded and in November, he became Chairman of the new Communist government.

One of Lenin's more difficult problems was to blend together the various "Soviets" of the new Republic. Only by July of 1918 did his government decide on a constitution which applied to the Russian Federated Socialist Republic, including the vast territory of Siberia. Yet Ukraine, Belorussia, and Transcaucasia were still independent states allied loosely to the Russian Republic by various treaties. In December of 1922, the First Congress of Soviets of the Union of Soviet Socialist Republics (USSR) met in Moscow to agree to a union, while for the first time, many Russians would hear the name of Joseph Stalin. Stalin was an assumed name, appropriately meaning "steel." He had been made Secretary of the Communist Party and was now to become Commissar of Nationalities, and thus Commissar of the various Commissariats in the USSR. At about this same time, Lenin's health was beginning to fail him and his illness led to his death in 1924. This caused a severe national crisis, although already a "proletarian dictatorship" had been formed to secure "Soviet Democracy." It was then largely in the hands of the Bolsheviks who hoped to spread their ideals for revolution all over the world. But this was manifestly disappointed in Germany when the Communists were put down by the rising power of German National Socialism and many other parties with somewhat similar aims.

Lenin warned his followers about Stalin's inclination to abuse power, but when the Stalinist faction defeated his opponent Trotsky – and eventually had him murdered – he transformed the party into a monolith of power, ruthless in his schemes to industrialize the USSR, collectivize agriculture by force (something already urged by Lenin), and stamp out any opposition by sending thousands to the gulags in Siberia's wasteland where they worked themselves to death building railroads, cutting down forests, and doing the hardest of menial labor.

* * * * * * * * * * * *

Under Stalin's aegis the secret services flourished with the GRU (Chief Intelligence Directorate of the General Staff) and NKVD (Secret Police) the latter becoming the KGB (Committee for State Security) in later years, exerting their power ruthlessly and spreading their tentacles all over the world. Vassily Zarubin was a good example of the coming breed of those sent abroad to spy, manipulate, and create their own networks of spies (Romerstein and Breindel 2000, 3-4). An old Cheka man who worked under Lenin in 1920, Zarubin came to the US in 1934. But when WW II broke on Europe, he became involved in the "dirty work" of the NKVD, carrying on many interrogations of Polish prisoners up until 1940. It was evidently on orders from Stalin for the NKVD to murder 15,000 Polish prisoners of war via the direction of Lavrenti Beria, Stalin's hatchet man. In all, nearly 22,000 were shot and buried in mass graves, as mentioned before.

Many of the early Soviet visitors to the US were not illegals, and some had legitimate jobs as journalists and the like. Later on, an illegal "Rezidentura" was set up in the US with Iskhak Akhmerov, Rezident in charge working with Zarubin (Romerstein and Breindel 2000, 34-35). Akhmerov had joined the OGPU (originally Cheka) back in 1930 and in 1934 was assigned to the US. By 1935, Akhmerov was active as a spy in the States and became intimately acquainted with Earl Browder of the US Communist Party. Connections to Moscow could be made via telegrams enciphered with the One-Time Pad which remained unbroken for many more years.

During much of the 1930s in America when many were trying to recover from the Great Depression, Soviet operatives had arrived, looking for left-wing-minded young men to more or less absorb into the Communist fold and work for Moscow. All this was being monitored by a supersecret US organization called "Venona."

One of these people was the young Laurence Duggan, drawn to Communism by his liberal training and by the aura of Roosevelt's socialist policies such as the "New Deal." Before long, he was recruited and handled by Mr. Akhmerov, who already had taken into his little cell others sympathetic to the Soviet Union's aims. Before long, Duggan was able to give up information gleaned from his New Deal friends in Washington, D.C., such as US diplomatic dispatches and comments made at meetings.

But before long a defector from the NKVD began to reveal facts about Duggan among several others. This was Ignaz Reiss who was promptly done away with by a squad led by the later well-known Sudoplatov, expert at such things.

While the terrible 1936-1939 pogroms (massacres of suspected people) went on in the Soviet Union, Duggan quickly lost some of his enthusiasm for his new job. But Akhmerov, informed of Reiss's murder, continued to work with Duggan who evidently relented and continued to work for the USSR, having obtained a job working for the State Department's Latin American division (Weinstein and Vassiliev 1999, 10-11).

All apparently went well until the spring of 1939 when the State Department began to deny information to Duggan. Later on in that year he was told to find another job. This he did and began working in connection with Secretary of State Hull. Feeling a certain amount of heat, although having a low opinion of the FBI, he quit the State Department and joined a UN Relief Administration effort as an advisor. But after the FBI questioned him in 1948 about Alger Hiss of the State Department, only nine days later he was found dead in the street, evidently having fallen 16 stories from his window (Weinstein and Vassiliev 1999, 21). Whether this was a suicide or he had some help from others remains unknown.

In September of 1944 while the World War still went furiously on to its final fiery ear-splitting conclusion, the intricate espionage apparatus set up by the USSR in America suffered a serious setback. Igor Sergeievitch Gouzenko, a cipher clerk in the Soviet Embassy in Ottawa,

Canada, received orders from Moscow to return to the USSR. Knowing what often happened to those sent back to the USSR from clandestine work abroad, he decided not to go, but take his wife and small child into hiding in Canada. Choosing an opportune time, September 6, 1945, almost the same time as the end of the US-Japanese war, he made his dangerous move. He simply walked out of the embassy carrying a paper bag full of vital documents from the embassy files.

On returning to his apartment, he barely had time to lock the door before two burly agents from the Soviet consulate came stamping up the stairs and demanded to be let in. Fortunately, Gouzenko's neighbor, a Canadian Air Force man, gave him refuge and the two finally gave up and left.

Later at a local police station, he refused to talk until the police could provide reliable Canadian authorities. When this was finally achieved, he began to reveal a litany of information related to atom bomb secrets. One person exposed was Allan Nunn May, a nuclear physicist, plus nine others. May was arrested in 1946 using the code name ALEK (Polmar and Allen 1997, 239). There were other revelations on Soviet espionage produced at length in the next few weeks.

One of the exposures produced was the probably identity of "ELLIE," a name that kept appearing in decrypts produced by Venona. Tentatively, it was the code name of Kay Willsher, a Canadian government secretary. A more important revelation produced by Gouzenko was that an extensive espionage ring was working in Canada, sending information through the Canadian Soviet embassy to Moscow. One man in question was found to be a GRU "rezident" in Ottawa: Nikolai Zabotin, director of that spy ring.

A Canadian Intelligence officer soon visited President Truman in Washington D.C. to try and convince him of the seriousness of Soviet penetration into North America. At first Truman was reluctant to understand the importance of the Gouzenko case, but in time the president was impressed and decided to do something about it. It proved to be the beginning of a long struggle to ferret out the pro-Soviet Communists in the United States.

Although the lid was thus coming off the Soviet spy rings in the United States and Canada, Soviet spying in Europe never became known in detail until 1963. One of the most important spy rings there was centered in Switzerland, remaining neutral throughout WW II. This was the so-called Rote Kapelle or Red Orchestra. It was only one of three big spy rings in Europe, but was probably the most effective of all.

The Red Orchestra consisted of several spy cells in Germany and had as many as several hundred members. Many were exposed by the Abwehr early in the war and either turned around or simply killed. But the most durable ring was that called "Lucy" in Switzerland (Norman 1973, 140-143).

The ring was run by a Hungarian named Rado, code name: Dora. Messages were sent to Moscow by radio in enciphered code from one of two places: Lausanne or Lucerne, usually in groups of numbers which remained undecipherable for several years. Messages were converted from English language reports through a complex of encipherments so that at the time their code was unbreakable.

From 1940 to 1942, almost all German military moves and often the plans for these moves were sent to Moscow. Although the crucial warning to the USSR that the Wehrmacht would soon invade Russia was sent, Stalin chose not to believe it, possibly because he thought he was being sent false information. Perhaps he thought that the international character of the ring was suspicious in itself. The gang consisted of Rudolf Roessler, a German, Alexander Foote, an Englishman, Rado the Hungarian, and Lucy, real name Karl Sedlacek, a Czech military intelligence officer (Polmar and Allen 1997, 343).

Rado and his friends kept up their clandestine game until late in the war. By this time there was pressure on the Swiss government to end the operation. Using radio direction finders from two different locations, they could draw on a map the two directions, and where they crossed was their transmitter. Also they occasionally shut off the electric power to certain parts of Lucerne or Lausanne to find out when the signal from the transmitter dropped out. Swiss police then decided to raid their location and caught the lot of them, complete with their cipher system, messages to be sent, and those received.

After the war, Rado was thanked by Stalin, although he had the Hungarian put in prison soon afterwards, Rado staying there until 1953 when Stalin died. It seemed to be the modus operandi of Stalin that whether a man was trusted or not it was best to be rid of him, often for no reason at all (Grant 1989, 83).

* * * * * * * * * * * *

With the end of the war coming in sight and Allied landings made in June and July 1944 in France, OSS (Office of Strategic Services) men were slipping into France via neutral Switzerland. By 1945, following the failed bomb plot led by Klaus von Stauffenberg, Hitler gave up his reliance on the German military command and depended almost entirely on the SS to carry out his policies. By mid-1945, German General Karl Wolff, Supreme Commander of the SS in Italy, strove to end the war by agreeing with the Allies to declare an armistice.

But Field Marshal Albert Kesselring, in charge of southern European operations, explained to Wolff that he, Kesselring, owed his rank to Adolf Hitler and besides, there were two well-armed SS divisions behind him to make sure he carried out Hitler's orders. Then in March of 1945, it became evident to Wolff that Heinrich Himmler, overall head of the SS and Ernst Kaltenbruner, a faithful National Socialist, knew about Wolff's dealings with Allen Dulles, an officer of the OSS.

Hitler, meanwhile, kept talking about the development of a "wonder weapon" to end the war in Germany's favor. This could have been the atomic, or "implosion" bomb. The Germans had built a plant for production of heavy water (D_2O) in Norway, but a British commando squad had attacked it and blew it up. D_2O was used in the production of fissile material for the atomic bomb or for other purposes.

By mid-1945 Wolff was striving to end the war with the Allies, but Heinrich Himmler, overall head of the SS, somehow got wind of what Wolff was doing and asked him to come to Berlin to do some explaining. Meanwhile, Germany's Foreign Minister Joachim von Ribbentrop was making overtures to the Russians in meetings in Stockholm but without success, later hung after conviction by a postwar jury for his troubles.

By August 12th, 1945, the date when Roosevelt died, Wolff decided to tell Himmler that he was seeking an honorable end to the war. Following Himmler's order, he flew to Berlin, avoiding many hostile aircraft and met with Hitler. Himmler himself was trying to make connections through Sweden with Count Bernadotte for a peace agreement. Meanwhile Wolff arrived at Hitler's bunker in Berlin. At first Hitler berated Wolff for a "colossal disregard of authority," but then listened to Wolff's explanations and let him go. Wolff survived the war but as most of us know, Hitler committed suicide in his bunker. For a detailed account, see Dulles's book "Secret Surrender," Harper & Row, N.Y. 1966.

Chapter 3

The New Enemy: The Soviet Union

With World War II coming to its bloody, ruinous end, Americans generally felt they had won while the Germans and Japanese had lost. This simplistic view ignored the fact that the Soviet Union had taken over much of Europe including eastern Germany, Czechoslovakia, Hungary, Bulgaria, and Albania as well as Manchuria, Southern Sakhalin, and the Kurile Islands. Most Americans, if they knew of it, assumed that the USSR would be content with all this success. Yet what Americans did not understand was that the Soviet takeover of eastern Europe while meddling in the Middle East, was merely the beginning of an attempt to control all of Europe and eventually the whole world. The Germans of Hitler's time once had a marching song that included the words: "Heute Deutschland und Morgen die ganze Welt!" (today Germany and tomorrow the whole world). Now it was the turn of the USSR to follow these unwritten aims.

When the war was finally ending, Roosevelt, Churchill, and Stalin went through their much-publicized charade at Yalta by the Black Sea. Stalin was said to have worried that the British might team up with the Germans. However, the condition in Britain of acute Germanophobia that grew up during the ruinous war, made it highly unlikely that Britain would join with an exhausted Germany against the USSR. It was with this, and a philosophy of World Communism that a number of young Brits undertook to spy for the USSR, which some had already done.

Steeped in the radical theories of Marx and Engels in their schooling, they envisioned a new world controlled by Communism that would bring peace and contentment to everyone for evermore. Initially there were four of these Britons that later bore famous —or infamous — names: Kim Philby, Donald Maclean, Guy Burgess, and Anthony Blunt, called the "Cambridge Four." Later on, two other Britons were added: John Cairncross, sometimes called the "Fifth man," and later on a sixth man, or woman, were initially unearthed by the American Venona decrypts.

By 1944, Philby had been made head of Britain's "Section IX" for anti-Soviet Counter Intelligence while retaining his deep belief in Communism. Philby had been involved in the Spanish civil war in the early 1930s, making out that he was assisting the right wing General Franco, supported by the Germans and Italians with money and weapons. Philby's activity was evidently planned as a cover for his real connections to the USSR which were expanded later on.

Besides Philby in Counter Intelligence, the other three of the four were well placed to glean information for the Soviet Union: Maclean as First Secretary to the British Embassy in Washington D.C., Burgess with the British Foreign Office, and Blunt in the Joint Intelligence Committee of MI5. MI stood for Military Intelligence and the whole code-word MI5 was considered "Counter Intelligence," while MI6 was supposed to handle "Foreign Intelligence."

In 1945, Blunt either began to have qualms about feeding information to the USSR or to escape the tension involved in spying, he took on the position of "Surveyor of the King's Pictures," a relatively relaxing profession. The other three only became more deeply involved in espionage.

The "Cambridge Four" had a lot in common. They all had attended Trinity College in Cambridge, England, a few years before WW II and had been members of the exclusive "Apostles" club. Maclean was appointed in 1944 to the British Embassy in Washington, D.C. A handsome young man bearing some resemblance to James Bond of film fame, he probably was influenced toward working for the Soviets by his close friend Guy Burgess. Guy, in the early years of his work, was a boyish appearing young man with a manner that belied his combative nature. In fact it was Burgess who helped to recruit his friends into working for the USSR. But Burgess had a way of often falling out with his superiors, while keeping his secret position of feeding information to the USSR. For years he went undetected (Grant 1989, 83).

In the meantime, Blunt had developed a close relationship with the

Royal family, and prided himself in showing the Queen herself through the galleries as "Surveyor of Pictures." He not only developed a close relation with the Royal family, but unlike the other three, Blunt managed to keep his cover for some three decades after WW II. Yet he was finally arrested while trying to load up his car for a fast escape, probably on the ferry to France.

When the Gouzenko case broke about the time that the war was coming to an end in 1945, the various Soviet spy rings in the US and Canada went into a state of panic, Gouzenko destroying much of their webs of espionage. While Gouzenko was being questioned in Canada, an MI6 representative at the meetings sent his reports to Philby. These included the exposure of Nikolai Zabotin a "Rezident," and Allan Nunn May, a nuclear physicist. Fortunately for Philby, Gouzenko did not mention him in his revelations.

Philby had initially married a Soviet sympathizer: Litzi Friedman and it seemed to be no problem that she was suspected of spying for the USSR (Page, Leitch, and Knightley 1968, 53). After divorcing her, he met, lived with, and then married Aileen Furse, producing three children. That Philby was already working his machinations with the USSR, went unnoticed after his assignment to Istanbul under the aegis of MI6. He then proceeded to reveal to the USSR the names of several British agents working for MI6 who had been sent into the USSR. This resulted in the disappearance and probably deaths of those agents. Yet MI6 did not get the word and following this, he was posted to Washington D.C. as MI6's liaison to the CIA and FBI. It was there that Philby became acquainted with James Jesus Angleton, chief of the CIA's Counter Intelligence. Philby had already known Angleton in London and were by now old friends.

Finally in 1950 the British Foreign Office sent Burgess to Washington where initially he went to live with Philby. By then Maclean, in London, had taken to drinking and was talking too much in bars and other public places. But Venona was working its wiles and warned MI5 that a certain "Homer" seemed to have connections to the USSR. Venona decrypts indicated that Homer was the code name for Maclean. How the Soviets got wind of this can only be guessed at, but they sent Burgess to Maclean to warn him of developments and plan an escape to the East. In May of 1951 the British Foreign Office gave MI5 permission to cross-examine Maclean. But Burgess acted fast to find Maclean at his home in Surrey and plan for the two of them to take the ferry at Southhampton for France, thence to the USSR.

As a result, Philby was recalled to Britain to answer some pertinent questions. By now he had been given the thumbs down by the head of the CIA, Bedell Smith. Yet Philby stood the gaff and denied all accusations. All this time, Philby was completely unknown to the US and British public.

Another interesting case of spying for the Soviet Union was that of Elizabeth Bentley. This was of sufficient importance to transcend the difficult and persistent other Soviet attempts to spy on the United States during and just after WW II. From 1938 to 1944 she took US government documents and passed them on to her lover Jacob Golos, a US citizen although only recently immigrated from Russia (Polmar and Allen 1997, 56).

Elizabeth had joined the Communist party USA while Golos worked for the "Society for Technical Aid to the USSR," which was actually deep in industrial espionage. As for Elizabeth, she was then working for the Soviet NKGB, although she seems to have heartily disliked it, mainly working for Iskhak Akhmerov. He was quoted as saying Bentley was a "rather complicated and controversial character," although much admiring her, calling her a "tall and strong beauty."

In March of 1944, she met up with Earl Browder, head of the Communist Party USA and was told to make contact with other Communist agents (Weinstein and Vassiliev 1999, 97). But the NKVD operatives in New York City and Washington complained about the openness of her approach to Browder who was under some degree of surveillance by the FBI. Browder evidently tried to convince her to focus more on espionage and not on "business connections," like those to the US Shipping Corporation which was by now a front for Communist activity (Weinstein and Vassiliev 1999, 99).

Elizabeth's apparent restlessness led the Soviet powers-that-be in the US to try and find a suitable mate for her, urging her to accede. It was hoped this would have the effect of calming her down since she was getting "careless" in her many activities.

Bentley's casualness toward her work, along with her admitted need for male company, may have led her to become romantically interested in a Peter Heller, a reserve officer in the US Army (Weinstein and Vassiliev 1999, 100). Evidently unknown to her, he was in some way connected to the FBI. As a result, there was talk in Soviet Intelligence of deporting Bentley to the USSR. Heller, meanwhile, tried to interest her in working for the FBI while her handler Gorsky told Moscow she had gone too far and they could no longer rely on her. As might be expected,

Moscow authorities began to think of ways to "eliminate" her. But Bentley was already beginning to cooperate with the FBI. Naturally, she was asked by Gorsky about her association with Heller, while Gorsky himself had apparently been put under surveillance by US authorities. Bentley was said at the time to have called the Russians "gangsters, only caring for Russia."

Into this increasingly tense situation, came one "Kim" Philby who quickly informed the New York Soviet station chief about Gorsky's difficulties with Bentley. The FBI's Hoover then informed Stephenson (mentioned before in this chronicle) as MI6 representative in the US, about Bentley's possible defection.

In November of 1945, Bentley went direct to the FBI and talked, revealing her activities with the Global Tourist Corporation (actually run by Golos), also about the Shipping Company (Weinstein and Vassiliev 1999, 104). All this information went as high up the Soviet hierarchy as Stalin himself. All station chiefs were told to cease connections with all persons known to Bentley and all KGB activity in the US stopped. This move was apparently made to keep "Homer" (Donald Maclean) intact and in place. Meanwhile Gorsky asked for "liquidation" of Bentley. After considering many different schemes of assassination, nothing came of it, apparently on order of Stalin's man Beria who had his own reasons for not upsetting the Soviet espionage apple cart.

* * * * * * * * * * * * * * * *

In the last few months of WW II and leading into the postwar period, the atomic bomb was the subject of intense activity among the various Soviet spies. One of the most diligent of these was Emil Julius Klaus Fuchs. The name Fuchs was appropriate since the word means "fox" in English. He was one of the most active people working with others on the atomic bomb as well as working secretly for the USSR.

Born in Germany, he took an early interest in physics but also in politics as he emerged from the local "Gymnasium." He became interested in the German Socialist Party and later joined the German Communist Party, soon to be outlawed by the rising tide of National Socialism under Hitler. A wanted man, he escaped Germany to Britain where he continued his studies in physics to achieve a doctorate in 1936. (Polmar and Allen 1997, 223) But when the war came in 1939 he found himself an alien in Britain, his new country. Along with many others he was packed off to a British concentration camp and later sent to Canada.

Yet somehow he escaped to return to Britain where he and some fellow Germans worked on the British atomic bomb project. Later he became a British citizen, but his communist sympathies led him into linking up with the Soviet GRU, sending them reports via a courier (Polmar and Allen 1997, 224).

In 1943, with World War II at its peak, he went with a British group to the US to work on the atomic bomb. At Oak Ridge, TN, he met with those who were overseeing the building of the gaseous diffusion plant, an enormously long building that survived for many years after the war. The purpose of the building was to separate uranium 235 from uranium 238. From this was produced plutonium 239, the material that became the atomic bomb, set off by a powerful implosion from exploding dynamite, sometimes called the "implosion bomb."

Fuchs was not content to assist the British-American effort, and in 1944 began to seek connections with Soviet espionage in America. In late 1945, Fuchs left the US for England where the NKGB made contact with him in 1946 after the German Communist network restored communications with him (Weinstein and Vassiliev 1999, 311-312). Fuchs's courier for feeding information to the USSR on the atomic bomb was Harry Gold who later was to fall under the scrutiny of the FBI.

Fuchs next appeared in Los Alamos, NM, and was able to contact Gold in Santa Fe, giving him details of the A-bomb. About this time the FBI was wondering why Fuchs was going off on so many trips, some to New York City. In 1949, Venona analyses identified Fuchs as the most important spy that they had revealed (Grant 1989, 92). Yet Fuchs in 1950 had left for Britain to assist in the British attempt to build the A-bomb. It was about this time that the FBI received enough information from Venona to label Fuchs as a spy for the Soviet Union. Fuchs was also involved in the development of the "thermonuclear" or hydrogen bomb, combining deuterium with tritium gas, set off by an implosion. On 8/12/53, such a bomb was exploded, yielding a force of 400 kilotons.

The British authorities, meanwhile, were ready to call in Fuchs for questioning and already in 1949, William J. Skardon of MI5, who bore a remarkable resemblance to the TV British detective associated with "Hercule Poirot" the French master sleuth, patiently examined Fuchs at length. After many long conversations, Skardon convinced Fuchs that it would be best to tell all. Fuchs then fingered Gold and others in the Soviet spy apparatus in the US, including Julius Rosenberg who stole a highly important radar secret for the USSR. Yet after a term in prison, Fuchs survived all this and in 1959 was made Director of the Central Institute for Nuclear Physics in West Germany.

Soviet penetration of US government activities had gone on even before WW II, as previously mentioned. Meanwhile, President Franklin Roosevelt's "soft on Russia" attitude, plus the naive, or purposeful, activities of his wife Eleanor had encouraged the penetration of Soviet spying into the US government. In time, Alger Hiss of the State Department was under much suspicion, while clinging stubbornly to his innocence into old age and along with Elizabeth Bentley was the subject of much controversy in the US media. While Bentley had confessed, Hiss insisted on his innocence, at one time explaining his mysterious trips into the swamps near the Potomac river as merely bird expeditions while seeking to find the wily Prothonotary Swamp Warbler that appeared there every spring. But Bentley was more interested in men than song birds and did her own singing for all to hear.

On July 31, 1948, Bentley and another alleged spy Whittaker Chambers, appeared before the House Committee on Un-American Activities to describe the depths of Soviet spying in the US and the activities of the NKVD. Led by the stubborn and articulate Senator Joseph McCarthy, the committee brought before it all kinds of people. Hardly a day went by into 1950 when the radio waves were not filled with the doings of the committee and the shouts of Joe McCarthy: "Point of Order!" in trying to stop the rude expostulations of the liberal politicians. Some State Department officials tried to refute McCarthy's attempts to expose those working clandestinely for the USSR. And McCarthy too was publicly attacked, then in later years seemed drained and often ill before he died May 2, 1957 (Herman 2000, 119).

Whitaker Chambers turned out to have a long and deep attachment to Soviet espionage, going back to 1932 when he was recruited by someone in the Communist Party USA (CPUSA) (Weinstein and Vassiliev 1999, 38, 41). Chambers, a plumpish man who often wore, as many men did in those days, a felt hat and seemed constantly glancing to the right or left, was dreaming by 1934 of penetrating the mysteries of the various US military organizations. Apparently he acted mainly as a courier for the GRU, working closely with Hiss, some of their material coming from Harry Dexter White in the State Department. But by 1947, Chambers began planning his defection and became a major source of knowledge about Soviet spying in the US. When Chambers was asked by his superiors in Moscow to come for a debriefing, he decided to defect, planning it carefully with certain others. Chambers later was hired by Time magazine and became an editor. He finally retired to a farm in

Maryland.

* * * * * * * * * * * * * *

By June of 1948, friction between the USSR and the western powers: Britain, France, and the US, was beginning to produce so much heat that many observers thought it could turn into war. The Soviet government made out that it had been insulted by the western powers concerning Berlin. As a result, the USSR initiated the "Berlin blockade," in which rail, road, and waterway access to Berlin from the West was severed. As bait to gain their ends, the USSR offered to supply the Berlin inhabitants through East Germany with food and other supplies if the western powers pulled out from that city —otherwise Berliners would run out of food and fuel.

Although President Truman's cabinet counselled caution, Truman felt that Berlin must be supported. In the meantime General Clay, in charge of US forces in West Germany, without consulting his superiors, began sending supplies by air to that city. But Truman did not reprimand Clay and gave him the go-ahead for an immense airlift of supplies into Berlin, assisted by the British Airforce.

The fuel consisted mostly of coal, brought in at the rate of two tons per aircraft on transport planes, flown from various parts of the US to Germany and to France. The Soviet reply to all this was promptly to encorporate their Berlin sector with East Germany (Gelb 1986, 35-36).

The Berlin airlift went on all through the winter of 1948-49, often interrupted by bad weather: fog, mist, snow, and cold. Sometimes the airplanes would take off from West Germany then be unable to land at one of the three airports. In this case they could either return to West Germany or to southern France where they could land safely. The Germans were jubilant; the Soviets privately dismayed. By spring, some 2,300,000 tons of supplies had been ferried into Berlin in 276,926 flights. Following talks in May of 1949 between US and Soviet delegates in the UN Security Council, the USSR agreed to lift the blockade, although the airlift went on until September 30, 1949 (Prittie 1973, 516).

Also by about this time, the USSR had successfully constructed a workable atomic bomb, probably known to Morris Childs, FBI man Hoover's spy in Moscow. Childs had been a trusted Soviet devotee, but turned coat in 1946 to assist the FBI in reporting on the atom bomb threat (Romerstein and Breindel 2000, 459).

When the USSR decided to include their East Berlin zone into the

Deutsche Demokratische Republik (DDR), Berlin was basically submerged in that DDR. In spite of this, Berlin remained a gateway to the West through which floods of refugees poured. One West German told the writer in Germany about this time: "The difference between the Russian zone and the western ones was the difference between night and day, the Russian zone clearly in the dark."

Even so, West Germany was also in poor condition. The writer, who had gone in 1950 to study at the University of Munich, found a generally impoverished populace. Despite an American Army plan to feed the Germans in the American sector, food was a scarce item. The Army plan was evidently to start rations at a low level, then gradually increase them with the idea that there would he less complaining. Yet there were signs of bombing everywhere, while the aim of many was to leave Germany, preferably for America. In Britain, things were not much better, giving rise to the German saying: "England hat auch den Krieg verloren." (England also lost the war.)

* * * * * * * * * * * *

In June of 1950 Americans found themselves suddenly involved in a war in Korea. The causes of this war were little understood by most all Americans and it seemed too far away to be of much importance. Before the end of WW II, Korea had belonged to Japan, but in a conference in Cairo, the British, Chinese, and Americans announced that when WWII had ended, Korea should be made free and independent. This was called the "Cairo Declaration," reaffirmed in Potsdam in July of 1945. However, the USSR had managed to butt in, persuading the Allies that Soviet troops should accept surrender of the Japanese north of the 38th parallel, a temporary line of demarcation. Following this, the USSR refused to accept the Cairo declaration. By 1947, the UN established a temporary commission to hold elections, but the Russians would not allow UN people into North Korea from the zone in the south. While the United Nations placed the capital at Seoul, they claimed all of Korea was included. But again the USSR, mainly in the form of Stalin, declared all this illegal and North Korea subject to the USSR as a "puppet state," its capital to be at P'yongyang. To pacify the UN, the USSR claimed that they had withdrawn all their troops. Yet they had left "advisors" for the new North Korean army. The North Koreans then launched a campaign of propaganda and sabotage against the South.

Secretly, Stalin and Mao Tsetung agreed to try and unify Korea while the USSR built up a modern military force there of some 10 divisions (10,000 to a division), as well as Russian-built tanks and the latest aircraft. These airplanes were flown, it was found out years later, by Russian pilots in the war-to-come in June of 1950. The pilots were instructed not to admit their Soviet nationality if shot down and captured.

On June 25, 1950, seven infantry divisions of North Korean troops with Soviet-built tanks suddenly burst across the 38th parallel. In only a few days they were in Seoul (Natkiel 1986, 142). American forces in neighboring Japan were quickly alerted and soon transported by U.S. Navy troopships and other warships to Korea. These troops, used to the soft life in Japan, were hardly ready to be thrown into a World War-like hell of fire and brimstone. The best they could do was to make a gradual retreat to the southern end of South Korea and await better equipment and more men.

There was, nevertheless, a well-kept secret that was soon to turn the war around in favor of the Allies, later including British and Turkish forces along with US and South Korean troops. Conceived and carried out by General MacArthur, despite the doubts and resistance of the powers-that-be in Washington, the plan was to land US and Korean marines at Inchon just west of Seoul, then cut in and cut off the North Korean troops that had invaded southward almost to Pusan on the southern tip of Korea. With the assistance of the U.S. Navy, the landing was so timed to come at high tide, thus escaping the extensive mud-flats on the coast at low tide. It proved to be a shattering blow to the North Korean troops, many of whom barely escaped to the north (Dupuy 1973, 470).

Another well-kept secret of the war was one involving the Chinese who planned, at the urging of the USSR, to make a sudden drive south into Korea. In December of 1950, some 300,000 troops, called the "Chinese People's Volunteers," (a cover name for regular troops), struck suddenly across the Chinese-Korean border and drove south a few miles beyond the 38th parallel in January of 1951.

Only by July 27, 1953 did the ruinous, bloody war end with a cease-fire agreement. The Chinese had suffered as many 2 million casualties (Natkiel 1986, 147), the UN troops having literally slaughtered them in their attacks. Stalin was said to have been shattered by the outcome of the war when the Chinese were so badly mauled and turned back.

Soon after General Eisenhower had become President of the United States in January of 1953, strikes and riots were beginning in East Berlin by workers of various professions (Crozier 1999, 162). By June, things had quieted down, but only after severe penalties were put on the strike leaders. There were rumors at the time that Stalin was extremely ill and on September 17 Joseph Vissarionovitch Dzhugashvilli, known as Stalin, died of a brain hemorrhage at the Kremlin in Moscow. Soon afterward, one Nikita Khrushchev established a department for "terrorist operations" on the capitalist states, including a mention of carrying out assassinations of enemies of the USSR. It was not long until Khrushchev became, for better or worse, the new Soviet dictator (Crozier 1999, 79).

* * * * * * * * * * * * *

The Vietnam problem, as it became in the halls of the US government, grew gradually over the years to entangle other foreign countries, especially the US. The geographical area known as Vietnam (The "Southern Land") had a long history said to go back at least to the days when China was expanding, hundreds of years ago. Towards the end of the 15th century when Columbus thought he had discovered the "Spice Islands," Vasco da Gama of Portugal sailed eastward to S.E. Asia in search of gold and spices and possibly to convert the natives to Christianity. He succeeded in arriving at least, and even sailed up the Chinese coast to establish trading centers, an extraordinary feat for that age.

In later years during the time of Napoleon III, the French came to search for treasures and "colonize" what was then called "Cochinchina". Striking into what is now North Vietnam, they discovered the fertile Red River valley and claimed it (Karnow 1983, 53, 66).

After WW II when the Japanese had come and gone, there was a growing mood in Vietnam, Laos, Cambodia, and Thailand (Siam) to win independence from foreign control. Communism then spread into those countries and began to have the influence to encourage the natives to drive out the French and their Catholic religion. But the French brought in troops to fight many difficult battles with the Communist-influenced natives. Finally, at the battle of Dien Bien Phu in northern Vietnam, the natives, with assistance from the Chinese Communists in the form of artillery and ammunition, finally defeated the French in that battle in 1954. The French, supported by some volunteer ex-Wehrmacht troops, had hoped for support from US aircraft, but it never came.

Apparently, France's Mendes-France, a radical Socialist then in power, wanted to end the war. The idea of German troops supporting the French was not to his liking (Crozier 1999, 128). At the same time it was Eisenhower who refused to send US aircraft to Vietnam, although stating that southeast Asia was of "crucial importance" to the US. As a result of all this, the French agreed to partition Vietnam, the Communists to the north of the 17th parallel and the Vietnamese Nationalists to the south, according to the Geneva Conference.

The North Vietnamese revolutionists then undertook to destroy the "foreign imperialists" beginning a campaign of murder or incarceration of those that had supported the French (Karnow 1983, 224). Few in America knew anything about this at the time, and the pogroms went on for many months in North Vietnam. Also unknown in the US, and probably much of Europe, a large number of South Vietnamese were being trained in North Vietnam for guerilla fighting against the powers that be. These guerillas later secretly returned to South Vietnam, mostly via the Ho Chi Minh trail in Laos with the plan to kill government officials, calling themselves "Viet Cong" (Viet Communists). Behind all this was the USSR (Karnow 1983, 228).

Thus began a civil war that seemed to have no end. Actually it was partly a war to cast out foreign influence and partly to spread Communism to the south.

No precise date can be given for the start of the Vietnam war, but generalized fighting began in 1957 (Crozier 1999, 244). About this time a US military mission was established in Saigon, South Vietnam, strictly in an advisory capacity for about a decade thereafter. Also in the 1950s, when John F. Kennedy was elected as a Senator from Massachusetts, he made some broad comments about how the US should defend southeast Asia against the Communists. Kennedy said: "Now we have a problem in making our power credible and Vietnam is the Place" (Karnow 1983, 247). Yet MacArthur warned Kennedy against committing soldiers to the Asian mainland and then in early 1962, Kennedy recommended a policy of "peaceful negotiations," according to Theodore Sorensen in his massive book: "Kennedy" (p. 640).

In February, 1965, the "second" Vietnam war began when President Johnson made the anguished decision to send US forces to defend South Vietnam from the obvious aggressions by Viet Cong (Viet Communist) forces. Although a Demilitarized Zone (the DMZ) was formed to prevent an invasion from the north, it was conveniently ignored by the Communists. At the same time, all sorts of restrictions were put on the US forces under General Westmorland. Certain areas in North Vietnam were outlawed as possible bombing targets. Not only the center of Hanoi was taboo, where small arms were manufactured, but more importantly Haiphong seaport was out of bounds for the bombers. The seaport was of extreme importance since Soviet war supplies were poured in for the great benefit of the North Vietnamese troops. This remarkable situation was generally ignored by the liberal US media which was against the war from the start.

Not surprisingly, many young American men saw no purpose in going off to fight a futile war on the other side of the world. This attitude led many of them to defy the draft, rioting, and even migrating to Canada. Yet generally unknown in the US, the North Vietnamese were forced to apply Communist theory and turn over large landholdings to peasants who then farmed small parts of their former employers' lands. Like the Kulaks of the Ukraine who were forced to give up their big farms to their former workers or face being killed, the Vietnamese that balked against these Communist measures were likewise executed (Karnow 1983, 225).

Early in the war in the late 1950s, the Communist leader Ho Chi Minh warned his forces against making armed attacks on the Diem regime in South Vietnam. He also claimed that rash attacks on the South, while calling for a general uprising, would be "jumping the gun" and putting the Minh forces in too much danger.

As 1959 went into 1961, attacks against South Vietnam government officials increased and forced many like the Catholics, into enclaves where they surrounded themselves with barbed wire and block houses placed at strategic locations. Then by 1960 the Ho Chi Minh faction in the north formed a new organization to pursue the war more vigorously while giving up much of their guerilla tactics. This was the NFLSV or National Front for the Liberation of South Vietnam, although they tried to pass it off as autonomous and unrelated to the Communists in North Vietnam.

During the early 1960s the attention of Americans was absorbed in the latest Berlin crisis engineered by the USSR, then by the Kennedy assassination in 1963. As much for this reason, plus the masterful chicanery of the North Vietnamese, the war went progressively against the US, (Crozier 1999, 243) still handicapped by bans on bombing certain regions of North Vietnam.

In 1964, the event of the Tonkin Gulf hit the US media, in which units of the North Vietnamese navy attacked US warships. President Johnson was incensed while Congress was in an uproar willing to give Johnson the power "to take necessary measures to repel any armed attack on US forces to prevent aggression" (Crozier 1999, 147). By 1966, Johnson's policy of bombing declined in popularity amid new cries to end the war.

In 1967 the war between Egypt and Israel occupied the world public's attention while the Vietnam war went on largely neglected by the US media. Yet by now there were MiG fighter aircraft flying over South Vietnam from Chinese bases as in the Korean war. And ominously, the Chinese government stated that it would not let North Vietnam down in "its war of liberation."

A new distraction occurred in January of 1968, most likely again engineered by the USSR. This was the incident of the US spy ship "Pueblo," captured off the Korean coast by the North Koreans. This completely occupied the attention of the media and the US government. President Johnson then appealed to Moscow to have the ship released. This may have seemed a naive move by Johnson, but it pointed to the probable hand of the USSR in the Pueblo capture. Nevertheless, nothing much then happened. It was only months later in December that the Pueblo's crew was returned to the U.S. Navy. According to information received by the writer from an ex-Navy man, the crew of the ship, during the attack, failed to throw overboard their encoding machine and their ciphers. The cipher books were kept in a weighted bag which would sink, but were captured also, he claimed.

In February of 1968 the North Vietnamese began the "Tet" offensive," although the US media was more interested in national elections. While Richard Nixon was running for President, Johnson announced that he was stopping the bombing of North Vietnam and that he would not run for President. Then in April of that year, Martin Luther King, a black leader, was shot. The perpetrator escaped. There was speculation in later years that the KGB was behind the job, carried out with the aim of stirring up a black revolution in the US. And in fact, burning and looting did occur in several cities, especially in Los Angeles where there was, and still is, a large black population. In the meantime, Vietnam peace talks languished as the USSR's government had probably hoped.

By March of 1968 severe fighting was going on in South Vietnam around the city of Saigon, while the morale of US forces continued downhill. Also, supplies were brought in by the North Vietnamese via the trail that went through the rain forest of Laos. Then like a bombshell, came the assassination of Robert Kennedy in June of 1968 by an immigrant from Jordan. It was only toward the end of the 20th century that evidence was gleaned from Soviet files that the KGB was involved in the killing of Robert Kennedy.

While the US defense budget rose by leaps and bounds to $70 billion a year from 13 billion in 1950, the numbers of US troops in Vietnam had gone from 53,500 to 542,000 in 1969. Again there was talk in the US of bombing Haiphong harbor where Soviet supplies were arriving daily, but nothing came of it until the presidency of Richard Nixon, which by then was too late to make much difference.

When Nixon became president, stronger measures were taken in Vietnam including the bombing of factories in Hanoi and the Soviet ships in Haiphong harbor. In fact the Soviet government complained mightily about their ships being sunk in Haiphong's seaport and the US media echoed the complaints along with diatribes against Nixon for continuing the war. Yet Nixon felt that the US and South Vietnamese forces might have stopped the North Vietnamese. But under pressure from the media and congress, as well as the decline in American interest in the war, the long, tedious, and bloody war was practically ending as 1973 closed with the North Vietnamese triumphant.

Chapter 4

The Soviet Union Confronts America:
Kennedy Vs. Khrushchev

When John Fitzgerald Kennedy was inaugurated as President of the United States and its possessions on January 20, 1961, most of the populace seemed full of hope for the future. But in Berlin, Germany, things were hardly in a settled state. The problem of that large city grew out of a policy of the USSR to control all of Germany. To begin this process, the Allies would be ejected from the city.

Berlin then became a testing ground for Soviet power. Supposedly, Berliners had free access throughout the various city zones and the "Grenzgänger" (border-goers) rode back and forth on the S-Bahn (surface railway) or the U-Bahn (underground railway). Yet the Soviet government saw Berlin as part of East Germany and knew that to control Berlin was to control Germany. Consequently, the Soviets hatched out a plan to drive the Allies out of Berlin. As a beginning to this complicated process, East Germany's Ulbricht suggested setting up a barbed wire fence and later a concrete wall between East and West Berlin, partly to stop emigration from East to West Germany that was rapidly becoming a flood.

Meanwhile, the Soviet government saw Kennedy as the youngest man and first Catholic to gain the presidency and felt he could probably be bullied into yielding. By the summer of 1961, a Hungarian revolt against Communist domination had been cruelly crushed by the USSR led by Nikita Khrushchev. He was now in a position to go further afield and see if he could bully young Jack Kennedy at a meeting in Vienna into giving up West Berlin. At first, Khrushchev buttered up Kennedy with all sorts of good will then came out with a statement that unless the West agreed to a German peace treaty, the USSR would sign a separate one with East Germany while West Berlin (controlled by the Allies) would have to be strictly neutral. No one would be allowed to cross East German territory from the west to Berlin. The Soviet leader then gave Kennedy a six month deadline and told him that war would result from any interference in the Soviet plans.

Kennedy, already suffering from back pains and certain other ailments, was appalled. Some said he looked stunned, although commentator Peter Lisagor simply said that he looked kind of tired and a bit used up. After due consideration, Kennedy said he would not accept such a plan. Khrushchev replied to this by threatening nuclear war. Pierre Salinger, Kennedy's mouthpiece, gave out nothing about all this except to say: "talks were frank, courteous, and wide ranging." Kennedy, on parting from Khrushchev, is supposed to have said: "It's going to be a cold winter."

On returning to the US, Kennedy decided that he had to tell Americans about Berlin. In a brief TV and radio address, he told his audience that US rights to West Berlin "are based on law and not on sufferance and we are determined to maintain those rights." According to polls, Americans agreed, but alot of the talks were not revealed.

At the same time, it was a well-kept secret that Kennedy was not a well man, suffering from Addison's disease, characterized by shortness of breath after mild exertions and was said by some to have syphilis, possibly associated with his frequent excursions into bedroom antics with various young ladies.

On June 28, 1961, Dean Acheson, a trusted liberal of ivy-league background once Secretary of State, suggested declaring a national emergency and ordering a rapid buildup of nuclear and conventional forces. In early July, a month after the Vienna summit, Newsweek magazine reported that the US Joint Chiefs of Staff had drawn up detailed proposals to strengthen America's military capabilities: evacuation of a quarter million military dependents in Europe, sending US forces into Europe to combat positions, calling up the National Guard, and stepping up the draft. Somehow this report leaked out and Kennedy was furious, trying to find out where the report came from.

Simultaneously, Khrushchev was running around threatening the British, French and Germans, rattling his nuclear saber. He then pompously announced that he was increasing the size of the Soviet Armed Forces. Interestingly, a poll reported by U.S. News and World Report showed that 71% of Americans were willing to risk war to back Berlin. In the midst of this, one of the most puzzling spy cases that came to light at this time seemed to involve the USSR's GRU and one Oleg Penkovsky. Back in 1960 he had tried to contact the CIA but they turned him down, apparently thinking he was just a nut. Actually, both the CIA and MI6 had been running him while P gave the details of Soviet equipment sent to Cuba. After MI6 accepted him as genuine, he arrived in Britain in April, 1961 (Grant 1989, 129-130). As many as 10,000 secret documents including details of the latest missile technology were handed over to the British and Americans. These indicated that Soviet missiles were far behind those of the West and that Khrushchev in the Berlin affair was bluffing.

On July 25, 1961, Kennedy addressed the nation on TV to say what he intended to do about Berlin. He made it clear that the US "cannot permit the Communists to drive the allies out of Berlin." Further, he stated that he would improve the Army's strength as well as conventional weapons, then activate certain Reserve and National Guard units and improve Civil Defense.

Soon after this, John McCloy, Special Assistant for Arms Control in Kennedy's government, was wined and dined by the USSR at Sochi on the Black Sea. But when Khrushchev heard what Kennedy had said, the Russian leader ranted and raved, telling McCloy that if America wanted war, it could have it! All this remained unknown to the outside world at this time. But Kennedy's statement had been heard in Berlin and it was said that everyone in East Germany was getting "Torschlusspanik" (panic to escape before the door closed) to leave East Germany for the West. It is estimated that 4 million might have gone through Berlin to the West by year's end. The Marienfelde reception center in Berlin was swamped.

In July, generally unknown to the US public, Kennedy had created a new organization to deal with the Berlin crisis, mostly under the tutelage of Dean Rusk, at one time Assistant Secretary of State under Truman, now Secretary of State under Kennedy. This was to be the "Berlin Task force" including an Operations Center under the State Department and Pentagon. Assistant Secretary of Defense Paul Nitze was the guiding spirit. Representatives of West Germany and France were included.

In early August of 1961, there were rumors that Ulbricht of East Germany had gone to Moscow to consult on the Berlin problem. There were other rumors that the KGB had penetrated the halls of NATO and knew exactly what was going on in western governmental circles. All sorts of plans were being made and rejected by the NATO powers, such as harassing Soviet shipping headed for Cuba or setting up a blockade around Cuba. But nothing much happened while by mid-August the barbed-wire fence was being completed between East and West Berlin. As if this were not enough, the Soviets began to build a concrete barrier with the barbed wire on top. Soviet authorities stated that anyone trying to go over the wall would be shot. Berliners were outraged, but their cries seemed to be lost in Washington.

Kennedy was said to have been infuriated when he realized Berlin was divided and the US had no contingency plan to offer. Kennedy then asked his advisor why we did not know. The barricade was against the Four-powers pact and therefore illegal. Kennedy talked about making vigorous protests while Berliners were stunned by the US lack of response.

Nevertheless, things were churning in Washington D.C. Kept secret at the time, US Air and Ground Forces had been put on alert and a plan made to run a column of troops from West Germany to West Berlin, thus crossing East German territory then strictly controlled by the Soviets. The First Battle Group of the 8th US Infantry, consisting of 1500 men under Glover S. Johns Jr., soon advanced from West Germany to drive along the corridor to Berlin. Six columns of 250 men each with 40 vehicles were included (Gelb, 1986, 226). Each column had a radio link to a command post on the East-West German Border and to General Norstad in Paris. When the news of this leaked out, the Soviets did nothing.

Even in 1961 American B-52 Bombers were flying missions around the globe, loaded with thermonuclear bombs, ready to reply to any Soviet nuclear attack on the US. These flights were continued for many years afterward (History Channel 2003, February 7).

In West Berlin a reviewing stand had been set up with American and German leaders: Vice President Lyndon Johnson, General Clay, Chancellor Brandt, General Watson and others including an Army military band ready to receive the column. When it arrived, West Berliners were there in force, shouting and cheering approval. The band played Sousa's "The Stars and Stripes Forever", Speeches were made, and Johnson said all the right things while being King-for-a-Day in Berlin to the delight not only of Berliners but Americans who saw it on TV. Nevertheless, despite these dramatic responses, the Allies had done nothing to break down the wire and the growing appearance of the concrete wall.

On October 25, 1961, the Americans once again showed their determination to ignore new East German regulations. In Berlin there were three check points labeled A, B, and C: Alpha, Bravo, and Charlie in radio and Army terminology. It was at Checkpoint Charlie that two military police officers of the US Army in civilian clothes tried to drive through into East Berlin, something agreed on in the 4-Powers Act. Although turned back by "Vopos" (Volks Polizei) for failing to show passports, the Americans turned around, this time supported by three US Army jeeps loaded with soldiers and guns. All four vehicles drove past the check point. A half an hour later, anticipating a Soviet response, a number of M-48 US tanks and armored personnel carriers came up and took positions nearby (Cate, 1978, 93).

The next day, 33 Soviet tanks appeared in the evening and took up positions near the Brandenburg Gate. Other Soviet tanks came down the Friedrich Strasse and faced the American tanks. The tension was so extreme it seemed it could be cut with a knife. Later on it came out that General Norstad in Paris was enraged that he had not known about this US sortie but Berliners at Checkpoint Charlie cheered the US vehicles as they came through.

In February of 1962, Robert Kennedy, JFK's brother and then Attorney General, visited Berlin. He faced an enormous crowd of Berliners to say in English that an armed attack on West Berlin was the same thing as an armed attack on Chicago, New York, London, or Paris, and that Berliners were our brothers and we would stand behind them. The cheering was tremendous and prolonged.

Khrushchev's government then invented a new stunt to squeeze the Allies out of Berlin. It demanded that West Berlin be turned into a four-power city where the USSR would station its own forces. But the Soviets were summarily turned down. By mid-February the Soviets announced that they were reserving the air corridors across East Germany to Berlin at certain times of the day for military aircraft. Seeing no reaction from the Allies, Soviet airplanes began buzzing commercial airline flights into and out of Berlin. Although Clay suggested sending US jets through the corridor, General Norstad rejected this. The British too, expressed anxiety over such a move.

It was about this time when, little known to the news services of the world, a Cuban delegation went to Moscow to sign an arms agreement. Somehow, apparently through the observations of the CIA, President Kennedy got wind of it and became worried about possible arms shipments from the USSR to Cuba. The Americans then officially protested to the USSR's Andrei Gromyko who stated that the weapons were just defensive and Americans had nothing to worry about from tiny Cuba.

Things drifted on into the heat of summer in an America worried now about Soviet intentions. However, an affair of another sort emerged from the depths concerning the Kennedys. It seemed of little national importance, nonetheless, when the popular star of the moving picture screen, actress Marilyn Monroe, died. She was rumored to have been taking drugs of some kind, and this was blamed for the cause of her illness and death. She had been one of the innumerable feminine friends of J.F. Kennedy in the late 1950s, but for some reason fell under the scrutiny of the FBI. Later on, JFK was warned by Director Hoover who was worried about information leaks through Marilyn in connection with Mob activities being investigated by Attorney General Robert Kennedy. Furthermore, Bob Kennedy was rumored to have dated her shortly before her demise, possibly to obtain information on the Mob with which Marilyn was said to be connected. She had, in the months just before her death, been concerned with possible wire taps on her phone line and did not trust the use of her home phone.

In those days wiretaps were legal according to standards used as late as 1969. The law was then changed and the Attorney General had to submit an application for tapping to a Federal Judge (Haig, 1992, 222). The FBI's Hoover seems to have allowed break-ins as late as the 1950s and wire taps were made on various suspicious organizations using a law passed as early as 1938. In fact, Hoover's taps were probably conveyed to Joseph McCarthy in his search for subversives.

In October of 1962 John F. Kennedy had bigger problems. The Soviet-Cuban affair now loomed large. The President came on TV to state that there would be an American naval blockade put on Cuba to prevent missiles from the USSR from arriving there. But he said he would not cut off food as the Soviets had done in Berlin. He further stated that if any nuclear missiles were launched from Cuba against any nation in the Western Hemisphere, it would be regarded as an attack by the Soviet Union on the United States, requiring a full retaliatory response upon the Soviet Union. This extraordinary statement stunned Americans as well as many others all over the world.

Khrushchev's answer to all this was to warn the US that Soviet submarines would sink any vessels trying to interfere with trade to and from Cuba. Nevertheless, Britain's MacMillan and France's DeGaulle backed up Kennedy to the full. At the same time, practically unknown to most all Americans, US nuclear missiles were primed and ready for launching, troops flown to southern Florida, and the Strategic Air Command (SAC) put on full alert. Strategists in Washington D.C. thought at the time the Soviets would move on Berlin. And there was not much the Western powers could have done about it. But they did not move.

The order was then given for the U.S. Navy to search all ships approaching Cuba. They would be looking for nuclear missiles, since on October 14, a U-2 aircraft had photographed a missile site under construction at San Cristobal, Cuba (Crozier 1999, 243). It was not long before Soviet ships were sighted headed for Cuba. Following a few desperate moments of anguished suspense, as US warships approached them, the Soviet ships turned around and headed back eastward.

By October 28, the popular notion was widely accepted in the US media that Khrushchev, eyeball to eyeball with Kennedy, was the first to blink. Actually, the whole standoff had been a bluff by the Soviets and it was more a case of wilting than of blinking. Yet Gromyko, never to be outdone by the Americans, suggested to Rusk that they trade off the missiles in Cuba for giving in on the Berlin standoff. Dean Rusk would not even consider it. The Soviets then agreed to dismantle their missile bases in Cuba.

While all this was going on, and a lot of it was in the news, many Americans were rushing to supermarkets to stock up on food in case of a nuclear attack on US cities. For several years back, the government had urged people to build rudimentary "fallout shelters" in their cellars or buried in their back yards to protect them from radioactive fallout and possible bomb-blast. Now it seemed that they were not needed.

One of the reasons for the US willingness to stand up to the USSR probably came from the information provided by the defected spy Penkovsky. He had given large amounts of information to the West about the weakness of Russia's arsenal, as mentioned before in this chapter. Just why he returned to the USSR remains mysterious, but on arrival there he was arrested, tried, and sentenced to death October 22, 1962. Possibly he had some influence on Kennedy's advisors in the NSC and was of assistance to the NSA (National Security Agency) about cipher systems.

It also came out years after the missile crisis, that Air Force Chief Curtis LeMay claimed JFK had made a deal with Khrushchev to withdraw US missiles from Italy and Turkey, provided the USSR would take theirs from Cuba, this information coming out on August 9, 1976. The date when this deal was made was October 27th, 1962, one day before the missile crisis was essentially over (Haig, 1992, 104).

****

During the desperate days of the early 1960s, spying went on at even a greater frenetic pace. The story of Anatoli M. Golitsyn, a major in the KGB stationed in Finland, was a rare case of a KGB officer who was evidently a genuine defector to the West. In December of 1961 he went boldly to the CIA offices in Helsinki, Finland, offered to defect, and promised to tell many tales of Soviet spies in the West. Although suspicious of him at first, Angleton of the CIA was delighted at the exposures he made. Golitsyn claimed, contrary to what the Americans had assumed, that there had been no break-off in Russo-Chinese relations. Also he confirmed the long-held suspicion in MI5 that Philby was spying for the USSR. MI6 later sent Philby to Istanbul where he openly stated his sympathies for the USSR, then left for that country to become an advisor to Yuri Andropov, head of the KGB. Philby died in 1988, evidently much admired by the Russians.

Still, there were many unanswered questions and new events. The case of Igor A. Ivanov in 1961 achieved much publicity. He was assistant Soviet Naval Attaché in London when he became embroiled in a ring providing "girls" for rich clients. Soon he became linked with a John Profumo, Secretary of State for War. One of the girls was asked by some unknown person to provide information about nuclear weapons from Mr. Profumo. But early in 1963, Profumo realized to his dismay that he was deeply entangled in Soviet espionage and promptly resigned amid highly embarrassing publicity, all of which reflected badly on his superior Prime Minister MacMillan. This situation may have led to the Conservatives losing the 1964 election (Grant, 1989, 133).

Also, there was the strange case of the Soviet agent Konstantin Volkov of the NKVD. After turning coat on his Soviet masters, he began to tell all to Britain's secret services. But somehow he was sent to Istanbul and, becoming associated with Philby (a serious mistake on his part), he was packed up in tight bandages and shipped off to the USSR, never to be heard from again (Grant, 1989, 90).

The Nosenko Case was more complicated and difficult to solve. The CIA's James Angleton, after nearly three years of interrogation, was never able to make the Russian admit his connections to the subsequent case of J.F. Kennedy's assassination on November 22, 1963. He may have been a KGB disinformation agent.

Other exposures were made in the 1960s. Despite attempts to pre-vent the publication of Peter Wright's book "Spycatcher", it embar-rassed a number of people in British Intelligence. Even MI5's Director Hollis did not escape suspicion (West, 1987, 87, 91).

While both Alexander Haig and Cyrus Vance abhorred the idea of political assassinations, it seems not to have inhibited Bob Kennedy's hopes to rid the world of Fidel Castro who continued to preside as dicta-tor of Cuba. Castro's confidence had been increased by the disastrously-fumbled "Bay of Pigs" invasion by Cuban exiles from Florida. Much of the disaster was caused by the failure of US forces to back the Cuban landings. This may have encouraged the USSR to build up formidable numbers of men and equipment in Cuba by August of 1962.

On June 19, 1963, President Kennedy OK'd a plan to resist Castro's government in Cuba, including commando raids on electric generating plants and the like. As many as three or four operations a month were carried out in Cuba with the assistance of the CIA. Bob Kennedy was al-leged to have been the boss. Although the plans were directed at under-mining Castro's government, the plans were said to include the idea of bringing about Castro's death. It seems possible that Bob Kennedy failed to realize there could be a mole in his own crew of anti-Castroite Cubans. As a result, Castro was informed of the plan to take his life and this may explain why Castro reminded an Associated Press reporter that, in effect two could play at that game. In other words, Robert Kennedy's life was in danger as well as Castro's, but also the life of John F. Kennedy (Haig, 1992, 110).

* * * * * * * * * * * * *

John Kennedy's visit to Dallas Texas was not widely noticed by Americans when it started. It was billed as merely a speaking tour to help certain Texan politicians and hopefully assist Kennedy's popularity. Like Franklin Roosevelt, Kennedy liked to ride around in a big open car, waving at the excited crowds as he slowly drove along. Such a tour would give Texas governor Connally some free publicity. They were ac-companied in the car by Kennedy's and Connally's wives. A chauffeur driving the car was a White House Security man, while a Secret Service man sat in the other front seat.

Just after passing the Book Depository building, the bystanders heard a shot, or perhaps a backfire. This first shot evidently missed, but a second shot from the rear passed through both Kennedy and Connally.

The third shot was thought to have hit Kennedy in the head, but this was uncertain at the time. Two bullets, one shattered, the other intact, were later found in the limousine. The police guessed that the three shots came from the Book Depository building where on the 6th floor were found three shell casings and a rifle with telescopic sight. A fourth shot had been heard by some, and several witnesses saw police running toward the Grassy Knoll that was ahead of the car at the time.

Connally was only wounded and survived. But Kennedy, rushed in his car to the hospital, died soon afterwards that day. When a policeman caught up with the suspect in a movie theatre, the policeman was shot with a hand gun and killed. But others soon caught and subdued the runaway. The assassin was jailed for a time but when let out, a gunman, Jack Ruby, stepped forward and shot and killed him. Ruby was arrested, jailed, tried, and found guilty. He later admitted his connection to a Chicago mob and to people in Cuba and languished for some time in prison, refusing to bring out further details in the apparent plot.

How many books, some say 2000, how many millions of words spoken and written, how many documentaries on TV shows have emerged after this event, can only be guessed. A week after the assassination, the Warren Commission began its investigation. Although much criticized in later years, months later after many more hearings and searching, it came to a conclusion in September of 1964. It claimed that two bullets had hit Kennedy and they were fired by the suspect, Lee Harvey Oswald, one of the bullets hitting Connally. No evidence of a conspiracy was discovered (Posner, 1993, 323).

But in later years, it became probable that a second gunman had fired a shot from the Grassy Knoll in front of the approaching car and hit Kennedy in the head. Many studies were made of the sound track recorded at the time as well as of the Zapruder film taken by an amateur photographer. One study of the sound tracks in the 1990s showed that four shots had been fired, the last one probably from the Grassy Knoll, this one thought to have hit Kennedy in the head to cause his head to snap backwards as shown on film.

Of course there were still endless questions. For example, who hired Ruby? He was thought to have Mafia ties and speaking of that, the name of Sam Giancana came up as one who admitted his hatred of the Kennedys. This goes back to Bobby Kennedy's investigations as Attorney General into organized crime. Santos Trafficante, allegedly stated on his deathbed that he only wished "we" had killed Bobby before Jack. He and Sam Giancana had been closely associated in Mafia operations.

Bob Kennedy had been plaguing Giancana for years, putting FBI men on his trail to follow him wherever he went. One story went that the Mafia, to which Giancana was allegedly connected, had supported Jack Kennedy's election. But then he was snubbed by Jack once he became president.

In later years, the "Soviet Theory" come more to light when the files of the Soviet KGB and GRU were opened following the collapse of the USSR toward the end of the century. The assassin, whose name was confirmed as Lee Harvey Oswald, was found to have strong connections with the USSR. At one time living in Russia, he had bragged about how he would someday kill John Kennedy. Married to a Soviet citizen and trained in the US Marines as a sharpshooter, even taking a shot at General Walker, he was a likely aspirant for the role of a killer. His visit to the Soviet embassy in Mexico City just before the deed was revealed soon after the assassination, a point often ignored by the liberal media.

The apparent defection of the KGB agent Yuri Nosenko to the US only strengthened the idea of Soviet complicity when he failed a lie detector test while denying any connection to the Kennedy killing. Further information of this came out on December 17, 1973, March 23, 1977, and November 1999, according to various news sources, pointing to Nosenko's complicity in the JFK killing, but not proving it.

Soon after the JFK assassination many more details appeared. Ex-cop Curry of Dallas, TX, said that several overpasses where the motorcade was going were supposed to be cleared and police stationed there, but were not. He further remarked that Oswald seemed to have had previous experience in being interrogated. Also, they let Ruby into the station, partly because the cop detailed to keep out people at the door, disobeyed orders and left his post. It was released later in the 1990s that Ruby had figured out a way to escape through the basement by a little-known passageway, but was soon caught and arrested to languish in prison. In 1964, he was tried and found guilty on charges of complicity, although later found technically not guilty, in any case to die in prison of cancer. At least it seemed clear that he had had connections with the Mob and with the Cubans.

Studies carried out in 2000 verified the idea that a second gunman had shot Kennedy in the head from the Grassy Knoll and had managed to escape into the crowd, in some way hiding the weapon. It is even possible that the order to kill J.F. Kennedy came from the top: Khrushchev himself. As once remarked by a CIA director, an order like that could be given by merely a nod of the head and "was like water on sand."

It is also probable, but difficult to prove, that the "Mob," some say the Cosa Nostra headquartered in Chicago to which Sam Giancana was allegedly attached, may have asked Ruby to silence Oswald after the deed was done.

* * * * * * * * * * * *

The year 1963 was also notable for the news that during WW II the USSR had operated three big spy-rings. One of these was the "Rote Kapelle" (Red Choir or Red Orchestra) consisting of several spy cells or groups in Germany with several hundred members in all. Many of these people were exposed by the Abwehr and either turned around to work for the Germans or killed. Another spy ring was operated by Richard Sorge, mostly in Japan. A third was the Lucy ring in Switzerland, perhaps associated with the Rote Kapelle.

The Swiss operation was run by a Hungarian named Rado, code name: Dora. Messages were sent to Moscow by radio from either Lucerne or Lausanne, Switzerland, where their transmitters were located. Messages were converted from English language reports through a complex of encypherments so that at the time (during WW II) their code was unbreakable (Norman, 1973, 140). If someone copied their transmission it would appear to be nothing more than a series of numbers in groups of five.

From 1940 to 1942 almost all German military moves were received, enciphered and sent to Moscow. Although the crucial warning to the USSR that the Wehrmacht would soon invade the USSR was sent, Stalin chose not to believe it, probably because he thought he was being sent false information.

The Swiss spy gang consisted of Rudolf Roessler, a German, Alexander Foote, an Englishman, Rado, the Hungarian, and Lucy, real name Karl Sedlacek, a Czech military intelligence officer (Polmar and Allen, 1997, 343). Rado and his friends kept up their clandestine game until late in the war when the Swiss decided they had had enough. Using radio direction finders along with occasionally shutting off the electric power to certain parts of Lucerne and Lausanne to find out when the signal dropped out, they finally discovered their hideaway. Moving fast, the police caught the lot of them complete with their cipher systems.

In later years, Rado was officially thanked by Stalin, then slapped in the clink until 1953 when the dictator died. Probably Stalin simply did not trust him.

* * * * * * * * * * * *

Lyndon Johnson, then Vice President, soon succeeded Kennedy in the Presidency. At once he felt the weight of responsibilities, primarily that of the Vietnam war, while his pet programs of tax reductions and new civil rights bills languished in Congress. He did, however, sign an "Immigration Reform Act" which made it vastly more easy for immigrants, legal or illegal, to enter the US, something that many Americans learned of to their great regret in subsequent years.

In the meantime, Johnson heard of the FBI's and CIA's suspicions concerning British Intelligence. Consequently, in the strictest of secrecy he ordered a review of British espionage leaks to the USSR. The London-based CIA then began a process of visiting the inner sancta of Britain's security agencies. What they found was what they suspected: laxness in communications, softness in vetting (examining) personnel, and other dealings that seemed highly questionable to the Americans.

When the British found out what was going on, they objected strenuously. But MI5's Director Hollis, probably knowing what was going to happen, resigned before the investigation got under way. There had long been a question in overseas transmissions as to who was "Ellie" mentioned before in this chronology concerning the Gouzenko revelations. Possibly, this was Hollis, and in later years, MI5's Peter Wright still suspected Hollis following Wright's own private examination of the facts plus some undercover sleuthing. But nothing of substance was found, according to the powers that be, to prove Hollis' complicity in dealing with the USSR. Even Prime Minister Thatcher made a public statement on TV and radio intended to clear Hollis, which seemed to lay the whole thing at rest, at least in government circles.

* * * * * * * * * * * *

It was 7:00 A.M. eastern US time on June 5th 1968, when Americans tuned in the radio news to find out who had won the California primary: Robert Kennedy or Eugene McCarthy. But this was no longer of importance. All the radio could report was that Robert Kennedy had been shot and that he was in "critical condition". CBS radio then ran a recording of a post-election celebration party in which Kennedy was participating. Suddenly, from the milling crowd, a young man, dark-haired, swarthy complexion, fired a .22 pistol at Kennedy. With all the shrieking and yelling, a listener to the tape could barely hear the shots. Just where the celebrators' cries of joy left off and the wails of anguish began was difficult to determine. It seemed like JFK's fate all over again.

The next day it was clear that the assassin – for Robert had died last night – was a Jordanian immigrant, disgruntled over the aid the US had given to Israel. The assassin had three or four 100-dollar bills in his pocket, suggesting he was a paid gunman. The police literally stuffed the killer into a squad car and refused to let the press near him, trying to prevent a repetition of the Oswald – Kennedy assassination. The media, printed and spoken, pointed to the "sickness of the nation", but the fact that the gunman was a foreigner deflated the idea that he was something homegrown.

Only by the end of the century did evidence turn up from the files of the USSR that the KGB was involved in the Bob Kennedy shooting. The USSR had for years used assassination squads to kill unwanted people, such as Leon Trotsky, hunted down in Mexico and shot, thus to destroy the Trotskyite faction in the USSR that had vied with Stalin for power.

A few days later, about June 7th, Robert Kennedy's killer, now known by the name of Sirhan Sirhan, was found to be a regular attendee at the local Du Bois club, a Communist Front organization. Although the press stated that Sirhan had no accomplices, there was a young woman apprehended, evidently involved. But little more was said of this.

As for those in the general public that had admired Bob Kennedy, the grief was profound. Although Robert Kennedy was a true liberal in many ways, he was keenly anti-Castro and against the Communist cult that planned the destruction of the US government.

****

By early July of 1968, Czechoslovakia reappeared in the news, well-known in the history of WW II. The nation was said to be facing military intervention by the USSR while the Soviet government itself talked of mobilization of its armed forces. But by now a militant West Germany had become a factor in the equation since it had gained much strength in recent years. Then too, Poland was becoming restless, Hungary wanted more internal power, and Romania sought freedom from the USSR.

Although in early August all the publicity about Czechoslovakia had fizzled out like a wet fuse, by August 22nd suddenly came the news that the invasion of that country was being carried out by satellite troops of the USSR. The Czechs, however, were not taking it lying down, any more than when Heydrich's SS men came through in the late 1930s. Civilians joined in against the invaders and Soviet tanks were set on fire while many Czechs were shot.

In late August, Johnson met with his Security Council and nothing much was decided; but in the UN, a move was made to condemn the USSR for the invasion. This was quickly killed by a Soviet veto. Refugees, in the meantime, poured across the border into neighboring Austria to create a new kind of disaster.

In early September US experts in missilry learned about a Soviet test of a long range missile capable of carrying several warheads of atomic bomb potential. Senator Jackson stated that this could threaten US missiles in underground silos. It was said, although supposed to be secret, that there were 1000 minuteman missiles in place to counter incoming missiles. Yet is was soon found that the entire disposition of US missile sites had been given away by spies. In fact, it was then wellknown that the USSR found out about the US A-bomb before it was tested and that all the secrets of the "plutonium implosion bomb" had been quickly given away by spies. By 1964, the Soviets had learned that in case of war, the US planned to bomb certain factory sites and that no land invasion by military forces was expected. But the Soviet government found all that hard to believe and continued to think in terms of moving large land armies as in WW I and II.

By mid-September, 1968, the Czech affair lingered on. Deutsche Welle, the German short wave radio, then revealed a jitteryness in Europe about the USSR's invasion of Czechoslovakia. However, a "Western Intelligence source" said that the Soviet division involved in the Czech invasion amounted to hardly anything and was now being replaced by East German troops, apparently aimed in the direction of Munich and Nuremberg. One German radio commentator recalled the statement by John F. Kennedy that the US would defend West Berlin if attacked and that he had said that he himself was a Berliner (Sorensen, 1965, 601). This statement probably galvanized a great many Germans, east or west into a greater confidence in their future.

The real reasons for the Soviet seizure of Czechoslovakia were most likely for espionage gleanings, military advantage, and to prevent the spread of anti-Soviet upheavals in its satellite nations.

* * * * * * * * * * * *

While all these events went on not only in the US but especially in a Europe struggling to stay clear of Soviet domination, the so-called "Cold War" between the US and the USSR went on not so much on the land as in the sea. The story of Navy officer John P. Craven, later published in 1998, revealed many of the secrets of the deep that involved the attempts of the U.S. Navy to keep track of Soviet submarines, mainly in the Atlantic Ocean.

In the early 1960s, submarines could only descend to about 1500 feet deep before suffering from the extreme pressures that could cause them to implode, or at least spring enough leaks to flood the submarine's compartments. The unfortunate case of the USS "Thresher" only proved this point too well. On April 10, 1963, she had dived to 1300 feet when certain pipes ruptured causing her to sink deeper and then implode, killing 128 men. Craven, who had been put in charge of a project called the "Strategy of Deterrence" went to work on a plan to build rescue vehicles for deeply submerged vessels. The idea of sending cameras into the depths had already been put to work during World War II, so why not build a camera that could go into extreme depths to photograph sunken ships? However, surface ships doing this sort of work would be too obvious to the USSR, so the idea of having the cameras sent down from a submerged submarine was developed (Sontag and Drew, 1998, 196-197).

Such a ship was the "Halibut" classified as a "research vessel". The Oceanographic Institution in Woods Hole, MA, had already helped to develop the "Alvin" for deep sea research under ONR (Office of Naval Research) auspices. Based on this, the "NR-1" (NR standing for Naval Reactors) was constructed, 137 feet long and capable of descending to a depth of about 3000 feet.

In 1966 a B52 bomber over Spain managed to lose several Hydrogen bombs, most of which fell on the mainland and were recovered, but one other had fallen in the ocean just off the Spanish south coast. With the aid of a local fisherman who had seen it fall, the bomb was discovered with the NR-1 at a depth of 2200 feet. Although Alvin had failed to grapple with it, the "CURV" or Cable-Controlled Underwater Recovery Vehicle, brought up the bomb even though the parachute was entangled in it.

By 1968, the Navy in cooperation with a US manufacturer, constructed a steel cable some seven miles long with a "fish" at its end. This transmitted sonar impulses that could be "read" at the receiving end. In July of that year the "Fish" apparatus was lowered from the "Halibut" and eventually found a lost Soviet submarine lying on the bottom at 16,800 feet in the central Pacific ocean.

Although the Navy wanted nothing to do with trying to lift the submarine to the surface, the CIA became involved and conceived a way to hoist the entire Soviet submarine lying on the bottom at about 3 miles deep. After consultations with multimillionaire Howard Hughes, the CIA hired his shipping company to build what looked like an enormous freighter, the "Glomar Explorer". This had an immense gap in its center, through which cables could be lowered into the depths. Massive grappling hooks were supposed to clamp on to the ship and hoist it to the surface my means of attached steel cables.

Remarkably, the grappling hooks succeeded in clamping on to the submarine. But then some of the several hooks broke and the sub fell back. Five of the claws still surviving tried again, but two more of them broke and a section of the sub fell back into the depths. There were still 3 nuclear missiles in that section, two of which were damaged already. The undamaged one fell back into the mud at least not exploding to cause a disaster of unimaginable proportions. Supposedly, the code books were also lost, but a part of the sub was retrieved, including a few bodies of the Soviet crew (Sontag and Drew, 1998, 206-207).

Chapter 5

The Rise And Fall Of Richard M. Nixon

Tonight at 6:45 P.M., October 31, 1968, Lowell Thomas was again reading the news on the radio as he had for the past 30 or so years. He said President Johnson would address the American people again tonight. At 7:48P.M. Johnson was on the radio and TV to declare there was now a bombing halt in Vietnam.

Richard Nixon, then running for president, pointed out that this was only ANOTHER bombing halt, thereby airing some needed publicity for the Republican campaign. By November 6th, California had gone for Nixon in the voting and Ohio soon followed. At noon Hubert H. Humphrey, the Democratic contender for the presidency, conceded the election. Actually, Nixon only had a slight plurality in total votes, despite the media's claim that he was a minority President, and had gotten elected by the electoral system without a true majority.

Although not yet President, Nixon was to inherit the incredibly difficult Vietnam problem. "Peace talks" had again bogged down, perhaps to await the arrival of the new President while arguing over the shape of the peace table.

The "Peace Talks" were something like the Mad Hatter's party in Alice in Wonderland, everyone trying to decide where they should sit. The Hanoi faction made out that their troops approaching Saigon in South Vietnam either were not under their control or simply did not exist. It probably occurred to the beleaguered US delegation that the North Vietnamese did not need to make concessions when they were obviously winning.

At least it was a counteractant to the failures in Vietnam, when the Apollo 8 space mission was launched on December 21, 1968. All systems were soon "Go"; the 3rd stage rocket had shut off and they were 3000 miles into space headed for the moon. After circling the moon they splashed down in the Pacific about 1000 miles southwest of Hawaii on the 27th. It seemed as if the Americans had finally done something right, although greatly assisted by the borrowed rocket expert Wernher von Braun, having barely escaped from the Russians.

In February of 1969 Nixon found himself in another Berlin confrontation. The USSR intended to prevent all surface travel of German government officials from West Germany to West Berlin. On the 23rd, Nixon left for Europe to arrive in Brussels in the evening. Amid cries of "Nixon go home!" he was assured that this was only a handful of dissenters. Nixon spoke about peace and of his aim to cement ties with NATO. In Paris, crowds, probably spurred on by the Communists, ran wild in the streets.

The Soviets then urged the East Germans to close off Berlin during the next elections, but Allied ambassadors had assured West Germany's Kiesinger that he would be supported in a Berlin confrontation. Yet the East Germans threatened to close all surface roads and harass airlanes from West Germany to Berlin. A new Berlin stand-off seemed imminent.

A few days later in March, Willi Brandt of West Germany appeared on CBS TV's Face The Nation. He said that it was his impression that the Soviets would not make a big confrontation out of the latest Berlin affair. But he admitted that he had been wrong in forecasting the Czech invasion which showed, he said, how difficult it was to forecast what a committee of rulers would do, let alone the volatile Mr. Khrushchev. As it turned out, the whole thing over Berlin was soon forgotten and the Soviet threats faded like the mists of dawn.

On returning to the United States, Nixon decided to approve a limited form of ABM (Anti-ballistic missile) system concentrated around the big missile-launching sites in North Dakota and Montana. In March, Defense Secretary Laird, in a Senate hearing, defended deployment of a limited ABM system. It was leaked out during the hearing that the USSR now had a superrocket that was capable of carrying 3 or 4 20-megaton bombs which could be delivered in a single rocket. The bombs would be scattered over the landscape, presumably nuclear bombs.

It was by this time known that the USSR had acquired two nuclear submarines that could fire long range missiles. The US also had evidence that the Chinese would soon have 10 or so ICBMs (Intercontinental Ballistic Missiles) by mid 1970s. It came out later in 1978 that John Haldeman, Nixon's Chief of Staff and advisor, said that the USSR had invited the US to join in on the atom bombing of China. Evidently, Nixon turned down the Russians.

On March 28th, 1969, Dwight David Eisenhower died. Said by reporters to be a do-nothing president, he was often found on the golf course or at his Colorado ranch. At one time he had wondered out loud why the US did not knock out Hanoi and the Haiphong seaport where Soviet supplies poured in, and he felt that the Chinese would not have attacked. Johnson, however, did not agree.

In the spring of 1969, it seemed as if the whole world was planning for war. On April 22nd, the Soviet ambassador to the US Mr. Dobrynin called on Nixon's Elliot Richardson to express concern over 23 US warships in the Sea of Japan. At the same time Soviet naval vessels had passed through the Dardanelles into the Mediterranean to give the Soviets an edge over the U.S. Navy. Simultaneously, the Egyptians were carrying out commando raids across the Suez on Israel, and China was threatening India, while Czechoslovakia was growling at the Russians' unwanted domination.

In July, it was a boost to Nixon's presidency that the Apollo 11 rocket left for the moon. The hopes of the whole moon-project, costing millions, then depended on its success since now they had planned to put men on the surface of the earth's only satellite. The Soviets too, were said to have launched a moon rocket in secret but it was thought to have crashed and nothing more was said about it.

On the 21st the astronauts were on the moon, jumping around effortlessly like jack-rabbits while planting the US flag. It could only reflect favorably on the Nixon presidency, although this was not mentioned by the media. When Nixon asked for another 30,000 US troops to be brought home from Vietnam, the media claimed that this was only a small force.

Just what China might do to intervene in Vietnam was always a question. Actually, China had troubles enough confronting the USSR, complaining that Soviet troops had attacked the Chinese along the Sinkaing border. Both sides took losses, but fighting soon died down. Marvin Kalb (CBS Television, 12/6/69) asked Nixon's man Averill Harriman if he thought it would come to war between China and the USSR? Harriman, an honest man, said that he did not know, but called Thieu of South Vietnam an incompetent, which summed things up as well as could be expected.

On September 20th, 1969, the Chinese secretly sent up and fired off their ninth atomic bomb, this one reckoned at 3 megatons, exploded in the atmosphere. This was quickly detected by satellites and then by raised radioactivity recordings in the US. Even more secretly, the Americans had set off numerous atomic bombs in the Nevada desert during the 1950s and into the early 1960s. Many of these were underground and did not produce much of any radioactivity in the atmosphere. Information on this only emerged some 20 years afterwards.

Another of Nixon's problems was that the Vietnam war seemed to be insoluble. In December of 1968, Henry Kissinger had become National Security Advisor under the new President now in office. Following the death of Ho Chi Minh in September of 1969, by early 1970 Kissinger was meeting secretly with a representative of North Vietnam, a connection that continued until 1973. This man was Le Duc Tho, an important personage well-known to his own people back in the 1950s when the Communist northerners were trying to drive the French out of North Vietnam. Tho, now in his 50s, was functioning in a clandestine way as leader of the Freedom Faction (Crozier 1999, 291).

Apparently at Kissinger's suggestion, Nixon in October 1970 sought a stand-still cease-fire. This was approved by Congressional leaders and seemed like a beginning to the end of the war. At the same time, Kissinger was carrying on highly secret meetings in a Paris suburb with Le Duc Tho. But Tho was determined not to make any compromises, something that Kissinger excelled at. Finally, in 1973, Kissinger gave up his plan for a mutual withdrawal to the old borders and Nixon then acquiesced to an effort to stop supplies being sent south to the Communists in South Vietnam. This could only be accomplished, it seemed, by allowing our troops to invade Cambodia and Laos. However, a Congressional amendment prevented this incursion of US and ARVN (Army of the Republic of Vietnam) troops. The result was that supplies continued to pour down from the north on the Ho Chi Minh trail and passed to South Vietnam from the west. By this time (1970) US morale, as mentioned before, was sagging while the war seemed more and more useless to the South Vietnamese and the Americans.

By mid-1972, large numbers of US forces had departed Vietnam for the states, leaving the ARVN to do the best it could to confront the NLF (National Liberation Front) troops. In that same year the NLF began a powerful offensive, entering south of the DMZ from Laos and Cambodia on the Ho Chi Minh trail, while South Vietnam forces retreated down

the East side of South Vietnam to defend Saigon. (Natkiel, 1986,154)
During 1974, the ARVN troops had fallen back to just west and
north of Saigon to try to keep the enemy from taking that city in April of
1975. By May of that year it became an utter disaster for the defense. A
truce was agreed to between the NLF and the South Vietnamese authorities.

****

A story was leaked to the New York Times which printed it on June
13, 1971. This was that a certain Daniel Ellsberg, having taken some
documents from Pentagon files, soon afterwards sold them to the Times.
Republicans immediately questioned the legality of Ellsberg's apparent
thievery, although not denying the truth of the contents of the documents. Part of the article in the Times stated that President Johnson had
deluded Americans in promising to take the US out of the Vietnam war
while actually planning to get it deeper in. These revelations were soon
to be called the "Pentagon Papers".

While the Ellsberg case seemed to have been filed away for some
future reference, it reappeared on July 16, 1971. John Ehrlichman of the
Nixon entourage undertook an investigation of Mr. Ellsberg and the pur-
loined papers, allegedly stolen from the Pentagon files. Little more was
said of this in the news.

In Britain, news from the USSR seemed more important. The London "Evening News" published a dispatch from Moscow by reporter
Victor Louis that implied that a Kremlin reshuffle was imminent. At the
same time Leonid Brezhnev, the current Soviet leader was said not to be
well, having high blood pressure and forced to stay at home. His condition was probably not improved by news at the time that Nixon had left
for a trip to Beijing. Observers abroad saw it as more cooperation with
the Chinese and therefore a worry for the USSR.

Back late in the year 1970, the British Secret Service, MI5, was receiving information from a KGB agent stationed in London. This went
on for about a year until August of 1971 when he was arrested for
drunken driving. But before the police could get far at interrogations, he
was "rescued" by agents from MI5. Continuing the interrogation with
MI5, the agent, Oleg Lyalin, fingered at least 105 Soviet agents in Britain who had penetrated the Labor Party. MI5 reasoned that if Lyalin had
remained for so long an undetected defector in Britain without the KGB
suspecting anything, this suggested that MI5 was clear of any moles

(Grant 1989, 150).

In America, meanwhile, politically-inspired violence suddenly appeared. Presidential candidate Wallace had been doing well in his campaign, especially in the South where he had been speaking. Then came the news that he had been shot. But he refused to die, although three bullets had entered his body and he then lay near deaths door. Doctors predicted that he would survive but would be paralyzed from the waist down. Wallace's assailant was seized but not before he had shot and wounded several others. He was finally subdued and held by local police. Evidently, the would-be assassin was paid, but otherwise had no visible means of support. It has remained a mystery as to who his backers were ever since the deed was done.

Despite Wallace's near-assassination, Michigan and Maryland went big for him in the voting. Wallace had stood up against the liberal craze to bus school kids from all over the place so as to bring the "disadvantaged" into contact with the supposedly "advantaged".

Perhaps in some way related to the Wallace shooting, three former high ranking FBI agents: Director Patrick Gray III, Acting Director W. Mark Felt, and Assistant Director Edward S. Miller were believed by certain un-named people to have authorized "black bag" jobs. These entailed searches of homes of friends and relatives of fugitive radicals. Beginning in May of 1972, and continuing in their clandestine work into May of 1973, they were indicted in April, 1978 for this activity. Although the government dropped the case against Gray, Miller, and Felt, they were convicted in 1980. Nevertheless, President Reagan pardoned them, saying: "they were just doing their jobs as agents."

Political problems of another kind broke on June 17, 1972. Although unknown to the public at the time, the so called "Plumbers", of which there were five, were arrested for breaking into the Watergate apartment building where the Democratic National Committee had its offices (Polmar and Allen, 1997, 441). A security man, checking the doors, noticed that a door lock had been picked and reported it. It seemed insignificant at the time, but about 10 days later, J. Patrick Gray, Acting Director of the FBI, was said to have told President Nixon about it. As the story came out and was put widely into print, it was said that some of Nixon's people had entered the Watergate building with the expressed intention of finding out the plans of the Democrats in the upcoming election.

In retrospect, Nixon would probably have won the election anyway, so that it seemed strange that he would have pulled off a stunt like this.

Whether he had initiated the break-in or not became a great bone of contention in later years and to rock the foundations of the presidency.

When the national presidential elections were over by November 8, 1972, results revealed that the "Solid South", once Democratic, was now solid Republican. This was a remarkable turn of history since the days of the Civil War. It was back in 1962 that Nixon, who had lost an election, said bitterly to the Press that they would not have Nixon to kick around. He then lost to John F. Kennedy. Today, Nixon had won by one of the biggest land-slides in American history at least since the days of Lincoln. West Germany's Willi Brandt congratulated Nixon and said that his reelection was of extraordinary significance for the world's future.

But all was then not sweetness and light. Only a few days later after the election, a two-engine airplane from Toronto, Canada, was hijacked and forced to fly to Knoxville, TN, not far from the Oak Ridge atomic energy experimental area. Although at the time the huge "diffusion plant" was shut down, there were other facilities there, such as those for teaching, that were continuing. As a result of the threat, the reactors at Oak Ridge were shut down. The plane, however, went on to Orlando Florida where the banks gave the hijackers about $2 million, but they still refused to release the passengers. Although FBI men shot out the tires, the plane took off anyway. The copilot evidently resisted and the kidnappers then shot the copilot in cold blood, although he was only wounded. From all that could be determined afterward, the plane finally landed in Cuba and the hijackers held there while passengers were returned to the US. One of the passengers had died of a heart attack, however. He had been old enough to remember the Wright brothers' first flight, but he had never flown in an airplane before.

As a result of this hijacking, airplane pilots in the US went on strike on November 15, 1972 to protest the lack of effort to protect passenger aircraft from hijackers. Evidently, in those days before the great disaster of 9/11/01, the door from the pilots' cabin into the passenger space was not legally supposed to be locked. Also the door was made of thin material to save weight and easily broken through, and the pilots were not allowed to carry handguns. Nothing much came of the strike.

While all this was going on, the Paris peace talks on Vietnam were recessed until early November 1972. In the interval, Le Duc Tho ranted against the "chicanery" of the US while Kissinger smiled as if to let the words run off like rain-drops. Also the powers that be in Saigon, South Vietnam, had blamed Kissinger when it was actually Saigon's fault that the war dragged on.

As if hijacking airplanes was now a popular thing, another one occurred in Frankfurt, Germany. While the aircraft sat on the tarmac, the hijacker held a stewardess hostage for two days. The hijacker's patience was wearing out when a German sharp shooter picked off the man as he tried to close a hatch. He had demanded release of convicted spies in Czechoslovakia. But the Soviets branded him a mental case, a standard explanation.

As 1972 came to a close, as many as 100 US B-52 airplanes attacked the Haiphong-Hanoi areas and dropped enough bombs, according to the North Vietnamese, to sink a Polish freighter and damage some buildings, failing to mention that North Vietnamese airfields were heavily bombed and made useless. By the 25th, Nixon called for a bombing halt, although on the 30th of December another bombing was carried out with the aim of crippling Hanoi's factories, something that should have been done decades ago, but had been declared out of bounds. On the 31st, the bombing was halted and the Paris peace talks resumed. Nevertheless in January of 1973, the bombing was resumed, this time on suspected military concentrations in Laos and Cambodia, while the US pressed for a compromise settlement.

But the media was by then adamantly lined up against Nixon's policy in Vietnam. Time magazine declared its stance against Nixon, taking him to task for dominating Congress and becoming a virtual despot. According to Time, the US Congress (predominantly Democratic) was trying hard to start a revolt against the Nixonian tyranny. Also liberal factions had begun a drive to shut off the money that fed the Vietnam war. Although Nixon vetoed the bill, the Democrats hoped to override the veto with a 2/3rds majority. In any case, the war was ending.

Riots occurred in Europe, protesting the Vietnam war. The Swiss had to use tear gas to disperse a mob protesting the US bombing and in Germany 10,000 university students stormed the US embassy in Bonn in protest. Years later in 1999, it was found in the ex-Soviet files that such riots were organized by the Soviet KGB. In early 1973, Nixon ordered an end to the bombing while Thieu in Saigon agreed to accept a ceasefire. Many years later, Nixon made the comment that if the bombing had been allowed to continue a little longer, a settlement might have been made favorable to South Vietnam.

January of 1973 was notable for the death of Lyndon Johnson and the reported end of hostilities in Vietnam. Toward the end of January, Secretary of Defense Laird declared the draft ended.

Despite all the fanfare over these events, Admiral Moorer, Chairman, Joint Chiefs of Staff, repeated Kissinger's warning that this was a very complicated war and difficult to stop abruptly. Furthermore, the North Vietnamese had long been operating from a secret sanctuary. The implication was that they would continue to do so. As it turned out, Kissinger and Moorer were right: reports of new fighting in Vietnam were coming from Saigon. Nevertheless an internationally supervised cease-fire was to begin January 27, 1973 (Crozier 1999, 291), although fighting continued until 1975.

* * * * * * * * * * * * *

The Watergate bugging incident had remained largely in the background for some time, but on January 30, 1973, it came out that McCord, in Nixons entourage, was found guilty of "trespassing". McCord had been head of a Republican "intelligence" group. The Democrats were determined not to let all this go unnoticed, although the media was already making much out of it. True to form, Ted Kennedy, brother of John and Robert Kennedy, saw his chance to shoot down Nixon by turning the Watergate bugging incident into a "Cause Célèbre". Already, about this same time, a certain Segretti had been revealed as one involved in the break-in plot. But as it turned out, this was only a bubble on the top of the whole stew pot, to be eagerly stirred by the Democrats. Not long after this, Maurice Stans, chairman of the Republican National Committee, and John Mitchell, Attorney General, were fingered by the so called "plumbers" as the source of their finances.

Unknown at the time to the US public on March 21, 1973, Nixon ordered an investigation into the "Watergate Affair", ostensibly to find out if his aides had been involved in the break-in of the Democratic headquarters. Later on, Nixon, under increasing fire from the media, stated that not until March 22nd, 1973, did he know about the break-in.

At the same time, major parts of the media were trying to spread the idea that the present administration was the most corrupt in US history. They compared it to the "Teapot Dome" scandal ca. 1922, in which Republican President Harding's Secretary of the Interior became entangled in "renting" oil to big oil companies, much of the profits allegedly going to the Republican campaign fund.

In April 1973, the Watergate affair, like a flood, was licking ever more closely at the feet of a number of people in Nixon's entourage. Not only John Mitchell, but one of the White House staff, John Dean, were named as being involved according to certain New York and Washington newspapers. But Dean stated that he would not be the fall guy and had been fingering several others in Nixons staff.

Later in the month, US B-52 bombers were again over Cambodia dropping bombs while the mining of Haiphong harbor was resumed. But all this produced little publicity while the Watergate case took over the headlines. Haldeman and Ehrlichman, Nixons top advisors, were now implicated in the break-in, according to the Washington Star Newspaper. Mitchell, under fire, claimed not to know anything about any attempt to find out details of Democrats' plans. Toward the end of April Nixon continued under siege in the form of articles in the Washington Post and CBS TV. Evidence had been discovered that Nixon and his staff, including Haldeman, were up to various schemes to influence voters during Nixon's election for governor of California 11 years ago. Yet it also was claimed that President Johnson was not quite clean either in obtaining votes during his early political days.

Toward the end of April, Patrick Gray, Acting Director of the FBI, resigned amidst the gathering Watergate storm. Nixon also said goodbye to Jeb Magruder, long a Nixon campaigner. Gray was alleged to have burned several documents before leaving his post. On the 30th, Nixon announced a number of resignations: Haldeman, Ehrlichman, Kleindienst, and others less-known in Nixon's circle of advisors. Elliot Richardson was made acting Attorney General. Shortly afterward in the evening Nixon was on TV saying essentially: I was away when the story broke. Somebody goofed. They were good men and true. Sorry to see them go. He added that he was appalled (at the story) and said that Richardson would appoint a special prosecutor to pursue the case. He finished by saying that the responsibility was his.

On May 4, Ehrlichman and Haldeman were called to the witness stand. Prosecutor Jaworski and supporters, obviously out to get convictions, planned to at least embarrass these two and also indict Dean and Mitchell. Not all the newspapers were out to shoot down the "President's Men". A story came out that the investigators themselves were found to be wire tapping, but this was all quickly forgotten. Certainly wire tapping between US and Soviet secret services was widespread all through the post WW II era up until the collapse of the Soviet Union in the 1990s.

Also in May, Daniel Ellsberg, having lifted secret government documents, was by this time off and Scott-free. At the same time, Nixon's aids were only getting in deeper, lately accused of photographing the files of Ellsberg's psychiatrist.

This was evidently brought out to reveal that Ellsberg was an unbalanced person. Yet the leftist media pounced on it as damning to Nixon's aides. Despite the efforts of Sam Ervin, one of the Nixon prosecutors, who said that Secretary of Agriculture Butz's claim that Watergate was a political inquisition, was ridiculous.

But Nixon did have some support from ex-FBI man J. Patrick Gray who claimed that Nixon did not know of the bugging at the time it happened. Nevertheless, the Nixon-detractors claimed that Gray was tainted for reasons that were not made clear. Evidently, Richard Helms, who had become DCI in 1966, did not want the CIA to be dragged into the Watergate scandal and refused to help out Nixon. The President felt that Helms had betrayed him, so had him fired, softening the act by making Helms ambassador to Iran (Polmar and Allen, 1997, 207).

What, actually were the "plumbers" looking for at the Watergate building? A number of possibilities have been proposed: 1) they did it to find out what information the DNC chairman had about Nixon, 2) to discover the DNC deal with a rich Greek tycoon, 3) to learn the connection between prominent Democratic clients and a call-girl ring, thus to embarrass the Democrats, 4) to find out if the CIA was involved in trying to prevent the exposure of the call girl ring, and 5) John Dean was seeking to cover up a connection of his fiancée to the call-girl ring (Hayward, 2001, 335). The last of these was favored by Colodny and Gettlin in their book "Silent Coup" (Colodny and Getlin, 1991, 156-160) which some regard as the last word on the subject, although seeming rather farfetched to many writers.

On May 17, hearings were started on the Watergate case, as if Richard himself were on trial. It promised to be a field day for the TV and the press, something like a glass menagerie open to the public.

During late May 1973, all the news was Watergate. Richardson chose a Harvard law professor Archibald Cox to be the investigator into the Watergate break-in. Shortly afterward, Nixon admitted that there had been an attempt by some to cover up the Watergate affair, much to the satisfaction of CBS TV. This information came out when tapes of Nixon's conversation had been released. Nixon also admitted to covering up the break-in at Ellsberg's psychiatrist's office. As a result, Ellsberg became somewhat of a hero for allegedly stealing important government documents.

On the 24th, Nixon managed to be in Vietnam where he spoke to a large contingent of ex-prisoners of the NLF. When Nixon mentioned that it was about time that we stopped making national heroes of people who steal secrets from pentagon files, he got a standing ovation that lasted for several minutes.

There were, actually, defenders of Nixon in the US government. One of these was Secretary of Interior Morton who, on CBS's "Face the Nation", defended the President, saying that Nixon was too busy to be bothered with bugging the Democrats and added that anyone trying to do that ought to have his head examined.

Reports on the case that came out in June stated that the FBI knew of the break-in right after it happened and investigated it, their results evidently kept to themselves. When the FBI's J. Edgar Hoover died May 2, 1972, Nixon appointed J. Patrick Gray Acting Director the next day. According to one story, Nixon asked the CIA to stop the FBI investigation of the break-in. But then Gray resigned in April of 1973. Perhaps this started the rumor that the CIA had revealed the break-in. One story went that the FBI had been asked to do the break-in but had refused with the result that Nixon's own "people" decided to do it. So, neither the CIA nor the FBI were involved in the break-in and wire tapping. Nixon, when he heard of the break-in, referred to the wire tappers (for this is what some think they were up to) as "those jackasses."

A curious side-issue to all this, especially including the Ellsberg affair, was that he was somehow connected to the "Fedora" case, Fedora probably a Soviet agent who was a "defector in place". One suggested reason for Nixon to cover up the Watergate Affair was to protect the identity of Fedora, an important source of Soviet information. Yet Fedora himself might have been a source of "disinformation", also feeding important information to the USSR. Fedora later returned to the USSR and evidently died a natural death ca. 1983 (Polmar and Allen, 1997, 207)

By mid-July, Nixon's health was breaking down, perhaps under the strain, with a case of virus pneumonia. Yet old Sam Ervin went on trying to "expose" Nixon's doings and even tried to issue a subpoena to the President. The only difficulty was that there was no President at home in the White House. Republican Barry Goldwater could only say of the whole thing that they ought to forget Watergate. He added that there were much greater problems than Watergate, such as inflation, the falling dollar, and the energy crisis. But then on the 13th, a former Nixon aide stated that Nixon had made tapes of his conversations in the Oval Office with various of his staff.

As a footnote to all of this, it came out at the time that the FBI's

Hoover did not think much of the Haldeman-Dean efforts in working for Nixon some years ago and had to quash a couple of their bizarre schemes before they got out of hand. But Hoover did not live long enough to protect the President from their antics and Watergate came to pass.

In mid-August Nixon stated publicly that he had no prior knowledge of the Watergate break-in and added that he had not tried to cover it up and that only one of several witnesses contradicted his statement. He went on to say that there were seven people planning the operation but he had no indication that anything was going on throughout the summer of 1972. He claimed that Dean was supposed to produce a written report (on attempts to learn about the aims of the Democrats), but failed to do so. He added that the whole thing was turned over to Peterson in the Justice Department. As for the tapes, Nixon claimed that private conversations could not be compelled to be made public, so he refused to give up the tapes that supposedly concerned Watergate.

Lowell Thomas in his evening radio program said that approval of Nixon's speech was favorable 5:1. But TV scenes were shown such as a bar-room full of men busy bending their elbows over their beer and agreeing with each other that Nixon was all wrong.

After Henry Kissinger was made Secretary of State, Nixon held a press conference on August 22. Nixon regarded Watergate as behind them now. He blamed Magruder and Dean for the flap, exonerated Haldeman and Ehrlichman, then said that if he had been running the campaign instead of running the nation, the Watergate thing would never have happened.

Toward the end of August, ABC in its review of the week's news said that Johnson, during his term in office, initiated a program of sleuthing, using the FBI to gather data on several rivals such as Barry Goldwater. But this was soon forgotten by the main-stream press and TV.

In September, the question became: could the courts force Nixon to give up the tapes of office conversations? Nixon, meanwhile, seemed to have recovered from his illness and appeared relaxed and at ease like his old self. Since the anti-Nixon media seemed to follow the old dictum that the majority is always right – in contrast to playwright Ibsen's theory that the majority is always wrong – it was simply a matter of convincing the public that the anti-Nixon bias was representing the majority.

Even certain foreigners detected the unfairness of the Democrats and their media adherents toward the break-in, especially since this sort of thing went on all too frequently in the USSR and modern Europe. One of these was the Soviet novelist and Nobel-prize winner Solzhenitsyn. He called the Democrats in the US "hypocrites" in their attack on Nixon's Watergate caper. He accused them of affected loud mouth wrath and pointed out that previous presidential campaigns were full of mutual deceit and misuse. S also stated that the US was going through the stages that the Czarist regime went through before the 1917 revolution. Interesting it is that it takes a perceptive foreigner to see through the fog of criticism blowing over the White House.

A new Watergate theory, as if there were not enough, was that the CIA did not approve of the group that hung around the President and for this reason James McCord allegedly led Liddy and Hunt into a trap which resulted in their getting caught. By mid-September, a new casualty of Watergate was Vice President Agnew who was said to be resigning, concerning certain income tax problems.

* * * * * * * * * * * *

At least some relief from the Watergate controversy was achieved when on October 6th, 1973, CBS radio announced – after a long pause – that the Israeli army was in action on both its fronts. The Syrians had evidently chosen Israel's Holy Day to make their attack. Then also there was fighting in the Suez between the Israelis and Egyptians. The Syrians were attacking in the Golan Heights on a 60-mile front and gaining ground. While the US Joint Chiefs of Staff met in emergency session, the Egyptians claimed that the east Suez bank was in their hands. But then the Israelis destroyed several of the Egyptian bridgeheads thus leaving the Egyptians marooned with 400 tanks unable to return to the mother country. Although not known at the time, the Israelis claimed to have shot down 114 Arab aircraft and the Egyptians on the ground were in great disarray.

Not known to the US public at the time, Nixon had been in communication with Moscow trying to agree on a cease-fire. Nixon knew quite well from CIA information that Syrian tanks and aircraft were of Soviet manufacture. A report from Damascus said that Israeli planes bombed that city and managed to hit the Soviet embassy killing several people.

On the 10th, Iraq decided to join the war on Syria's side while the USSR continued to secretly pour supplies into Syria, also sending land-to-air missiles which were effective in shooting down a few Israeli aircraft. But Russian tanks could not stand up to the Centurians made in

Britain, and the Israelis soon invaded southwest Syria and were well on the way to Damascus, despite having encountered some 15,000 Syrians on the Damascus road. In the air the Israelis had the edge, using French Mirage, US Skyhawks and F4Es while the Egyptians had mostly MiG-21s plus some fighter-bombers (New York Times, 1973, October 12). On the 17th, a huge tank battle occurred near the Suez canal, when some 400 Egyptian tanks were said to have been destroyed. The Arabians felt they should support Syria and threatened to close down their oil export to the Western Powers. When it was found in Washington that 70 Soviet submarines had been sent into the Mediterranean, President Nixon told Kissinger to send the Israelis everything that flies.

By the evening of October 18th, when the Israelis claimed to have destroyed 110 Soviet-built tanks, Nixon and Kissinger were agreeing with the Soviets for a cease-fire. It was found out later that North Koreans were piloting Egyptian aircraft and the North Vietnamese were helping the Syrians with SAM missiles. On the next day a big artillery duel was going on in the Golan Heights.

It was not known at the time and only came out in 1974 that Nixon had warned the USSR not to bring in two parachute divisions to fight against Israel and then pressured the Israelis to end the war.

In spite of all this near approach to a World War, the effort to bring down the Presidency continued on with Judge Sirica demanding that Nixon hand over the White House tapes. But then the judge could not be located, having gone somewhere overseas, all this greatly to upset Senators Weiker (D-CT) and Inouye (D-Hawaii) who thought that they would finish the deal. Possibly, at this juncture, Nixon could have been another de Gaulle and dissolved Congress, but this had no legal precedence, and Nixon had no real military backing.

On October 22nd, Egypt had accepted a cease-fire "standstill" but artillery duels continued. Then to astound the American public, the radio reported at 7:00 AM US Eastern time that a General Alert for all American Armed forces had been made (CBS Radio 1973, October 22). Intelligence sources had reported that the Soviets were flying infantry into Syria and Budapest, Hungary. But all this came to nothing and the UN agreed to send peace-keeping troops to the Middle East. Britain's Sir Douglas Hume stated that there was no further Soviet military action.

On October 26, 1973, Nixon faced a press conference consisting of a hushed and obviously hostile press corps. Nixon described how intelligence reports had shown unusual Soviet military action and this was why he had alerted NORAD and SAC as well as Armed Forces throughout the world. He added that he hoped for a cease-fire at home, but this remark fell on deaf ears and complete silence. The press people there seemed horrified that he had put the armed forces on alert. But Kissinger then came on and produced a detailed explanation of how it all happened, and how he had tried to come to an agreement with the USSR's Kosygin, apparently succeeding in this.

The UN, meanwhile, voted to send international forces to the Middle East with Finnish, Australian, and Swedish troops. This was soon accepted by the nations involved. These amounted to a force of some 7,000 men and was approved by the Security Council.

After things had settled down and the smoke of the battle blown away, Golda Meier stated that the cease fire came at Nixon's insistence and that under this pressure, the Israelis acquiesced. Yet it seemed likely that the Soviets called off the war the minute it seemed that their side was losing.

* * * * * * * * * * * *

Returning to Nixon's problems at home, the now famous tapes of Nixon's office conversations were seized by the faction trying to shoot him down. It turned out that the part where Dean was supposed to be saying to the President that the cover-up was coming undone, was never recorded, much to the frustration of the anti-Nixon faction. But surrender seemed in the offing when a delegation including Goldwater was said to be preparing to ask Nixon to resign.

So, while the Nixon faction seemed ready to surrender, Senator Guerny, a member of the Watergate committee, said that the prosecution was of no use. In fact all it had accomplished was to force down the stock market, raise the price of gold, lower the confidence of the public, and generally make a mess (Rather and Gates, 1974, 299, 309).

Toward the end of November evidence appeared that the USSR had master-minded the whole Middle East war. All that US threats to retaliate against the Arab faction had brought were new threats from the Arabs, creating a serious oil shortage. But by December, Arabians controlling most of the oil production in the Middle East, suggested that they might ease the oil embargo, especially if Israel gave back lands taken from Arabs (presumably including the Egyptians). The oil shortage, however, stimulated some new ways of escaping its consequences, such as Polish coal being imported to Massachusetts to generate electric power. Likewise, the Germans were offering fuel made from coal to the beleagured Dutch.

As for the Soviet Union, the much-bally-hooed "détente" with the US proved to be much ado about nothing. Soviet reactionary Solzhenitsyn, recently defected to the United States, claimed that dissention exsisted in the USSR and it was vocal and serious. At the same time, Willy Brandt in West Germany was losing popularity and was about to resign, not only because of economic problems but because of rumored connections with the USSR.

In the April 1974, Nixon was on TV explaining his role in the Watergate flap. He said the FBI had made a thorough investigation of the affair and he invited certain people to come to the White house and listen to the tapes. One thing that emerged from the tapes was that Dean probably lied frequently in his version of the break-in. The worst part of the tapes was where Nixon was saying that he planned to pay out hush-money.

Were the eastern liberals the cause of Nixon's downfall? Democratic President Truman once said of them that in his experience, "they were also very unpleasant people... Behind their slogans about saving the world and sharing wealth with the common man, lurks a nasty hunger for power" (McCulloch 1992 on Truman).

During May of 1974, the West Germans were having their own exposés and troubles with spying. Willi Brandt suddenly resigned, saying he would take the blame for harboring a communist spy in his government. Helmut Schmidt, a Social Democrat, perhaps in comparison, was said to be the only honest man left in the Western world. He was then nominated for West Germany's top job. Soon after this, Brandt's aides began fighting over who had covered up for the spy Günter Guillaume, Brandt's personal assistant and a STASI agent who was reputed to know Brandt's innermost thoughts. Brandt then decided to leave office, his "Ost Politik" a shambles. Guillaume had been arrested in April and sentenced to 13 years in prison. His wife too was arrested and imprisoned. A few years later both were exchanged for certain West Germans held in the East (Polmar and Allen, 1997, 247).

How many and how important were the secrets that the Kremlin got from Guillaume? It seemed that the BND (Bundesnachrichtendienst) knew about G for a year and used him to feed the Soviets false information and to find other links with him. It later came out that the French Secret Police had seen G in southern France making contact with a Soviet embassy official. They then informed the BND and the cat was out of the bag.

A recent newspaper article in the New Haven Register (CT) (New Haven Register, 1974, May 17) alleged that there were three newspapers that determined the press opinion in the US: The Washington Post, the New York Times, and the Los Angeles Times. Also, certain of these were linked with big broadcasting companies.

Out of the blue came the case of the Symbionese Liberation Army in California. This was a desperate gang of revolutionists, bombers, and thieves. The California State Police and the FBI had been looking for months for the leaders of the gang. On a hot day in September, 1975, an elderly unnamed woman had gone to call on her daughter to discover that the daughter had been staying with a certain unsavory collection of characters in exchange for $100. The mother, realizing the desperate nature of her daughter's friends, left the hide-away as calmly as she could. She then went directly to the police. In only a few minutes it seemed as if every cop and FBI man in Los Angeles had arrived on the scene. Police commander Fagan called it war. Even machine guns were used by the gang in defending themselves. Then the house caught fire and five or six of the "Army" were burned up in the flames. This included "Marshal Cinque," chief of the crew. The much-publicized Patty Hearst was thought to have been among them, but after the Hearst family investigated, she—or her body – could not be found in the ruins. Only in 1979 was she finally caught, tried, and jailed for 6 months, allegedly sprung by her parents. In later years she claimed that she had been forced to work with the gang.

Even Ireland, with its capital in Dublin, was not free of Communist meddling. In June of 1974, the Irish government in Dublin opened diplomatic relations with the USSR. This allowed some 150 Soviet "diplomats" to take up headquarters in that city. MI5 was alerted, knowing all too well how the Soviets operated, and concluded that the Irish Republican Army could be getting help from the USSR.

In England itself, the strange case of Hugh Gaitskell proved related to the doings of the Soviet Secret Services. Gaitskell, preceding Harold Wilson, was Prime Minister and had a short career, evidently because of a trip to the USSR. On returning to Britain, he came down with a rare tropical disease, or so it was diagnosed. However, there was a greater probability that he had been somehow inoculated with a substance or organism that produced symptoms like the tropical disease. This theory was supported by James Angleton who came from the US to warn MI5 that it was a case of murder. Angleton also passed along the information from the CIA that Harold Wilson, who followed Gaitskell as P.M. was a

Soviet agent (Grant 1989, 154). But nothing came of all this at the time. MI5 already knew the Soviets had deeply penetrated the British Labor Party and as a result, MI5 undertook to drive Wilson out of office by various means. Whatever the cause, Wilson resigned in 1976 under a cloud.

Back in the US, the Watergate catastrophe went on into July of 1974. The Supreme Court decided that Nixon should give up the tapes of his office conversations. How much of it had been erased remained uncertain. If Nixon refused to give up the tapes, it was said to be an impeachable offense, eagerly pointed out by NBC and CBS Television. On August 5th, the leftist faction of the media was triumphant that more of the tapes were delivered to the House Judiciary Committee. These suggested that Nixon did cover up conversations about the break-in. Dark clouds were gathering for the President. Soon afterwards, Vice President Ford met with Nixon on the 8th and the President decided to address the nation at 9:00 P.M. eastern US time. Kissinger was also said to have urged Nixon to resign.

At 9:00 P.M. eastern US time on the 8th, Nixon was on the TV and radio. He said he was resigning. He quoted Theodore Roosevelt to the effect that one should at least try to succeed at doing good for the country. Nixon added that he had succeeded at some things and failed at others.

The media's reaction to the abdication was mixed. Some press writers were picking already on Ford, saying he was appointed, not elected. Otherwise, many in the media seemed to be shedding crocodile tears for Nixon's plight. Walter Cronkhite, CBS anchor man on TV as far back as many Americans could recall, seemed sad and almost sheepish. Dan Rather, also a TV commentator for years, said it was sad no matter how one regarded it. But Mr. Mudd of TV fame, said Nixon failed to say that he knew about the break-in all along, although this remained a matter of controversy. In the final view, one would think that Nixon had died, for after all, he had been elected by an enormous majority.

On August 12th, President Ford spoke to Congress and the American public that evening. He had a long list of suggested improvements and admonitions, including good relations with China, détente with the USSR, barring wire tapping and break-ins (much applause), and to finally say that his office door would be open to all Congressmen – if they didn't overdo it (much laughter).

During October, a leaked secret report claimed that during Nixon's last days in office, the military considered taking over the government, at least temporarily. The source of the information remained obscure.

Chapter 6

Soviet Terror And Turmoil In The 1970's

In May of 1975 a new international incident occurred that probably did more to puzzle Americans than get them upset. A US freighter was captured off the coast of Cambodia by Cambodian warships. President Ford then spent the night of the 13th discussing the problem with the NSC while keeping Senate leaders informed. Evidently, the US government decided to do nothing now.

The following day, US warplanes appeared off the Cambodian coast and fired rockets and machine guns at a number of Cambodian gunboats, sank three and crippled four to leave them drifting in the sea. The Cambodian government high handedly demanded that the US remove its marines, from their country. By 9:00 P.M., eastern US time, word came to Washington D.C. that the Cambodians were releasing the freighter. Actually, what happened was that a US destroyer had come alongside the freighter and US Marines had swarmed aboard to seize the ship.

The Chinese government in Peking promptly branded the US action "an act of piracy." But President Ford had already called the ship's seizure "an act of piracy." At this same time, the nation of Cambodia was in such a turmoil that it had no intention of doing anything about the situation, especially since US aircraft had pounced on a Cambodian air base and destroyed it.

By the 18th of June, the Cambodian ship incident was still reverberating around the world. According to TV commentator Peter Lisagor, the US government was worried that it could turn into another Pueblo incident. But the Cambodian freighter, the "Mayaguez" was 60 miles off its coast and thus in international waters, although the Pueblo was later determined to have been also in international waters.

* * * * * * * * * * * *

During the summer of 1975, the CIA learned through secret sources that the USSR was in worse economic shape than generally accepted in the western world. This situation was not helped by a wheat shortage this year. Nevertheless, there was criticism of the US Intelligence services for their methods of operation. But FBI Director Kelley defended those services, the FBI and CIA in particular, and claimed that attempts to find things wrong with them would end with the US in third place. He added that we should be willing to give up a little freedom to save the bulk of their activities.

In mid-August of 1975 the CIA had revealed that several million rubles a month were spent by the USSR to aid the Communists in Portugal. But it was not too surprising that Portugal's Catholics did not want to follow that path. When Kissinger was alerted to the situation, he warned the USSR not to try and assist the Portuguese Communists. That Communism was not all that popular in Portugal anyway was indicated by an incident in the town of Braga in which someone set fire to the office of the Communist party after the contents had been dumped out in the street.

The CIA, asked about the situation, repeated that the Soviets had poured altogether $4 million worth of aid to Portugal to overthrow the government. Kissinger then warned the Kremlin to stop meddling in Portugal and Ford added to his words. The Soviet government replied that Portugal's affairs should be settled by Portugal and the US should not meddle in them. Ford replied by saying that if the strategic weapons agreement with the USSR did not occur, the US would have to build up its nuclear force to a new level.

Following this, in early September an attempt was made to assassinate President Ford. For some time Manson, famous for the "Manson murders," had been in prison, but his various unsavory followers were wandering more or less aimlessly outside. One of them was a little red-haired girl named "Squeaky." For some reason known only to her, perhaps paid by some unknown party, she attempted to shoot Ford when he came down 10th Street in Sacramento, CA in a parade. When the President came in his limousine, she stepped forward in the crowd, raised her handgun, and pulled the trigger. Nothing happened. Apparently she had not cocked the gun or there was no shell in the chamber. Another theory was that a Secret Service man had grabbed the gun and put his finger in front of the hammer. Squeaky, dismayed at the outcome, shouted "It didn't go off!" and was quickly seized by the Secret Service man. She was then wrestled to the ground and cuffed. As if nothing had happened, Ford went on to give his speech. He talked about the need for gun legislation.

Editorials in various newspapers asked why the Manson gang was not under surveillance. But at the same time the CIA was under fire from Senator Church (D-ID) for being too forward in its operations. In fact a big Senate vendetta was occupying itself by picking on spy organizations, the CIA in particular. However Ford warned (by way of rebuttal) against exposing the names of CIA operatives. Leaks were common enough and there was a saying going around the nation's capitol that the CIA always made one copy for themselves for each report, one for President Ford, and one for Jack Anderson the columnist.

And the witch hunt for the CIA went on. Senator Church and his committee sat like judges deciding the fate of Joan of Arc, except that they were looking down from their podium on a number of sweating CIA agents. The fact that the Soviet organizations used wiretapping, listening in to telephone relay towers, using undercover agents, and even assassinations, was of course not mentioned.

Certain elements of the media were also critical of US Secret Services. In a British film, it was revealed that the CIA, with Britain's MI6, had helped to install the Shah of Iran as Iran's king and even supported the Daily Worker newspaper in order to keep track of Communist associates. Although the Shah effort was born of an attempt to thwart the spread of Communism, it proved to be a gigantic problem when the Communists took over in Iran under Khoumeini and brought about a revolution resulting in ejection of the Shah and the holding of American hostages in Tehran.

Shortly after the Ides of September, 1975, another attempt was made to assassinate President Ford. Again it was a woman, again it was a leftist, name of Sarah Jane More. The weapon, evidently a handgun, was concealed until she came close to Ford during a public occasion. But there was so much pushing and shoving that she lost her chance and the plot failed.

Another spy case came to light during the autumn of 1975. This involved a Virgil Tipanut, 37, third Secretary of the Soviet embassy in

Oslo, Norway. He had abruptly defected to Norwegian authorities. The Oslo newspaper "Aftenpost" reported that Tipanut had revealed the names of 40 Romanian intelligence agents who were stationed throughout Europe, specializing in diplomatic and industrial espionage.

In November, came the "Saturday Night Massacre," so-called by the media. (Newsweek 1975, November 2). James Schlesinger, Secretary of Defense, and Henry Kissinger, National Security Chairman, who were rumored not to have seen eye-to-eye on many problems, were out of office. Also William Colby, DCI, was out. Colby was said to have written to columnist Jack Anderson that Jack had been wrecking the credibility of their operations. Anderson had answered this in a column that he (Anderson) was the guardian of a free press.

Schlesinger's job was taken over by Rumsfeld while Kissinger's position was taken over by Air Force General Scowcroft. As for the directorship of the CIA, George Bush, a decorated flier in WW II, was installed while Morton's job as Secretary of Commerce was taken over by Elliot Richardson. Indeed a massacre.

By now, both the US and the USSR had "merved" (multiple warhead) missiles. With the older ones, a miss of a mile was standard, but now 0.1 miles were within the range of error. (Science 1975, July 12)

International espionage and assassinations were, by the mid-1970s becoming commonplace. "Carlos the Jackal" had long been known as an elusive murderer and kidnapper. Austrian officials were especially eager to get their hands on him. His latest escapade was to hijack an airliner in the Netherlands and hold the passengers hostage. Who was this "Carlos?" many students of espionage were asking. His real name was Illyitch Martinez, known to be an international spy. He was thought to be the ringleader of the latest kidnapping, this time of a group of OPEC ministers. Later on these people were released to various Mediterranean countries while the kidnappers fled to Algiers. But the Algerians refused to extradite the kidnappers to Austria, not surprising considering the reputation of the city of Algiers.

Apparently unrelated to this, Greek newspapers had published the name of the chief CIA operative in Athens. This, of course, exposed him to his enemies and he was murdered.

The United States itself was not immune to international attempts to bomb key government buildings. An attempt was made on January 12, 1976 to blow up the United Nations building in New York City. But the bomb was discovered just before it exploded. Later on about this time, a threat had been sent via the New York Telephone Company to bomb La

Guardia airport just east of New York City. Although the entire airport was closed, nothing happened. The originator of the call was never discovered.

The source of such attempted bombings was thought to be somewhere in the Middle East. Beirut, Lebanon was in a turmoil by the middle of June, 1976. Two US embassy staff people had been kidnapped in the city and then murdered. In spite of this, the Beirut government assured Americans and Brittons that they would have safe passage from that city. This announcement resulted in a sudden flood of evacuees, mostly US citizens. Landing craft were brought to the beaches and carried people out to waiting US warships. One of the evacuees commented that they had no idea what was going on and wondered why they had to leave. Nevertheless, there were about 1000 US citizens still in Beirut. These were destined to become sitting ducks for what was to come.

During the hot days of August, the US Socialist Workers Party was being infiltrated by one of the various Federal police forces, probably the CIA or FBI. Unfortunately, this was discovered and the SWP was beginning to complain about it. Clarence Kelley, Director of the FBI, was on the TV's "Face the Nation" (CBS). He was asked if the FBI should not "lay off" groups like the SWP now that the red scare was over. Kelley replied that it was CBS's opinion that the red scare was over, and added that if a reddish group has an espionage organization and it is dedicated to the overthrow of the US government, it would be investigated.

About this same time, details of the latest bomber aircraft had leaked out. The British, Germans, and Italians had together designed and built a swing-wing airplane called the "Wunder Waffe" (in German: Wonder Weapon), It flew just under the speed of sound and could reach higher altitudes than any conventional bomber. Britain would get 385 of them, Germany's Luftwaffe 324, and the Italian Airforce 100. Each would cost $19 million. Turbo Union (British), including some of Rolls Royce, some of MTU in West Germany, and 20% of Italy's Fiat, would build the turbo-jets in Britain. (UPI 1977, November 15).

In early September, as a sign of a disintegrating USSR, a Soviet jet fighter of the latest design, flew over the China Sea and landed in Japan —to the utter astonishment of Japanese authorities. The pilot asked for asylum in the US. Probably the DIA (Defense Intelligence Agency) would have liked very much to chat with him. Anyway, as could be predicted, the airplane was not returned. As if to counter the Soviet embarrassment for their defected airplane, the USSR leaked the information that they had tested "killer satellites" successfully, although security on this in the USSR was very tight.

On September 9, 1976, Mao Tse Tung was said to-have died during the night, aged 82. Kissinger was asked if this would affect the policy of the Chinese government. He said: "their policy was not the whim of individuals, but of a nation," and therefore evidently would not change.

Although "Western leaders" (just who they were remained a little obscure) were deluded enough about China to extol the virtues of the dead Mao, certain sources within China claimed that he had killed 900,000 Chinese citizens and other sources said it was more like two million. A whole upper class of Chinese was said to have been eradicated by Mao, resulting in a setback to technical progress since they were the intelligencia of China.

In the meantime, the USSR, never tired of meddling in faraway places to extend their power in the guise of spreading Communism, were busy training black guerillas for fighting in Rhodesia, a nation just northeast of South Africa. It began to appear to some people in Washington that troubles all over the world: in northern Ireland, Chile, Korea, Vietnam, Cambodia, and Cuba were all related to the machinations of the USSR. Intelligence sources agreed with that appraisal.

On November 3, the US presidential race was a close one between Gerald Ford and "Jimmy" Carter. Although Carter won easily in terms of the electoral vote, he only won 51% of the popular vote.

* * * * * * * * * * * * * *

In December the pentagon released information on missiles, although such secrets had already leaked out to some extent, claiming that the USSR had a missile launched from a submarine under water that could travel 6,600 miles while US missiles could only go about 2,900 miles. Only a few years ago Soviet missiles from submarines could only go some 700 or so miles.

At the same time the spy game between the USSR and the western world went on. A defector from the USSR, name of Myagov, 31 years old, claimed he was a KGB captain in Counter Intelligence and defected from East Germany to the British, presumably in West Germany, on February 2, 1974. He claimed that 8,000 West Germans were spying for the Soviet Union and other Communist countries. He added that 1,200 of the 1,500 KGB officers stationed in East Germany were engaged in espionage, mainly against West Germany, but also against US, British, and French troops stationed in West Germany. In a new book "Inside the KGB" he wrote that troops were exposed to serious radiation just east of Lake Baikal following an atomic explosion. As many as 70% of the troops were seriously affected and many were hospitalized for years.

As reported to the western world via a Japanese monitor satellite, China's Hua Kwo Feng, party chairman, was on Peking's TV. He had said the usual soothing sayings, the drift of which being that the "party" would undergo a thorough purge in 1977 in order to rid itself of the Mrs. Mao factions, at the time said to be plaguing China. Fukein province was said to be in open revolt, while near Peking, there was much "unrest" following the machinations of "the Four" led by Mao's widow. Finally, the Chinese army had to put down the upheavals.

Even Switzerland was not free of Soviet machinations. Her former Air Defense Chief, Brigadier General Jean-Louis JeanMaire was arrested for revealing to the USSR details of the Swiss Air Defenses. He could have gotten 20 years in prison. Following this revelation, the whole Soviet embassy staff in Bern quietly departed from Switzerland, perhaps to the Gulag. (New Haven Register 1977, January 1)

Although US borders were notoriously open to immigrants, often with visas that they soon overstayed, the FBI succeeded in arresting a Soviet immigrant on January 7, 1977 who was charged with attempting to slip classified Defense Department information to the USSR via a highly-placed member of the Soviet delegation to the US. The man, Ivan N. Rogalsky, was charged by the FBI with conspiring in 1971 against the US and was found in possession of documents from the RCA Space Center in Princeton, NJ. The FBI's Director Kelley said R's effort was linked to the case of Yevgeniy Petrovich Karpov, a ranking official at the UN in New York City. Karpov could not be arrested, but could be deported. As if in response to all this, a number of Germans and Czechs were arrested in East Germany and Czechoslovakia and accused of being CIA agents.

Also, during this month, the French Secret police arrested an alien: Abu Daoud, suspected of masterminding the murder of the Israeli athletes at Munich, Germany in 1972. But the French government, evidently fearing more terrorism, let him go, thus to make the Israeli government angry enough to recall its ambassador to France. The US government also expressed its annoyance over the release of Daoud. This only angered the French who called in the US ambassador for a "dressing down," telling the Americans, in effect, to mind their own business.

In early February, Intelligence reports stated that the Soviets had moved their new T-72 tanks into East Germany, formerly kept in the USSR. Also they moved up their new SA-8 radar-guided ground-to-air missiles, designed to destroy low-flying enemy aircraft. A Pentagon report stated that the USSR wanted superiority in weapons, not just parity.

While Gerald Ford took up his duties at Yale University as lecturer in history, Alexander Haig visited that center of learning to state that NATO forces in Europe still had the "vigor" to repel a Soviet attack on Western Europe. He also mentioned that we needed the B-1 bomber because of increased vulnerability of US missile silos. Asked about Watergate, he refused to talk about that.

Also in early February 1977, Admiral Turner of the U.S. Navy and former Carter classmate, was nominated Director, Central Intelligence (DCI). A Rhodes scholar, he had been an aide to the Secretary of the Navy, 1968-1970, and had directed Systems Analysis Division in the Office of the Chief of Naval Operations.

One of the curious secrets of the time that was leaked out during Carter's administration was that a converted 747 Jumbo jet, called the "Doomsday Jet" was Carter's command center in case of nuclear war. It was said to have a "long wire" some 5 miles long trailed from an airplane and emitted long wave lengths to penetrate the ocean depths to submerged submarines. Carter evidently saw no harm in releasing the information and said that the more assurance we have that all this command system will work, the more he could be sure that we would never use it.

By mid February, a secret manuscript was leaked, naming King Hussein of Jordan along with Kenyatta of Kenya, Thieu of Vietnam, Mobutu of Zaire, Burnham of Guyana, and Brandt of West Germany as those receiving aid through the CIA. According to the Washington Post, the CIA went to court to prevent the names from being published in the new book: "The CIA and the Cult of Intelligence." by Victor Marchetti and John D. Marks. While the book then had curious blank spaces where certain names were deleted, Jordan's King Hussein evidently used the CIA money for his own intelligence-gathering purposes.

But the CIA had worse luck in Britain where several publications blew the cover of Ed Proctor, CIA's station chief in London. Certain British journalists resented the fact that US Intelligence agents were stationed in Britain, although they had been there in one form or another for years (New Haven Register 1977, February 20).

Toward the end of February 1977 Idi Amin of Uganda, just north of Lake Tanganyka in east-central Africa, produced a mass of hysterical and extraneous verbiage that was faithfully repeated in the liberal US press. According to him, British, US, or Israeli troops were planning to descend on him from the skies. But other reports persisted that he was busy murdering thousands of African tribesmen. Carter, on hearing about this, said he did not approve of such antics.

During March the CIA was taking its lumps from the liberal media. Admiral Turner, then Director, Central Intelligence, was on CBS's TV show "Face the Nation" on the 20th. Turner countered complaints about the CIA spending so much money by saying that, compared to the amount of total foreign aid, the amount spent abroad as "foreign aid in secrecy" was infinitesimal. When asked about the morale of the CIA, he said it had held up well in the face of badgering by the press. Asked if there were Cubans involved in the Zaire invasion, he would not say.

Washington was also keeping its eye on Chile where Communist elements were working their wiles. It was known later on that Orlando Letelier was employed at one time in Washington D.C. at the Institute of Policy Studies, at the same time an official in the cabinet of the Socialist Allende government in Chile. On September 21, 1976, Letelier was killed in a bomb blast. Possibly he was working in favor of Cuban influence in Chile. Perhaps connected to this case, on October 6, 1976, a Cuban airliner over the Caribbean Sea exploded, killing all aboard. There was a published rumor that anti-Castro Cubans had caused it, in connection with the Letelier case.

On May 6, 1978, the FBI named three anti-Castro Cuban exiles as having planned to kill O. Letelier, namely: Sampol, Esquinel, and Romero. This outcome seemed to support the idea that Letelier was writing letters to Allende's daughter who was closely linked with the Castro Communists.

The Cubans did not confine themselves to meddling in South America. Zaire, for example, once known as the Belgian Congo in central Africa, faced a "foreign" invasion, probably financed by the USSR. However, native forces in Zaire put up a good fight and routed the enemy, capturing many weapons. Most of these were made in the USSR. Angola too, on the west coast of Africa, once known as Portuguese West Africa, had become a nesting ground for Cubans and fellow travellers of the USSR's KGB.

Most Americans were unaware of it, but the Soviets were often flying up and down the US east coast. In one case, they were checking on maneuvers of a US carrier task force. These Soviet aircraft were Bear class bombers, flying so close to the coast that fighter aircraft in North

Carolina were scrambled and drove them off. The Soviet airplanes were bombers of the TU-95 type, equipped with cameras, electronic intelligence devices, and two types of anti-ship missiles, probably based in Cuba. On January 11, 1977, Soviet bombers had flown out over the Pacific from Vladivostok to within 50 miles of Guam and were known to have operated in the South Atlantic flying from African bases.

In the spring of 1977, the big TV organizations were continuing to throw cold water on the Nixon-Frost talks, claiming that they would make a tidy profit. But Nixon came on, seeming suave and relaxed, hardly the ogre and bitter "King Richard" so-painted by the big networks. Telling anecdotes, bringing up recollections, and cracking jokes, one might wonder how this man had the fiber to withstand the Watergate era —which, in a way, he had not.

Many years later in 2001, Associated Press produced an article about Watergate, reporting that G. Gordon Liddy had testified that the Watergate "burglars" were seeking photographs linking John Dean's future wife to a call-girl ring, a theory already mentioned in the present chronicle. Liddy evidently thought that they were seeking political intelligence about the Democrats and admitted arranging the break-in. And the FBI later found the bug on a DNC phone line. Dean denied all this Liddy story. According to the A.P. article, Jeb Magruder, Nixon's deputy campaign director, gave the break-in order. Liddy added that the whole thing was "stupid." (Republican American 2001, January 30).

In late May, 1977, the Nixon-Frost talks continued. Nixon was asked about the overthrow of Chile's Allende. He replied that if Marxism had won in Chile, it would have put South America in a giant sandwich with Cuba and Chile as the bread at the two ends and the rest of the place as meat in the middle. Although Frost said he could not buy that, Nixon seemed undismayed and added that when the Republicans did something wrong every liberal Democrat was down on him; but if one of them broke the law, then it was "Ha Ha Ha" and forget it.

But the Russians too had their problems. The axing of Mr. Podgorny in the inner circle of the Soviet Politburo suggested a serious failure in Soviet foreign policy. The USSR's forces had failed to invade Zaire, and China was befriending South Africa.

For some mysterious reason, the US government suddenly declared itself alarmed by the widespread eves-dropping carried on by the USSR in telephone communications. As a result, President Carter planned to use special kinds of communications such as "scramblers" that distort the voice and can be unscrambled later on. US Intelligence agencies had found that when the Soviets listened in on telephone lines, they also gave off a signal so that US sleuths could tell when the line was tapped. Much of the phone conversations in these days were going on via microwave from tower to tower, so that they could easily be intercepted. Of course, underground and undersea cables had been tapped for decades, mentioned in this chronicle in WW I. But in the late 1900s, tapping undersea cables became the favorite occupation of US submarines, the case of the submarine Halibut in the Sea of Okhotsk told toward the end of the century.

By this time in the spring of 1977, the Minute Man III missiles had given the US an 80% chance of destroying their targets instead of 20%. The US was said to have now 500 Minute Man IIIs, each with three warheads, also 450 of the older Minute Man II (Science 1977, July 10).

During August, some reporter evidently leaked a story that claimed that there was a US scheme to let the Soviets have a third of West Germany in any European invasion. Probably as a result of this leak, Carter released "Plan 18" supposed to inflict "unacceptable damage" on any Soviet invasion force in Europe. But this created an understandably violent reaction in West Germany since the Germans quickly envisioned their country a battleground, all this according to CBS TV news.

West Germany was still suffering from Communist-minded terrorists. German industrialist Hans Martin Schleyer was kidnapped in August, The Red Army Faction thought to have been involved. Their main aim was to have other Bader-Meinhof gang members released from prison, but this scheme fell flat when Schleyer was found dead in a car trunk.

In the US, meanwhile, there were those that firmly believed that the media was strongly biased against the right wing. In a new book on the subject, Victor Lasky asked whether the US media was biased? Did they minimize or hide the scandals of the Roosevelt, Kennedy, and Johnson administration? Did they maximize the faults of the Nixon administration? Lasky's answer to all these questions was "Yes."

The Germans too were plagued with airplane hijackings. On October 15, 1977 a Lufthansa passenger airplane was hijacked during its flight from Mallorca to West Germany. It then flew to Cyprus, Bahrain, and to Dubas where the hijackers gave the Germans until the next day to hand over $15,000,000 and free certain of their kind being held in prison. But the Turks refused to release any of those people demanded by the hijackers.

By the 18th the plane went on to Somaliland. But unknown to the rest of the world, another airplane with a team of German commandos followed it. Using black uniforms and having blacked their faces, they approached the airplane as it sat at the airport in the dark. They then blew open the doors and charged in. The four hijackers started throwing grenades, wounding several passengers, but the commandos quickly shot down all the hijackers.

Sighs of relief were almost audible all over the world. Even Begin of Israel congratulated the Germans, although other terrorists were then threatening Chancellor Schmidt.

The Dutch police were not so easily taken in by terrorists. The police figured out that members of the Bader-Meinhof gang of Leftists would be hanging around the airport where Lufthansa airliners came often in to land, no doubt hoping to hit one of these airliners with a portable missile. The police, after a thorough search, found two of the missiles in a large apartment complex and one in a phone booth on the street. Soon after this, an airplane came in to land and pulled up to the usual place to unload passengers. A big shoot-out followed and two of the gang were caught, some evidently escaping.

In the United States, selling weapons to foreign elements went on as always. Two men were arrested this November, 1977 for selling the details of the gyroscope system used in missiles made by Litton Industries. One of them, name of Wieschenberg, was convicted of espionage and the other, Heiser by name, although accused of being a registered agent for a foreign government, was found innocent.

Jane's All the World Aircraft estimated that the amount of warning of an impending attack that NATO might expect in Europe had diminished from 30 days to 4 to 5 days. The article pointed to certain weaknesses in the cruise missiles' design. Evidently, it fails to "jam" enemy radar and also lightweight aircraft can shoot down cruise missiles. Nevertheless, it is possible to produce thousands of cruise missiles in contrast to the great expense of a single B-1 bomber.

In January of 1978, it was discovered by the US that the Soviets had a new missile, the SS-20, carried on a tank-like vehicle for use in intercontinental war. It seemed to be a 2-staged version of the SS-16 carrying three warheads with a range of about 3,000 miles. Carter publicly warned the western powers of this weapon, perhaps to counter Breshnev's complaining about deployment of the neutron bomb in Europe. This could be fired by a howitzer or a Lance missile.

* * * * * * * * * * * * * * * *

Most all Americans probably did not know it at the time, or even at the end of the century, where the Palestinians really lived. Around 1978 about three fourths of a million lived on the West Bank, nearly half a million in the Gaza strip, nearly a million in Jordan, a half million in Israel itself, nearly a half million in Lebanon, a quarter million in Kuwait, 150,000 in Syria, and 15,000 in Egypt (New Haven Register 1978, January 17).

While the deadlock over what constituted Palestine continued unabated, the Soviets were conducting maneuvers off the Egyptian coast with the Soviet aircraft carrier Kiev and the helicopter carrier Moskva, mostly to test out antisubmarine devices. The Kiev carried Yak-36 vertical takeoff aircraft. All this show of force seemed to be directed at Egypt.

In late January of 1978, the US media became much excited by the crash of a Soviet satellite in the wilds of central Canada. A mounted policeman stationed near Great Slave Lake said he saw a meteor-like glow streak across the sky. Breaking into pieces, some of it made it to the earth, including a grapefruit-sized nuclear energy source. Whether this was an accident, a shoot-down, or brought down on purpose remained uncertain.

Evidently the crash created a lot of radioactivity in the air. German rocket scientist Heinz Kaminsky at Bochum, Germany said that a radioactive cloud over a hundred miles long and a half mile wide was moving eastward from the Soviet satellite crash site. He called it a breach in international agreements.

By the 26th, the Canadians discovered a piece of radioactive material near Baker Lake that was believed to have come from the satellite. There was speculation by commentator Mel Elfin on the Agronsky & Company TV show that we might have shot down the Soviet satellite after they had done the same to ours.

Some four days later, more of the Soviet satellite was found, along with a large crater near Baker Lake, Canada. People nearby were taken to a hospital for possible radiation exposure. The Canadians released photographs showing a jumble of pipes, like plumbing from a house. Walter Cronkhite, commentator on CBS TV was not impressed, stating that it was known 10 years ago that "they" had reactors out in space as energy sources for taking pictures of ground installations.

About a week later in February, the West German Military Counter Intelligence Service was discovered to have been bugging numerous private dwellings. Defense Minister Georg Leber then resigned when he learned of this, triggering a cabinet reorganization. Leber's admission of involvement followed a parliamentary investigation into his handling of the case of three Communist spies discovered in Leber's ministry. Leber said the bugging was done without his knowledge or approval. He was then replaced by his protegé, Hans Apel, who was unique in never having done military service. He had been too young for Hitler's army and too old for the postwar era.

Also in West Germany, a Frau Renate Lutze, a 37 year-old secretary in the Defense Ministry, along with 15 other East German agents, allegedly copied hundreds of documents, telling the locations of fuel dumps and ammunition depots in West Germany. The documents were sent east. Asked if nuclear bomb storage depots existed, the article's author could not discover. Evidently, NATO had its own spy organization while each nation within it had its own apparatus.

Also in early February, a large scale spy network was uncovered by the Royal Canadian Mounted Police in Canada. Twelve Soviet diplomats would have to leave. The RCMP said it was the fourth such incident since WW II in which the Soviets had attempted to infiltrate the Security Branch of the RCMP in Ottawa. All the old tried and true spy methods were used: dead drops, passwords, false cigarette cartons, hollow pens, and so on. $30,500 in Canadian money was said to have been paid to the undercover Mountie.

While as many as 1000 Soviet pilots were flying Soviet aircraft in Ethiopia, billions of rubles were said to have been sent there by the Soviet government (Washington Week in Review PBS 1978, February 10). In the meantime, US Intelligence sources reported that Soviet pilots had been flying missions from Cuba because so many Cuban pilots had been sent to Africa, especially Ethiopia.

By the 24th of February. 1978, the Soviet Union had to all intents and purposes taken over Ethiopia. The US government's Brzezinski said today that there were 10 to 11,000 foreign troops in Ethiopia, led by one of Russia's top generals of 40 years experience. Furthermore, about 70 Soviet-built tanks had been used in Ethiopia and Somalia where Cuban and Soviet troops had been fighting the natives.

In Iran there were signs of a coming upheaval as indicated by increased espionage activity. One case was that of Boris Kabanov, Soviet Consul who would stop his car near the home of Major General Mogharebi in Tehran. Kabanov would push a button in his car and transmit 20 minutes worth of data in 20 seconds to Mogharebi who then taped it. This sort of thing went on for four years until agents of SAVAK, the Iranian Secret Police, moved in and arrested both sender and receiver. Mogharebi was said to have been executed and Kabanov asked to return to the USSR (Newsweek 1978, March 10).

* * * * * * * * * * * *

With the Democrats dominating the halls of Congress as well as the presidency, it seemed time to throw more cold water on the pro-Nixon survivors and on the FBI. Griffin Bell, the new Attorney General, initiated this new attack, indicting certain FBI agents for allegedly using wiretaps to listen in on the Weathermen underground, one of the most dangerous revolutionary groups to rear its head beginning back in the 1960s. Also, Patrick Gray, ex-FBI Director, was under fire once again.

Despite this US witch-hunting, a Soviet diplomat, Arkady F. Shevchenko, defected to the US, the highest Soviet official ever to defect. The Soviet government was greatly perturbed by this and demanded that the US "let" him come home, claiming that he was persuaded by US agents to leave his UN job.

Griffin Bell's plan seemed to be to limit the powers of the FBI by harassing it as best he could. However, the head of the FBI office in New York City decided to fight back at Bell's accusations, challenging Bell to a public debate. But Bell wormed out of it, saying that the FBI's charges were unrelated to the case at hand. The FBI pointed out that the "Weathermen" gang was connected to the machinations of the PLO, although they could not prove it. It also pointed out that Carter was trying to gain control of the FBI.

Bell excused his apparently destructive acts against the FBI by saying that he was trying to save it and had to think what was good for it. This evidently excused his bringing indictments against Former Acting Director Gray, Former Associate Director Mark Felt, Former Assistant Director Edward S. Miller, and still others. One of the others was J. Wallace LePrade who was removed on April 13th as Head of the New York FBI office. LePrade called a press conference and accused the Justice Department of waging a campaign to exert political influence over the FBI and destroy its independence. It was probable that Gray's, Felt's, and Miller's problems came from efforts to track down the Weathermen, the Feds allegedly breaking into homes of friends and relatives of that gang of desperadoes.

One ex-CIA agent on CBS's TV show "60 minutes" was willing to talk about how CIA advisors had operated in Angola, trying to thwart the efforts of the USSR. He reported that the anti-Communist side did not have the weapons to win and had to try some other methods, such as flying in prostitutes to influence Soviet agents. But the girls found the Russians impotent or with halitosis.

Turning to more mundane methods of secret agents, American embassy personnel, in Moscow, USSR, discovered bugs (listening devices) last May of 1978 in a chimney. Wires from the tiny microphones led down to a tunnel in the basement which led to an apartment building nearby. Here they found a man sitting quietly at an electronic console monitoring the various bugs. When accosted, he ran away (US News and World Report 1978, June 26).

It was about this time when the workings of NSA became more widely known. Originally as mentioned earlier in this book, the U.S. Army's Signals Intelligence Agency gave birth to Venona in 1943, later absorbed by NSA, the National Security Agency. Venona busied itself first with decoding and deciphering messages sent by telegraph. By 1978 NSA had obtained huge proportions, getting more than $1.3 billion a year. Computers at Fort Meade near the nation's capitol acted as a kind of vacuum cleaner to decipher and decode foreign traffic on the air and from cables. Satellites sometimes received signals from Soviet staff cars and relayed them to the US.

One might think by the late 1970s tanks would have become obsolete in warfare. NATO's modern tank was far from outmoded. But there was disagreement among NATO powers as to the best design. The West Germans wanted the highly motile Leopard tank, while the British had developed armor using layers of ceramic and steel that could hardly be pierced by the new artillery shells in a heavier type of tank. A compromise was finally agreed to between these two with the Chrysler corporation building it (Science 1978, July 25).

There is something about the heat of August that encourages more instances of crime. An attempt was evidently made to assassinate President Carter during his trip to Idaho where certain atomic energy work was going on. But the supposed gunman was surprised by a maid who came into the suspect's motel room. He promptly hit her on the head with his gun, then disappeared. Little more was said of the affair, but the Secret Service took the story seriously.

* * * * * * * * * * * *

In early September of 1978 the fiercest battle in nearly a month erupted in Beirut, Lebanon. On one side were the Syrians, reported to have 70,000 troops now in Lebanon; on the other were the Christian-rightist militia armed by the Israelis.

In nearby Iran, as if someone in Moscow had pushed a button, the revolution in Iran was becoming suddenly more acute, having become better organized than before. The Americans talked of sending troops, while the Iranian Marxists had changed from peaceful demonstrations to bloody confrontations (New Haven Register 1978, September 17).

On October 2nd the Syrians opened up the heaviest shelling of the Christian Militia in the history of the Middle East wars, most of this from mass-fired rockets of Soviet manufacture. By early November unrest in Iran was getting worse, probably urged on by agents of the USSR. Students at Tehran University formed a mob and threw rocks at Iranian soldiers. Thus began a real revolution.

On November 4th, unrest in Iran was beginning to fester, probably urged on by agents of the USSR. So-called students at Tehran University gathered into a mob including Communists and Moslems, to throw rocks at Iranian soldiers. The troops fired back and were said to have killed seven of the rioters. This sort of effervescence served to feed the flames of violence and were the real beginning of a serious revolution. The next day the Iranian government declared Marshal Law. Those killed in the rioting reached a total of 40 while Iran's Foreign Minister resigned, as reported by CBS radio on the 5th.

December came and the Iranian situation continued to ferment. Americans there were said to be crowding the airports to escape the turmoil. One woman from the US said they (the mob) had poured diesel fuel on her and tried to set her on fire, but diesel fuel is difficult to ignite and she escaped. A few days later, as many as 300,000 people marched in Tehran's streets, while the Iranian army did nothing to stop them.

Toward the end of December, Iranian terrorists murdered a US oil expert, Paul Grimm, ambushing him in his car with automatic weapons. His daughter said he had been an oil executive in Tehran. At the same time, the Shah offered to give up much of his power to a legislative body, but rioting continued. Oil production in Iran by then had fallen to about 15% of normal and even Iranians were running out of kerosene for their heaters and gasoline for their cars.

The Shah's whereabouts at the time was a secret, but was said to have handed over his power to a regency council. A new Prime Minister was already installed. Various wild reports in the US claimed in a "net alert" bulletin that the Shah was leaving Iran, but by 5:00 P.M. Tehran said this was not true.

On the last day of December, 1978, the US recommended that all nonessential US embassy workers leave Iran, their numbers put at between 15,000 and 30,000 people. But several Secret Service men were said to have been captured and hung by a mob. Presumably, these were Iranian Secret Service men. One observer reported that he had never seen such vicious mobs as those in Iran, running up and down the streets, screaming and yelling.

At the beginning of the new year, 1979, the Shah, after many false rumors, was said to have left Iran while a new Prime Minister promised to ban oil to Israel and South Africa.

Arthur Schlesinger in Carter's retinue claimed that if the Iranian oil cut-off continued, the US would suffer oil shortages within three months. But other sources claimed that there were secret oil reserves in Mexico that were enormous, while the true facts about it had been hidden from the public (Science 1979, January 4).

In mid-January, 1979, the question was debated on TV as to whether Iran was secretly being led into this upheaval by the USSR. The entire panel: Kilpatrick, Sidey, Will, and Rowan agreed that the Soviets were in it up to their necks. But the MC, Agronsky, did not agree, quoting Cyrus Vance who had said that the USSR had nothing to do with it. Yet a local New York newspaper reported that 1000 Communist Iranians had coordinated the riots. George Will on the panel pointed out that Iranians were shipped to Cuba, trained, and shipped back to Iran.

The Shah actually left Iran on January 16th, said to have piloted his own million-dollar airplane to Egypt, in fact shown on CBS TV sitting in his airplane nodding his head as if at his success in escaping. But some critics thought he was actually counting his money. "Newsweek" magazine recently reported that he had stashed away some $23 million in Morocco.

In mid January, President Carter wrote a letter (it leaked out) to Iran's new leader Khoumeini, asking to give the new government a chance to work. As might have been expected, K said that it was presumptuous of Carter to ask. Barry Goldwater (R-AZ) said the whole Iranian flap was Carter's fault and it showed that he had no foreign policy.

Khoumeini arrived in Tehran February 1st from his hideaway in the hills and the mob seemed to think their new Savior had arrived, but he had to be rescued by helicopter. Yet little did the mob know that he would bring them a long and exhausting war with Iraq, when thousands on thousands of Iranians would die.

Later in February Iran continued in its tortured turmoil, troops shooting at rioting civilians. According to a secret that emerged later on, helicopters were being made ready for a rapid evacuation of Americans from Iran. By 6:00 P.M. on the 10th, Iranian time, Iran's Army general realized that their military activities had failed and that Khoumeini's hordes had prevailed. Soon afterwards, Bakhtiar, who had been backed by Carter, was arrested while the military made a deal with Khoumeini to end the fighting.

On the 14th, despite an apparent end to the rioting, the so-called Marxists took over the US embassy in Tehran, then later Khoumeini's followers moved in, which only meant the Americans went from the frying pan into the fire.

In April, the CIA announced that the US would lose a number of secret radar tracking stations in Iran. These would take years to replace, and the revolution went on. Khoumeini then watched impassively as the 200th Shah supporter was taken out and shot after a kangaroo court condemned him.

The USSR, probably encouraged by the results in Iran, then set its sights on Afghanistan. This nation seemed a ripe plumb to be picked, lying just east of Iran and bordering on its northern frontier with the USSR. The Soviet government claimed that atrocities had been committed against their "advisors" and their families, now numbering about 1000. Thus began an attempt by the USSR to take over Afghanistan that went on for years without a clear victory.

By mid-May, probably related to the Iranian turmoil, US gasoline shortages had caused long lines at the pumps in many states. In California, people were waiting three hours to get served at gas stations. Carter and the Democrats wanted to have gasoline rationing, but most Republicans were against it. And other nations were suffering from such shortages. There were long lines at gas pumps in Ireland, West Germany, France, and Denmark. An independent study by a Mr. Ellis said that about 1/3rd of the gasoline price rise was the result of Iran's problems, 1/3rd due to dealers wanting larger profits, and 1/3rd due to withholding by oil companies.

On June 25th, 1979, an attempt was made on the life of General Haig on a Belgian highway near Brussels. Although Haig was an effective and progressive NATO commander, he had been threatened a number of times by terrorists, probably of Marxist-Leninist persuasion. Belgian police had advised him to travel with US Army guards and to change his plans frequently. He had complied — more or less.

Haig was travelling in a caravan of three cars, with his the second one, a big Mercedes 600 sedan. Cars were separated by about 100 meters. In his car were two US Army men, one the driver, Hans Hooker, the other, the aide Major Hudgens. They were on their way to Mons, Belgium, famous for WW I battles. The cars had to cross a small bridge which the first car passed over without any trouble. But Haig's car had barely cleared the bridge when a tremendous explosion forced the Mercedes to lurch suddenly forward while the rear compartment lid burst open. The third car, also going at high speed, fared the worst, resulting in wounding the occupants. Haig himself suffered afterwards from a temporary hearing loss (Haig 1992, 540).

A survey of the area by Belgian police showed that the bomb had been buried under one end of the bridge, set off by a wire to a hand-operated switch 100s of feet away. Haig later talked to the Director of the CIA who said the bombers were a branch of Belgian KGB-trained terrorists, probably linked to other such groups in East Europe, later said to be members of the "Red Army Faction." If the bomb had gone off a second earlier, Haig said he would not have survived. Fortunately, the driver had been going faster than usual.

* * * * * * * * * * * * * * * *

In mid-July of 1979, another kind of explosion hit the Carter government. At first in secrecy, then coming out on the 17th, all 12 cabinet members offered to quit. Only Vance, Brzezinsky and maybe Brown would stay (CBS radio 1979, July 17). In time, the upheaval began to look like a massacre worthy of the Ayatollah Khoumeini. Califano, Brock Adams, Schlesinger, and Blumenthal looked like fall-guys. And a couple of days later Energy's Brock Adams quit. Some Texan commented: "Good grief, they are cutting down the biggest trees and keeping the monkeys."

A reporter asked Adams how all this change would affect the energy situation? Adams scratched his head and said he did not know. Stevens, a senator from Alaska, said he doubted Carter's sanity.

And the struggle against the USSR's machinations went on. Congress continued its demands that the Soviets pull out of Cuba, but Carter remained silent and his spokesman Jody Powell clammed up on the subject. Retired U.S. Navy's Admiral Moorer said they (the Russians) should be told to get out. As for Senator Church (D-ID) on CBS's Face the Nation he was asked if it was the fault of intelligence that the Foreign

Relations Committee did not know earlier about Soviet troops in Cuba? Church said that it was very difficult to distinguish Russians from Cubans since they both wear Soviet uniforms. He was then asked how did the story get out? He could only say that he thought the Senate should have known about it and it was now up to Carter to act on it.

Castro, in answer to all this US discussion about Soviet troops in Cuba, said that the US was in Guantanamo for years and said it was known since 1968 that Soviet troops had been in Cuba. But the Soviets themselves claimed that there were no Soviet forces there and all the news about it was just a ruse to torpedo the SALT II treaty. DCI Turner, for his part, said he was very proud of his intelligence service (for discovering the Soviet forces) and for putting the pieces together. As for Carter, he was said to be "seething mad" at Church for releasing the information. A few days later it was apparent that the Carter government was not going to ask the USSR to leave Cuba, implying that Soviet troops were there for training purposes. Carter was then shown on TV inspecting ship yards on the Gulf coast.

On September 25th 1979, the Soviets formally announced that there were no combat troops in Cuba, although there were some advisors. However, there was new evidence from the recently defected Mr. Shevchenko from his position in the UN, that half of the Soviet UN staff was made up of KGB agents, and he named names (Polmar and Allen 1997, 508). Later on in October, Carter finally decided to increase surveillance of it, bolster US presence there in Guantanomo and speed more aid to Latin-American nations that felt threatened by the Cuban-USSR alliance.

Early in October it was revealed by unknown sources that the Soviet's missile targets in the US were not the big cities, but bomber bases, missile fields, and submarine support bases sprinkled all over the USA. These missile fields were launching sites, mostly in the western states: Arizona, Wyoming, North Dakota, Kansas, Missouri, and Arkansas (U.S. News and World Report 1979, October 2).

By November 1979, the revolution in Iran seemed unable to lie dormant for long. So-called "students" in Tehran took over the American embassy, threatening injury to personnel unless they returned the Shah. But the stark vulnerability of the US embassy, where several Americans still remained, was evidently not appreciated by the Carter government. And two days later, the US government realized that diplomatic and other staffers could easily be held as hostages. However, as seemed typical of the US presidency, Carter's wife Rosalyn was reported to be visiting Cambodia to check on the problem of the reputed starving thousands there.

By November 6th, the US government realized that those employees still in Iran were already being held hostage. No one knew what to do about it. Iran then threatened to cut off all oil exports and kill the hostages if any sign of intervention were attempted. Barsagan, the Ayatollah Khoumeini's minister, resigned while the Ayatollah instituted a "Revolutionary Government." The British embassy was also seized while later today Arafat, leader of the Palestinians, was said to have volunteered to act as a US-Iranian intermediary.

So it had come to pass that the Ayatollah had a firm grip on Carter's nose and he could give it a twist any time he wanted. Carter could then only think of calling for calm, while the US captives in Tehran pleaded for the return of the Shah. Carter ordered Iranian students in the US to report to authorities. Any Iranians living in the US illegally would be deported. There could be as many as 50,000 of them, many known to have overstayed their visas. As for the Iranian government, it cut off all oil exports.

By mid-November the Iranian revolutionists decided to release some of the Americans. These were said to be women and blacks, maybe 16 in all. The rest would be put on trial. Egypt's Sadat had one comment to make about the Iranian situation, although a Moslem himself, that the Ayatollah was a lunatic and a disgrace to Islam.

A few days later in Islamabad, Pakistan, mobs, probably urged on by Communist elements, crawled all over the fort-like US embassy building there. But US Marines fired tear gas at them and fortified themselves on the top floor. Some seven hours later, the Pakistan army arrived and laid siege to the building. Then the British military flew in helicopters and rescued all concerned.

Even in Saudi Arabia, certain relatives of the Saudi rulers were taken hostage, but later released. There was speculation that these revolutionaries were well-coordinated by the KGB. Evidence for this pointed to a Polish Army Counter-Intelligence chief, Michal Golienewski, who defected to the west in 1960. According to him, Khoumeini's activities on behalf of the USSR were discovered in 1960 when G defected. G told the CIA that Khoumeini was the most important of five top Soviet agents in Iran and that K reported to a high Iraqi government official, who then passed the information on to the KGB through its agents in Warsaw where G was Deputy Chief of Polish Army Counter-Intelligence. G was said to have sent 8000 secret documents on microfilm to

US Intelligence authorities from 1958 to 1960.

On December 1st, the Shah, now recovered from an illness in New York, asked to be allowed to travel to Mexico. But that country refused to take him. He replied to this by saying that he would leave secretly from the US.

Another well-coordinated act, probably again the work of the KGB, was the storming of the US embassy in Libya, North Africa. Although they burned the place, all US personnel escaped.

While it got very little coverage in the US, on December 6th, a counter revolution by other Ayatollahs in cities near Tehran was undertaken, apparently failing in its quest to take over Iran.

The US government, in reply to all this, moved three Battle Groups of the Navy into the vicinity of Iran. This included a Mid-East task force, a Midway (aircraft carrier) Battle Group, and a Kittyhawk (aircraft carrier) Battle Group, each of these with other ships. Their mission remained a secret and nothing came of the whole thing probably on orders from the top leaders of the US government. It leaked out later on the 26th that the USSR invaded Afghanistan with 6000 troops, the biggest troop movement by the USSR since WW II. Perhaps this move was timed to coincide with the upheavals in Iran.

As a result, the US State Department planned to file a formal protest to the USSR. Carter was said to have talked with Brezhnev on the "hot line" to Moscow, telling him basically to withdraw his troops. Nothing happened.

Chapter 7

Soviet Spies And Exploits In The Early 1980s

Secretary General Waldheim of the United Nations, a tallish, clean-cut sort of man that seemed as if he might have been an alpinist guide in younger days, arrived in Iran in hopes of solving the unsolvable. More exactly, he was hoping to reason with revolutionists and secure the release of the captives. From the start he was clearly unwelcome. On arriving in a big limousine, he was greeted by a yelling, screaming mob of rag-tag revolutionists that would not let him out to speak and if he had, his words would have been quickly drowned out.

At almost the same time on January 3rd, 1980, the US ambassador to Moscow left that city in protestation of the Soviet attack on Afghanistan. But the Soviet reply was only to move its troops deeper into that country even as far as Kandahar in the south-central region of the state. In the US, the Carter government could only talk of increasing aid to China, boycotting the Olympic Games, and decreasing grain shipments to the USSR. But the Iranian revolutionists, unimpressed by this US and UN posturing, dragged US employee Bruce Laingen before a kangaroo court and accused him of spying. Laingen's stay in Iran promised to be a long one.

Even the Soviet embassy in Tehran was seized by a group of Afghan nationalists, holding some nine Soviet citizens hostage until the Soviets got out of Afghanistan, according to demands. As for American hostages, the UN Security Council made this the last day for Khoumeini to give up the hostages. If nothing happened, the US would call for trade sanctions on Iran.

Also early in January, the US government put some new restrictions on the USSR. One of these was to remove their consular employees from their New York office. This had long been a hotbed of spying by the USSR. Carter also planned to fire several other Soviet employees working in the US. Even Americans at the Kiev, USSR, embassy would be withdrawn. Then too, instead of sending $2.5 billion worth of grain to the USSR as planned, the US would buy the grain from US farmers.

The UN's Security Council tried to pass a resolution to censor Iran for taking hostages, but the USSR vetoed it. Experts claimed that the USSR was planning to achieve a warm-water port to their south and the seizure of Afghanistan was a step in that direction. It may have been the USSR's "dream of the century," but like a lot of dreams it did not come true.

Soviet officials in the US might have wondered how the Americans knew so much about what was going on in Soviet affairs. They soon found out. Already in January, Soviet agents uncovered bugging devices in their own offices, residences, and cars in the cities of Washington D.C., San Francisco, and New York. Izvestia, in releasing all this, said they even found bugs in hollow bricks in the chimneys of their buildings in the US.

Once again, Soviet agents were caught red-handed in Canada, using the old mail-drop techniques to pass information. Usually, a tin can at the side of the road suggested a message was hidden nearby. As a result of this revelation, the Soviet embassy's Ottawa military attaché was removed together with his deputy and a chauffeur. Soviet agents had met secretly in Ottawa with an American during 16 months. The American was paid $100,000 for information. But the RCMP and the FBI together figured it out and released the information to the press which concluded that the American might have been a double agent.

At nearly the end of January, several US embassy people in Tehran managed to escape via a regular airline using Canadian passports. Iran's temporary leader Gohtbzadeh was beside himself with rage. He called it a brutal flouting of international law, a comment that seemed strange coming from an Iranian.

In early March, 1980, the hostages held in Iran expected to be transferred to the "Revolutionary Council." This was obviously a kind of kangaroo court to make publicity. Secretary of State Cyrus Vance would only say of it that he was watching the situation.

The Shah of Iran, like a wandering shadow likely to show up anywhere, appeared in Egypt toward the end of March, supposedly for an operation. The speculation was that this only put Egypt's leader Sadat in a more precarious political position, considering the large number of Muslims in that country.

Interestingly, in the light of developments toward the end of the 20th century, the harassed FBI warned the US public that as many as 50 Iranians a day were pouring into the US and these could be terrorists bent on bombing and/or sabotage. As pointed out before, most Americans had little knowledge of the flood of immigrants that were coming into the US with few checks on their activities, from simply crossing the borders at night to faking documents and claiming they were on student visas.

On April 7th Carter broke relations with Iran. Iranian diplomatic personnel in the US would be leaving tomorrow. One story appeared in the US media that the US would mine waters near Iran to cut off oil exports. In the meantime, Iranians leaving the US shouted inane and scurrilous remarks, perhaps to pave the way into the good graces of the revolutionists.

Around the middle of April, a Colonel Beckwith, in great secrecy, was sorting out his plan to rescue the hostages held in Tehran. He had discussed the plan with Carter, Brzezinski, and others. The plan was to fly in with several helicopters to the desert called the Dasht-e Kavir just south of Tehran, where they would establish "Desert I." Then transport aircraft would fly in to rendez-vous with the helicopters. At the same time, CIA-recruited Iranians would drive a party of commandos in old trucks to the city and they would go over the wall into the embassy. The helicopters would then fly them out to the transports. It all looked so neat in planning, but they miscalculated on one thing: the weather.

On the morning of April 25th, the radio news in the US reported that an attempt had been made by US forces to rescue the hostages in Tehran. But it had been a total disaster. It came out several months later that a desert sandstorm had caused all kinds of engine failures in the helicopters. Then in the strong winds, one of them crashed into a transport plane on the ground. The whole crash scene was a mass of flames. Eight Americans were said to have been killed in an explosion and subsequent fire.

In Washington D.C. at the White House, Vance was reportedly taken ill, most likely with an acute case of exasperation, having said he would resign if Carter went ahead with the Iran-desert operation.

The military involved in the rescue operations claimed that they could still have flown out some of the hostages, but the whole plan was scrubbed on orders from Washington. So everybody was mad at somebody. Congress was mad because it was not consulted, the US public was mad because the operation failed, the Iranians were mad because the Americans nearly carried it off, and the US military was mad because Carter scratched the whole operation after the collision. One is reminded of the age-old Chinese saying: Success has a thousand fathers, but failure is an orphan.

Vance did formally resign. Hodding Carter, the President's spokesman, considered resigning. The bodies of the US servicemen killed were to be given to an International Commission. At a news conference on April 29th, Carter said that peaceful means would now be used to pursue the hostage problem.

The FBI in early May released the information that four members of the Libyan embassy in Washington D.C. were probably acting as assassins to carry out Khadafi's wishes in the US. Fortunately, they were all expelled before taking action. Even the Libyan government agreed to this expulsion.

In the same month, as many as 31,000 Cuban refugees were said to have landed in the US. In fact, TV commentator Elizabeth Drew said the figure might go over 100,000. One newspaper suggested a quarter million. Just where they would go remained unclear but were sent somewhere in the western states. Later on it came out that many ended up in big camps somewhere in Pennsylvania. Others went to Arkansas where they rioted and had to be repelled with shotguns.

On the 1st of June the CIA stated that over the past 10 years, the USSR spent nearly 30% more than did the US on defense, last year amounting to $165 billion, while the US spent a total of $108 billion.

On June 3rd, a whole freighter-full of Cubans arrived at Key West, Florida, ready to be dumped on the US. Some politicians actually objected, like Jim Wright of Texas who suggested as firmly as he could on the radio that we should send the rioters back to Cuba. Some were not so outspoken, one Senator saying how it was uncertain what their refugee status was and asked only that the known criminals be returned.

It was later leaked out by two generally-unknown writers, Duncan Campbell and Linda Melvern, who claimed in the leftist weekly New Statesman that the super secret NSA (National Security Agency) was running a massive big ear spying operation on telephone and telex lines throughout Europe from an equally massive telecommunications center in northern England. But then the British Defense Ministry and the British Post Office, instead of denying it, readily admitted that the facility was a relay communications center for US forces in Europe. Its main purpose was to assure rapid and secure communications. It was located on a 562-acre base at Menwith Hill in the Yorkshire moors, about 8 miles west of Harrogate and 170 miles from London.

In mid-July when the central US states suffered from one of the worst heat waves in a century, the Shah died in Egypt where it was probably even hotter. The US ambassador to Egypt, Mr. Atherton blamed the treatment of the Shah by the present US administration for his demise. According to the ambassador, the Shah's father died in Johannesburg, South Africa, after a stormy war career. Iran was then left divided between the Soviet sector and the more southern British sector. In 1946, the British had withdrawn their troops, but the Russians had refused to withdraw theirs, laying the ground for the upheavals of the 1970s.

In August of 1980, Defense Secretary Harold Brown revealed what had been a dark secret for many years. Calling it a major break-through, he announced the development of a new type of aircraft called the "Stealth." The remarkable thing about it was that it had a skin that could largely absorb radio waves from radar detection devices so that they did not reflect normally back to the ground receivers. Although the airplane was not really invisible, it made the radar reflection from the plane too late for the enemy to shoot at it accurately. Also the flare from the back of the jet was so designed as to be hidden and the infrared from the flame was not detected. Apparently, the secret of the Stealth bomber was leaked as early as May of 1975 when the weekly newsletter Aerospace Daily released an article on it (New Haven Register 1980, September 14).

Then on July 23, 1976, the "Daily" gave a two-page account of the Stealth, mentioning Lockheed as the manufacturer. The article added that Soviet spies probably knew about it and their satellites had probably already photographed it on the ground.

However, Secretary Brown was called on the carpet to explain why the "Stealth" bomber was made public. Candidate Ronald Reagan took the opportunity to blame Carter for the release of the information. Evidently, Carter had hoped to show that he was doing something for US defense. In any case, the Stealth would not be operable until 1990.

The British, observing all these political antics, took some pleasure in pointing out that here we have "Ronald" who refers to his wife as "Mummy" while "Jimmy" sends his aged and decrepit mother off to act as an ambassador. They might also have mentioned that Jimmy sent off his son Chip to China as another kind of ambassador. The Chip to China caper got some feeble publicity without causing any known damage.

* * * * * * * * * * * * *

It is difficult to state where, why, and when the war between Iran and Iraq began. The location of its beginning was most likely along the length of their mutual border, according to a report by Iran's Bani Sadr on September 18, 1980. Also at about this time, Iranian civilians began to be evacuated from southern Iraq near the Persian Gulf via the Shatt-al Arab waterway while the Iranians had been holding war-games in their semi-desert.

As for the why of the war, there were marked differences in religions and customs, the Iranians more of an Indo-European origin, the Iraqis more Babylonian, more modern technically, and more homogeneous in religion, a majority of them Shiite Muslims (about 75% including many of the Kurds who lived mostly in the north). While the population of Iraq was only about 8 million, the Iranian population added up to about 25 million in a society that has long had a variety of customs, cultures and religious beliefs. Also, both countries had very different pasts, Iraq tracing its history back thousands of years to the days of Babylon and Ur perhaps even to 5000 B.C. Iran's history was not quite so ancient but went back at least to the days when "Persia" ruled most of the Middle East and fought a losing war with the Greeks around the 5th century B.C.

As for the when of the war, there had for many years been friction over the area where the twin rivers joined and flowed into the Persian Gulf, one big oil depot being at Al Basrah in Iraq and another large one just over the border in Iran, not far from the Persian Gulf.

In fact a lot of the early fighting, not widely reported, was near the Shatt-al Arab waterway where Iranian civilians were being evacuated from southern Iraq and later taken to Khorramshahr just northwest of Abadan. This occurred about the 21st of September, 1980.

Another factor in the cause of friction between Iran and Iraq was the influence of the USSR. Back in 1979, after the USSR had secretly sent more arms to Iraq, the Iranians in reply closed the Soviet consulate at Rasht in northern Iran. The USSR then retaliated by closing the consulate in Isfahan, some 200 miles south of Tehran. Possibly, the USSR then encouraged the Iraqis in their quarrel with the Iranians. But rumor had it that the CIA was helping Iraq.

On September 21, 1980 in the US, CBS radio announced that Iraq had officially declared war on Iran. Three hours later the Iraqis said that border skirmishes had grown into full scale war. The Soviet Union immediately blamed the war on the US which was said to be secretly in cahoots with the Iraqi government.

There was feeling in the US military that Iran would have problems fighting the war because of various military failings. A US military expert predicted that the Iranians would have problems because of lack of spare parts, the murder of many Iranian US-trained officers, and the loss of their own trained army and navy officers.

By the evening of the 21st, fighting escalated as Iraqi bombers were over Iran and six Iranian aircraft shot down. Also six Iranian warships were sunk in the Persian Gulf. In Tehran there was panic to obtain gasoline and food, and the whole city was blacked out at night, according to a source in Ankara, Turkey.

The US military was also alerted and SAC's 57th air division at Minot Air Force Base, North Dakota, was already earmarked for Middle East deployment.

By the 23rd, Iraqi troops were invading southern Iran. Tehran radio was heard asking their border guards to "sacrifice themselves." The current Iranian theory was that they would be assured thereby of going to heaven.

A British observer reported that he had watched the Iraqi attack on the world's largest refinery at Abadan, Iran, at the top of the Persian Gulf. Later on that day the Iranians attacked by air the Basra oil depot in south-eastern Iraq not far from Abadan. Four Americans and four Britons were killed, as reported by a British observer who had a radio-telephone conversation with a ship in the Gulf and thence to BBC in London. The tape of the conversation was then run by BBC for the evening news.

By September 24th, Iraqi forces seized the town of Quar-e-sharin, about 300 miles west of Tehran. The Iranians, as if in despair, threatened to blow up their own oil wells, while the Iraqis claimed 100 airplanes shot down. Later that day they claimed to have taken Khorramshahr, just north of Abadan. Iraq then offered a cease-fire.

It is not the purpose of the present treatise to follow the war, and although Baghdad itself was bombed, it claimed it was winning the war by the end of September. Whereas Baghdad's power plant was blown up on October 1st, things were worse in Iran. Iraq's Hussein told the Iranians that if they did not accept his peace terms, he would not be responsible. When Iraq declared a cease-fire on October 5th, the answer from Iran was a bombing raid on Baghdad.

On the 9th, the Iraqi's ground-to-ground missiles were used for the first time against Iran (CBS radio 1980, November 5). These were probably Frog-7s, made in the USSR, 30 feet long 20 inches in diameter, weighing 4400 pounds, and capable of going 40 miles.

Iran finally managed to find a friend in Libya, although far away in North Africa. The Libyans had lately been sending supplies by air to Iran. Syria too, was secretly supplying weapons to that country, the shipping boxes labeled in Russian Cyrillic letters so few could read them. By now the smoke from the burning refineries and storage tanks could be seen blowing southward for miles and no one could go into Abadan at the time, so dense was the smoke.

****

In this "modern" world there are spies that do not want to work only for one country against another, but find it rewarding to sell information to both sides. The story came out in the newspapers that David Barnett, a 12-year career employee of the CIA, took a job somewhere in southeast Asia in 1970. But he also undertook contract work with the CIA. In the mid 1970s, he was said to have been acting as a Soviet agent, thus burning the candle at both ends, neither side aware of the situation: selling Soviet military information to the US in the "HARBRINK" operation, while selling other information to the USSR on US manuals, weaponry, and the like, being well paid for his efforts. Recently, he was debriefed by the CIA to find out what he had given away to the USSR. According to information gleaned at the end of the century, he betrayed the identities of 30 CIA employees. On January 8, 1981, he was arrested in the US and given 18 years in prison (Polmar and Allen 1997, 305).

On November 4, 1980 by 7:30 p.m. eastern time it appeared that Ronald Reagan was winning the presidential battle. Reagan not only won most western states, but many others that seemed to have been a tie. By 8:45 Texas and Connecticut had gone for Reagan. Carter was ready to concede. Republicans also won a majority in the Senate.

In retrospect, Carter's occasional naïveté puzzled the Soviets while they got little useful information. But when a Romanian secret agent defected to the West in February, it was found that a senior US Democratic senator had employed a go-between to the USSR via Romania. As a result, the USSR knew most everything going on at the highest levels of the US (New Haven Register 1980, November 5).

Another spy case at this time involved Andrew Lee and Christopher Boyce. They were paid some $80,000 by the Soviets for the CIA's satellite surveillance system (Polmar and Allen 1997, 83, 305) while William Kampiles gave away the secret of the Big Bird for a paltry $3100. This was the SR-71 that could fly at 80,000 feet.

While the media fell into a state of great palpitation over events, agreements between the US and Iran on the hostage situation were signed in Algiers and Tehran. But the Iranians quickly snubbed up the leash. Apparently, they were waiting until Carter left office, and they would not have to wait long.

The next day, now in 1981, Carter was said to have spent the night on the couch in the White House Oval Office, hoping the hostage deal would have been concluded during his administration. Unfortunately for him, however, Ronald Reagan marched in and promptly took over. There was speculation in the media that Carter had gone out along with the couch, although this was not verified. Reagan then announced that the hostages had left Tehran for Greece and would then go to Germany for medical attention. Iranian newspapers told how the US had given in on all Iran's demands.

And the Soviet Union never gave up with its spy activity. It was discovered this year that the Soviets had tried to have a spy placed in the White House itself. A US Army man, name of Holbrook, was approached in Moscow, apparently by a woman proceeding to threaten him with blackmail if he did not follow Soviet orders. Holbrook was not so easily duped and went to his superiors for advice. They quickly transferred him to a quiet place in Virginia where he could not be reached. The Soviets had somehow found out that he was to become an aide to Vice President Bush and thus become their man in the White House.

In late February, 1980, Castro had run off to Moscow perhaps for some fresh advice as to what to do about the El Salvadoran revolution. Reagan was attempting by this time to stop the Cubans from assisting the Communists in San Salvador, but Breshnev was said to have given Castro the red carpet treatment, and promised the Cuban that the USSR would help him out – again.

To counter the Cuban game in El Salvador, tucked as it was between Guatemala and Honduras in Central America, U.S. Navy experts planned to enter El Salvador and help to organize a small Salvadoran navy. In this way, they would try and prevent the import of Soviet weapons and equipment.

In the US, the El Salvador situation fell under the criticism of CBS

TV, complaining of adventurism by the US government there. It was evident by now that US advisors had arrived in that southern nation. In fact, Reagan was considering a broad expansion of the CIA's authority in other fields: using break-ins, physical surveillance, and covert infiltration of certain groups of people and businesses. "Black Bag" jobs would be allowed (New Haven Register 1981, March 11). Although US liberals worried about this sort of activity, including deploying the neutron bomb in Europe (to which the West Germans greatly objected), Reagan's tough stance against the USSR and increased defense spending, brought warm words from China.

By the middle of March, 1981, a Senate committee asked Alexander Haig, now an important figure in Reagan's cabinet and NSC meetings, to enlighten it on US dealings in Central America. Haig pointed out that even Soviet tanks had been sent from Eastern Europe into Nicaragua. In fact the President of Costa Rica made it clear that the Soviets were trying to penetrate his country, supposed to be a model of democracy (CBS TV 1981, March 19).

That the activities of the USSR were being discovered in many parts of the world, was pointed out in various sectors of the US media by various columnists such as Jeffrey Hart (New Haven Register 1981, March 21) that implied the USSR was creating a world-wide network of terror and destabilization.

Nevertheless, the trend away from Communism could be detected in Britain, a nation that had included such people as Philby in its realm. Then the "Daily Mail" had claimed that Hollis was the most damaging spy in British history.

Another Briton that came out in his true reddish colors was Driberg, head of the British Labor Party and long-time member of Parliament. He was found to have been working for the Czechs, not, as formerly supposed, for the British.

On March 30, 1981 at 3:00 p.m. eastern US time, came the news by TV and radio that a gunman had shot President Reagan. Accompanied by James Brady and two others, they came out of the Washington-Hilton hotel in Washington D.C. to enter a limousine. But before they could get in, a young man stepped forward and shot at the President, hitting him in the chest as well as Brady in the head. One Secret Service man took a round in the stomach as he tried to protect Reagan. At this point they were all crammed into the Presidential car and taken to the hospital. The would-be assassin had escaped, despite other reports.

At 3:30 p.m. there was a net alert on CBS radio. It was announced that three people had been shot, although Reagan had been able to walk into the hospital. It came out later that a policeman was also shot. The suspect was found to be a John Hinkley from Colorado, white, male, and about forty years old.

Was it a coincidence that Reagan severely criticized the USSR about a month ago? At 4:00 p.m., the same day, Secretary Haig was on the radio and TV, looking somewhat ruffled up and sweating under the press lights. He announced that he was "in charge" since he was automatically third in command when the Vice president was away. Not surprisingly, the press and TV made a big stink about Haig's apparent excitement and made out he was panicking.

As for Hinkley, he was found to be the son of a Colorado oil executive with no police record. He had bought two handguns last October and when apprehended at an airport after running out of town, he had three guns on him. By 8:30 p.m. Vice President Bush arrived and spoke to representatives of the media in the Situation Room. Bush simply stated that he would meet tomorrow with Congressional leaders and continue Reagan's schedule.

On the 31st, Reagan was said to be in "exceptionally good condition," but Brady was not so good, in fact lucky to be alive. Hinkley was said to have had no job, no income, but had money to buy guns which he had on him when arrested in Nashville, Tennessee.

Foreign reaction was swift in coming: Thatcher was "distressed," Schmidt was "disgusted," and D'Estang sent condolences, as did Breshnev and Castro.

By April, the tabloids came up with a story that Hinkley had been infatuated with a moving picture actress, now a Yale student, and told her he would shoot the president if she would not "see" him. Jody, the girl, was told by her attorney to clam up after she said simply that she never heard of Hinkley. In time, the whole Jody story seemed to have been fabricated.

The bullet was finally removed from Reagan, having been difficult to find. It was said to have ricocheted off the door of the limousine and was flat as a dime.

On April 8th more on the Hinkley case emerged. A man with the name of Edward Richardson was arrested with a hand-gun in his possession. He had stayed at the Park Plaza hotel near Jody Foster's dorm at Yale. A maid had discovered bullets and threatening notes. All this suggested a wider conspiracy and not simply a lone assassin acting on his own.

There was a story printed in the press that Vice President Bush's life had been threatened. Several guns were discovered, one with a telescopic sight, but Secret Service men would not release details. Since the attempt on Reagan's life, it was said that the number of death threats to him had greatly increased (New Haven Register 1981, November 17).

As if the attempted assassination of Reagan was part of a worldwide plan to kill off anti-Communist dignitaries, another near-killing had occurred. At 1:00 p.m. eastern US time on May 6th, a radio news release said that the Pope in Italy had been shot, the act occurring in the late afternoon, Rome time. Later it was said that the Pope had been shot twice and bullets had penetrated his abdomen. Two American bystanders were also wounded. After the TV had gone through several minutes of recording the wailing and crying of the mob, they announced that the Pope had survived. The assailant was said to have been grabbed by a nun so to prevent further shots from hitting the Pope.

The assailant turned out to be Turkish and the Turkish government asked that the attacker be returned to them. As shown on TV, the attacker had the same glassy-eyed staring look that Hinkley had when apprehended, suggesting both these people had been on drugs. The would-be Pope assassin, called Agca, had a large amount of money with him, some $500 of it spent on an excursion to Spain before his attempt.

At least the US media was not trying to say Agca was just another weirdy. Israeli intelligence said that Turkish extremists and Libyan government agents had been in collusion lately to hatch out various plots. Also the Egyptian Foreign Minister Aly told the New York Post that the hand of Libya's Khadafi was involved in the Pope's shooting. Perhaps as a result of intelligence information, Reagan asked the known Libyans in the US to leave. The last batch of them was soon seen boarding an airplane at Dulles airport.

In early June the Israelis made an air raid on Iraq, specifically on Iraq's nuclear installation. Some US politicians complained, calling it an illegal use of US aircraft and US bombs. The Egyptians also complained about the bombing. The rumor was that the Iraqis were building a reactor that, with proper procedures, could not only produce electricity for Baghdad, but produce a form of uranium that could be further treated to produce plutonium for bombs. Kuwait also complained about the bombing by Israeli planes and called for an embargo on Israel in protest. Washington then put a freeze on sending new aircraft to Israel. All this turned out to be of interest to the events of late 2002 when the US involved the United Nations in trying to have inspectors go to Iraq and find out if nuclear bombs were being made there.

While Agca would soon be tried in an Italian court, Iran's Bani Sadr and friends, namely those that had not yet fallen before a firing squad, were thought to have blown up the building housing the Iranian ruling junta, killing 60 in all. Twenty of these were top brass in the antique government that then ruled Iran. Ayatollah Beheshti, Khoumeini's right-hand man, was killed in the bombing and many more with him. Also, four cabinet ministers, a deputy minister, and 20 members of Parliament were killed. Haig, asked about the bombing, firmly denied having anything to do with it.

After the CIA's loss of its Chief of Clandestine Services for playing the stock market, the FBI announced in mid-July, 1981, that a US Army man, Joseph Helmich Jr., had been giving away to the Soviets the whole coding system for the overseas transmission of secret information including some of the encrypting machine itself (Polmar and Allen 1997, 256). It was discovered that he had been made a colonel in the Soviet Army and was due for a "Hero's" medal. He was arraigned on July 15th, the press wondering why it took so long to catch him. It came out later in this connection that the Soviets might have been able to decipher the US Army orders during the Vietnam War, accounting for some of the serious US setbacks.

In mid-August of that summer, units of the U.S. Navy, conducting exercises in the Mediterranean, found to no one's great surprise, some sharp opposition from Libya. What had happened was that US aircraft had been fired on by Libyan jets, but the US planes promptly shot down two of their opponents. Reagan was apparently declaring US international rights within the Bay of Sidra, drawing the line of demarcation at the 12 mile limit, widely recognized. But the Libyans claimed the whole gulf as theirs.

At the other end of Africa, the Soviets had been making serious incursions into Angola, once called Portuguese West Africa. South African forces, attempting to prevent this Soviet incursion, themselves invaded Angola, killed a number of Soviet leaders of troops, and captured one of them to prove Soviet involvement in Angola. While the UN tried to sanction South Africa for this move, the US vetoed the ruling. This outcome was much to the anguish of the US liberals in Congress and the media, continuing their crusade to "liberate" the South African blacks from the partly-white government. In this way they could punish South Africa's government for their Apartheid (separation of the races).

In mid-September, more details came out on the Helmich case, mentioned above. He had evidently given away to the Soviets, for a price, "a top secret maintenance manual for the KL-7 cryptosystem" and a coding machine still used by the US armed forces. He even sold the rotors of the KL-7 system, along with certain classified documents. FBI agent Murphy said Helmich was supposed to alert the USSR if there was to be a nuclear attack on them. This would be done by sending a telegram to a lumberyard in Denmark. He also was suspected of taking top secret code material from the Signal Battalion's "Cryptoshack" of the US Army (United Press International 1981, September 6).

Well-paid for his troubles, Helmich spent lavishly on cars, a house, and rich clothes. But this affluence became too obvious and the army began questioning him. Finally, when in Canada, he was watched by authorities who then informed the FBI. He was sentenced to life in prison.

* * * * * * * * * * * *

On October 6th 1981, at 7:45 a.m. eastern US time, CBS radio and TV announced a net alert. A truck-load of soldiers, part of a parade in Cairo, Egypt, leaped from their vehicle and began shooting at people in the reviewing stand. At first Sadat was thought only to be wounded, as well as two US military people. But about four hours later, Sadat had died.

Kissinger said that the Libyans and the USSR could well have been behind it. Later on, the "Egyptian Liberation Organization" claimed responsibility. All this had put the US Fleet on "Level 5" alert, while Egypt's Vice President took over until elections would be held in a couple of months.

On the 13th, the US and Egypt decided to form a joint commission to combat Libya and keep the USSR from taking further African territory. But already, Libyan forces were massing near the Sudan border in Libya's southeastern corner.

By December of 1981, the new foreign problem of any importance was Libya. The US government stood by its position that Khadafi, the present ruler of Libya, was planning to assassinate Reagan and close associates. Senator Moynahan, head of the Senate Intelligence Committee, felt that you could turn everything Khadafi said around and you would get the truth. By now there was hard evidence that several hit-squads were being dispatched to the US. A Republican congressman from New York pointed out that Khadafi was just part of a larger picture that went back eventually to the USSR.

President Reagan realized the seriousness of the Libyan threat and gave orders to secretly cancel all visas on US passports for people planning to go to Libya. At the same time there was a story leaked out from Intelligence that a Libyan hit-team was in Mexico planning to kill Reagan. The team was said to include an Iranian and a German. In fact photographs of the men on the hit-team had been published, just where was unclear. But the sketches of these characters seemed to have come from customs offices and border patrol stations, according to columnist Jack Anderson. Two of these people were Iranian, one a Lebanese, one a Palestinian, and one a German. With all this publicity, no attempts were evidently made on the President.

As the new year of 1982 began, the CIA's director Colby had written a book soon to be published by Simon and Schuster. But it quickly became the center of a storm. The US government wanted a chance to approve of it first while trying to pass a law preventing further CIA secrets from being released. If the book were published in France, Colby would have to pay a fine, assuming he did not get US clearance.

One way that questionable people, bent on bombing, got into the US was via Aeroflot airplanes from the USSR. As a result, Reagan attempted to cut down on the number of Aeroflot airplanes landing in the US as well as Soviet ships landing at US ports. According to Robert Moss, author of various spy books, the Soviet GRU had been more aggressive than the KGB in playing a role in stealing scientific, technological, and industrial secrets from the West.

But things often worked both ways in the spy business. Recently, a spy known as Vadim to some, defected to the West and released information on the workings of the GRU. But, said he, the one thing the Soviets really needed was a way to make bread! As an example of the GRU's activities, the Boeing plans for building jumbo jets were stolen and sent to the USSR.

Another espionage report that came out in early January was from Washington, D.C. via A.P. It stated that the USSR had lately much increased its Intelligence operations in the US. This information was evidently supplied by a Mr. Yakushkin. After six years in the US as a top KGB operative, he planned to retire. He had directed about 500 agents in the US.

New York City was said to be a hotbed of Soviet spies, running around copying everything they could and shipping it off to the USSR. In fact the UN in New York was said to be one big spy center, besides various others in Manhattan. These included TASS News Agency, Polish

Consulate, East German Mission, Cuban Mission, Amtorg Trading Corporation, Soviet Mission, Czech Mission, and Polish Mission. FBI Agent McGorty stated that spies associated with these missions outnumbered US Counter Espionage agents 10 to 1.

Perhaps there was a sign that the worm had turned in the Libyan-US confrontation. The CIA verified a story in the press that a high-ranking military man took a shot at Khadafi and wounded him in the jaw. This must have inhibited his usual outflow of words, at least to some extent.

The problem of El Salvador continued. Secretary Haig claimed that the leftist Nicaraguans were guiding rebels in El Salvador by radio. Although the media mostly shot down the story, Haig said he had proof in the form of a Nicaraguan soldier that had escaped capture in El Salvador. Senator Byrd (D-WV) was not impressed and only feared that the US could become involved in some kind of revolution or war in Central America. Therefore he tried to push a bill through Congress that would prevent the US government from sending troops to foreign countries without Congress's consent.

But Admiral Inman, echoing the feelings of the CIA and Defense Intelligence Agency, said he was angry that the public did not understand the importance of a Soviet-sponsored build-up in El Salvador. He added that both Cuba and the USSR were active there. Under Secretary of State Enders sided with Inman and opined that Cuba was doing its utmost to spread violent revolution in Central America as well as in certain parts of South America. Enders pointed out that now-a-days drug traffic was assisted by all kinds of technological advances and was a serious problem in South and Central America, all of which added to the upheavals.

****

Unknown to the US populace in March of 1982, a story emerged, originating with Alexander Haig, that the British Ambassador Henderson had been given a letter from Lord Carrington containing information that a party of Argentineans had landed on South Georgia Island off the Argentinean coast.

On April 1, 1982, unknown to the US public, Reagan was on the telephone to Argentina to try to convince Galtieri that Britain would fight if the Falklands were invaded.

Despite many negotiations involving Alexander Haig, Britain declared a blockade of the Falklands. Shortly afterward, Argentinean Marines came ashore, but a British garrison, consisting of a small marine detachment, fired on the Argentineans, killed four and wounded two. Evidently, the small British garrison at Port Stanley was overwhelmed. The Argentinean news in Buenos Aires told how Argentina had "exercised its territorial imperative" and taken over the Falklands. It also told how the British had not resisted.

Although the United Nations Security Council approved a resolution to make Argentina withdraw its forces from the Falklands, it had no noticeable effect. But repercussions were felt in Britain and Lord Carrington resigned in the midst of a furor over the apparent loss of the Falklands. And already a British task-force had left Britain by April 3rd for the South Atlantic.

As if exasperated by the antics of the human race, three volcanoes made themselves well-known in 1982. Mount Saint Helens in the western US blew steam up about five miles into the air, a volcano in Java blasted off, and Chichen Itza rumbled ominously to send thousands of people fleeing their homes on the Yucatan Peninsula, crying "La Fin del Mundo!" (The End of the World).

On April 6th, the story was released that a US satellite had observed the Argentinean fleet at sea and warned the British government. But nothing happened in Britain until the 11th when it was evident that a blockade of the Falklands was planned by the British. Two days later, a British task force was off the Brazilian coast, headed south despite heavy seas.

On the 13th, Haig presented a plan to Argentina to form a tripartite government for the Falklands (Haig 1984, 283). But Argentina stated simply that the plan was "an insult." Yet Haig did not give up and seemed to have rapport with Thatcher.

The Argentinean claim to the islands was based on an antique Spanish claim made centuries ago. Although the British discovered the islands in 1592, the French established a colony on East Falkland in 1764. But the French signed over their claim to Spain. Then a year later the British formally claimed the islands and British citizens settled there. Soon afterward the Spanish, failing to negotiate an end to British occupancy, sent troops to expel the British from Fort Egmont. This ended up in a dual occupancy. But in 1816 the British expelled the Spanish and moved the capital to Stanley and had held the islands ever since (Embleton 1973, 473).

By April 15, 1982, the British fleet had reached the Falklands, while Haig flew to Buenos Aires for consultations. Haig was actually fighting two wars: one to stop the war between the British and the Argentineans (for reasons that remained obscure), the other against Reagan's "staffers" who did not approve of Haig's machinations. The Argentineans hoped to invoke a treaty which required the US to come to their aid, but the British were already approaching Georgia Island and stated that if the US did not support them in the war, it could mean the break-up of NATO. Hence Haig's worries about it all.

After the British, as reported by CBS from London, took over Georgia Island about 900 miles east of the main islands, some four days later British commandos landed in the main Falkland Islands near Fort Stanley. By then, Haig realized the situation was beyond outside control and announced that he would support the British and stop trying to mediate the dispute. The government in Buenos Aires was said to have been "stunned" by Haig's decision. A few days after April 29, British Harrier jets attacked Fort Stanley's airfield.

Although it was not the purpose of this book to describe the wars of the 20th century, certain events might be mentioned here. On May 3rd, British aircraft arrived at the Falklands, and helicopters attacked two Argentinean patrol boats, sank one and damaged the other. Next, an Argentine cruiser, once named "Phoenix" when she was with the U.S. Navy in WW II, was torpedoed near the Argentine coast by a submarine. Some 850 sailors and officers were left in the sea, many to drown. But the apparent loss of the British missile cruiser Sheffield brought consternation to the British public. The Argentine missile had flown just above the waves and the crew, with no means of defense against such a sudden attack, could only stand and watch the missile approach. Despite reports, the Sheffield survived the explosion and was towed to a seaport further north.

On May 29th, Fort Darwin and Goose Green fell to the British who took 900 prisoners. When the Argentine troops gave up, they marched out in ranks, came to attention, cheered, sang their national anthem, and laid down their guns.

The Soviets, not to be left out in all this, protested to the British that penetrating the war zone around the Falklands was unlawful according to certain obscure maritime laws and agreements. At the same time, the Soviets were sending low-orbiting satellites to photograph the British ships. The films were then dropped by parachute on some part of the Soviet land mass to be retrieved (Time 1982, May11).

Finally on June 6th, the passenger liner Queen Elizabeth ("QE 2") arrived and landed some 10,000 men before returning at once to Britain.

On the 11ᵗʰ, British troops closed in on Port Stanley and surprised the enemy to produce some fierce fighting. Soon, white flags flew over Stanley, according to a report from Britain's Mrs. Thatcher. In Argentina, the Peronists who had once supported Mrs. Peron, asked the military government to step down and return to civilian rule.

* * * * * * * * * * * *

Still, in late June of 1982, Beirut continued in its upheaval, while reporters watched a crowd of Americans scrambling for boats to take them out to a ship where it already had over a thousand escapees. By then, British, French, and US embassies were closed while British and French nationals were also evacuated. The war had gone on by now longer than any war that Israel had fought since the formation of the Palestine mandate by the British.

In July, it came out that Sidon in Lebanon was the home of one of the top schools for training terrorists, including Red Brigades, Japanese Reds, German Reds, and others. But the Israelis came along and drove them all out. The PLO people were also driven out of Beirut only to find that they had nowhere to go and the Syrians refused to accept what appeared to be several thousand of them.

Washington D.C. was having its own upheaval, although not widely reported. Reagan announced that he had accepted Haig's resignation. But it came out later according to Haig, that the acceptance of his resignation occurred before Haig could tender it. The press corps guessed, probably correctly, that the problem lay with Reagan's staffers, especially Baker and Deaver. The Israelis, however, called Haig's resignation a disaster besides the loss of a good friend. James Baker, for his part, said that Haig's failure on the Falklands problem was why Haig had to go.

In mid-July, Iran was preparing to invade Iraq, according to British sources, and was gathering some 80,000 troops near Iraq's border (Hartford Courant 1982, October 13). The Saudis were said to have pumped billions into Iraq, fearing a dominant Iran in the Persian Gulf. About 100,000 Iraqis were then poised to defend their border on Iran, although Iraqi troops were unenthused by the prospect of war.

Once more on the 14ᵗʰ of July, Iranian troops were mustered for battle and within a half hour were deeply penetrating far into Iraq near Basra. Most of their advance consisted of men on foot, while Iraq's dictator Sadam Hussein calmly predicted that Khoumeini's dreams would not come true. He was right: the next day the Iranians were stopped in their tracks and tried to regroup. Evidently, they had come in massed thousands, advancing against dug-in Iraqis only to be mowed down as in World War I, like sheaves of grain. Artillery, machine guns, rifles: they did their gruesome work on the flat battlefield. It was said to have been the biggest battle in the Iran-Iraq war.

Probably as a result of the disastrous attack against the Iraqis, Iran's Gohtbazadeh, a reasonable sort of man among desperadoes, was forced to confess his sins and failures and then on September 14 they shot him dead. Probably, the Ayatollah Khoumeini was looking for a scape-goat for the Iranian military failure.

* * * * * * * * * * * * *

The secret war between the US and the USSR went on as usual. Two big spy cases broke from the depths to spill their truths into the light of day. One of these involved a KGB agent, a big fish this time, who defected to the West. A second one concerned a British subject, name of Fein or Fine, who was caught giving away everything he knew about what the US Intelligence community knew about Soviet agents (CBS radio 1981, August 11).

Still another spy was revealed by the British government. He was evidently connected to the Cheltenham Information Center in the Cotswolds. The man's wife, apparently miffed by his playing around with other women, let it out that he was probably a spy. It was later discovered that he had been sending secret information via short-wave radio to foreign countries, probably enciphered "RTTY" transmissions (ABC Radio 1982, July 21).

As even the Soviet Communists must, Leonid Breshnev, top man in the Kremlin, passed away on November 11th, 1982. Some people in the western world suggested that this caused a panic on world gold exchanges and stocks fell in price. Polish civilians who were interviewed about his death said they were not much interested and one said that it was just one less Russian and was only to the good. The next day, Yuri V. Andropov, chairman of the KGB since 1967, was made President of the monolithic USSR. Probably as a result, Poland's Walesa would soon be released from prison.

In the wake of this upheaval, there was some hint of who was behind the attempted assassination of the Pope. Evidently Agca, who had tried to kill the Pope, had Bulgarian help and therefore probably had inspiration from the USSR which then dominated Bulgaria. As DCI Helms once implied, the order to do away with the Pope could have been given by Andropov's merely nodding his head.

Soviet machinations in Central and South America continued despite the change in Soviet leadership. In fact Soviet meddling in Nicaragua finally brought the Reagan government to close out all six US consulates in Nicaragua. This came after the ejection of two US diplomats from that country. On June 20th, Reagan sent an aircraft carrier and its task force to the Atlantic side of Nicaragua and another one to the Pacific side. Kissinger too was brought back, dusted off, and asked to be chairman of the diplomatic effort involved. Reagan pointed directly to the USSR and Cuba as meddlers in Central America. The Soviet reply to this was to state on short-wave radio from Moscow that Reagan was dragging the US into a war in Central America to prevent the normal course of events. After all this became public, things tended to quiet down, at least in Nicaragua. News wires were soon absorbed in the shoot-down by the Soviets of a passenger airplane going form Alaska to Seoul, Korea, thirty Americans were said lost in this shoot-down on September 1, 1982.

Another spy case broke into the news in October (New Haven Register 1983, October 19). One James D. Harper had been caught passing secrets to Polish authorities in Poland. Missile data were believed to have been sent. Evidently, Harper's third wife had disappeared and the investigation of it led to Harper's arrest. It came out in later years that Harper had provided the Poles and the Soviet KGB with US defense secrets, especially US strategic missile technology. Harper was thought to have had a girl-friend, named Schuler, who had secret clearance to military weapons designs. Allegedly, it was she who stole the documents and gave them to Harper who got $100,000 for a hundred pounds of documents brought to Warsaw, Poland, at the Soviet embassy there. When the Soviets found the documents genuine, Harper got a commendation from Andropov himself. Harper later continued his efforts in Mexico city, but the FBI and CIA became suspicious concerning the Andropov commendation, so tracked Harper down and sewed up a case against him. He was given a life sentence (Polmar and Allen 1997, 254).

Suddenly on October 23, CBS radio reported that a suicide truck-full of explosives had been driven into the Marine barracks at Beirut airport, Lebanon. As many as 76 marines were said killed and 100 or so injured. The French too were attacked with a car bomb and 19 killed. Reagan was awakened at 2:27 A.M. and flown to Washington D.C. for an NSC meeting. Only the day before there was said to have been an attempt on Reagan's life while he was playing golf. Secret Service men were all over the place, but the results hushed up.

On the 24th, Israeli Intelligence claimed that the Ayatollah had "inspired" the attack on the Marine compound, but it was Shiite Moslems from the Bekaa Valley, now in Syria's hands, that were the ones responsible.

* * * * * * * * * * * * *

Early in the morning of October 25, 1983, an amateur radio operator on the 14 MHz band sent out a report from the island of Grenada in the Lesser Antilles, He claimed that the island was under attack by what seemed to be Cubans. Newsmen in the US, trying to verify the statement, asked the Grenada representative in the US if the Cubans and KGB were involved? She answered that some people on the island had been associated with KGB officers but that was about all she knew. As for the radio operator, he guessed there were about 600 Cubans involved in the invasion.

The next day the operator said the Cubans were fighting off an assault by US Marines in a town near the capital. Castro, asked about it, claimed that Cuban troops there in Grenada were just Cuban workers and would fight to the end. At that time, the only source of information from Grenada was the amateur radio operators, one of whom was operating from under a table while bombs exploded nearby.

On the 26th, the US garrison at Guantanamo in Cuba was alerted, having been attacked by Cuban forces. As many as 30 Cubans were killed and shortly afterward their resistance crumbled. Some 200 Cubans were captured and some others committed suicide.

On the 27th, Castro told his men on Grenada by radio to fight and die. But somehow about 600 of them surrendered and were removed from the island as prisoners. The story went that they would be held in exchange for forcing Castro to take back the so-called "boat people" in a Georgia (US) prison. It also came out later that the islanders were glad to be rid of the Cuban invaders and gave credit to the 92nd Airborne and US Marines in helicopters as well as Rangers for their defeating the Cubans.

Although the United Nations disapproved of the US action, Reagan pointed to the connection between the timing of the Lebanon bombing and the invasion of Grenada. Secretary Weinberger then released information to the effect that the US invaders of Grenada had found all sorts of secret equipment and documents including ciphers, encoders, transceivers (to send and receive radio signals), plans for anarchy, and other espionage material.

Probably several hundred Cubans were still at large on Grenada. For safe keeping, some 5000 US troops planned to stay on the island, the War Powers Act allowing them 60 days to stay there.

By early November, Soviet personnel in Grenada were packing up and leaving with whatever they could carry, leaving behind all kinds of war material, including automatic weapons, pistols hidden in typewriters, radios built into cabinets, and other secret communication equipment. It turned out that North Koreans, East Germans, Hungarians, and Cubans were among the motley crowd that shipped out. Many later returned to Cuba.

* * * * * * * * * * * *

British sources claimed to know what misfortune had befallen Andropov, head man in the USSR. Apparently, Breshnev's son, after engaging Andropov in an argument, pulled out a gun and shot Andropov in the arm, thus adding to his other ailments including kidney and heart disease. The Soviet news simply said that he had a cold (New Haven Register 1983, November 17).

Toward the end of November the Pentagon released secret information gathered by intelligence that the Syrian Secret Service, not the military, trained the assassins that attacked the Marine barracks in Lebanon. They surmised that Assad of Syria must have known about these plans, although the people trained for the job were Iranians. Reagan finally decided to withdraw the Marines sometime soon.

When the New Year turned over its first few pages, the Marines in Beirut came once again under fire in January of 1984. But the Marines were better armed now and brought up tanks and bazooka squads to blast the building that had been the source of the small arms and rocket firing. The enemy building was totally disintegrated. In early February, the CBS TV announced that Reagan had decided to have the Marines make a phased withdrawal from Beirut, ferrying them out to ships standing off the coast, Military dependents were removed in helicopters which landed in Beirut's streets. At the same time, the battleship New Jersey continued to shoot its huge shells into positions in the Beirut hills as well as at Moslem or Syrian communication centers. British troops were driven in armored cars to the seaport and removed by small craft to warships. The French, however, decided to stay for the time being, while the Italians planned to leave soon. As a result of the shelling from the New Jersey, the Americans had ruined 30 Moslem gun emplacements and had killed the General of the Syrian forces and probably his entire staff.

On February 10, 1984, Yuri Andropov was reported to have died. No one in Moscow or abroad seemed to know what to make of it. As a former head of the KGB, he must have led a high-tension life. Since the whole Soviet structure had been so arcane, so Byzantine, and so mysterious to foreigners and natives alike, no one expected there would be much of any kind of political change. He had been in office only 15 months and was quickly replaced by Konstantin Chernenko (Crozier 1999, 402). The new Secretary General promptly made all the usual Soviet noises about Nicaragua and the Middle East. So apparently nothing in Soviet foreign policy had changed.

Even Chernenko was in office only a few months when he died in March of 1985. At this time, Michael Gorbachev came to rule the great sprawling USSR.

While all these change-overs in Soviet rule were going on, the Iran-Iraq war went its bloody way. The Iraqis claimed, by the end of February, several thousand Iranians killed near Basra, mainly from artillery fire. The Iraqis pointed out that "Iranian" artillery shells landing in Iraqi towns were Soviet made. They also had seen Iranian children sent out in front of the regular Iranian troops to trigger the mine fields. Each child had a little key tied his neck to gain entry into heaven. Photographs of the battlefield were more expressive: Iranian bodies lying all over the battlefield so mangled that they must have been hit by rocket or shell fire, not rifle fire. A British correspondent said there were so many Iranian dead that he lost count. The Iraqis claimed 50,000 killed in the past week. Iran's Khoumeini said it was not a territorial war but a religious one of Islam against blasphemy (New Haven Register 1984, March 5). Captured Iranians were said to have only complained that they were sick of the war.

In May of 1984 experts on the Iraq-Iran war said that Iran would soon launch another human wave offensive when the marshes of what used to be part of Old Babylonia would be dry enough to let the infantry cross them. Intelligence sources said that 600,000 Iranian troops were being massed on the Iraqi border for another human sacrifice en masse.

The Saudis by now had the new AWACS radar airplanes with the curious dish-like antenna emerging from the top of the fuselage and were able to take part in the shoot-down of an Iranian jet, perhaps to see how the radar worked. Other Gulf states applauded this action, adding that two Iranian fighter-bombers had been shot down after the AWACS had detected them.

US missile experts were at the time working on a way to stop intercontinental missiles. In mid-June an intercontinental missile was fired from Vandenberg Air Base, California, headed for Kwajalein. Although the first two tries to stop it had failed, a third try, consisting of an intercepting rocket, was successful. The anti-missile was said to open a huge net that caught the incoming missile and either spoiled its aim or blew it up – the experts were not saying which.

The changes in Soviet government did nothing to slow the spy business and attempts to steal secrets from the West. In Germany a large truck-load of documents appeared at the border that divides the East from West Germany trying to enter East Germany. It seemed suspicious to the West German border control and it asked for an itemized bill of lading. The Soviets, hearing about it, objected that it was diplomatic material, but the West Germans said no go. The truck then tried the Swiss-German border but was turned back by Swiss authorities. The West Germans then sealed the truck and were still holding it on the 21st of July. It was thought to contain plans for missile secrets, computers, etc.

Even the FBI had its turn-coats. One of their agents, Richard Miller, distinguished himself by having been the first FBI agent in history to have allegedly revealed US secrets to a Soviet agent. Miller had been working with a certain Ogorodnikov and his wife Svetlana who had, some 10 years ago, come to the US. FBI Director Webster said Miller had given out very serious material to the USSR. By this time he was quite overweight, claiming he was acting as a double agent with the KGB. But he had evidently passed a number of important documents to the KGB. An FBI search of the Ogorodnikov apartment turned up various secret means of communication such as one-time pads and a means of making microdots. To make a long and involved story short, Miller was finally found guilty in a second trial, after the first trial in 1985 was declared a mistrial (Polmar and Allen 1997, 369). The Ogorodnikovs were also tried and briefly jailed.

In early October, the CIA identified the people who recently blew up the embassy in Beirut. That agency also said their equipment came from Iran and their explosives from Syria. The bombers called themselves the "Party of God" or "Jihad." The British, regardless of who did it, decided to close down their Beirut embassy.

On October 31st, news came to the US that Mrs. Gandhi of India had been shot seven times by Sikh gunman, apparently three of them. They had been members of her own bodyguard.

The Soviet Union's government promptly accused the US of having been behind Mrs. Ghandi's assassination. The US then issued a formal protest to the USSR, leaving some to wonder if the USSR were not involved in it in some way. As a result of her death, 148 lives were lost, mostly in protest rioting about her killing. Following an ancient tradition that may go back thousands of years, her body was torched on a huge pile of lumber.

Spy cases continued to rise from the depths of darkness, hatched out by those that lurk there making their complex machinations for reasons only known to their kind. On ABC Radio New York on November 28th, the story was told that a recent Czech immigrant, having claimed a Ph.D. from Columbia University and one from Prague University, went to work for the CIA. It was found out recently that he was working for the Czech Secret Police, using his wife as courier to the CIS (Czech Intelligence Service). On the 29th, it was reported that the FBI had nabbed him. This was Karl F. Koecher, said to be the first European spy to penetrate the CIA. Koecher was arrested and later swapped for a Soviet "dissident" (Polmar and Allen 1997, 316).

As if it was about time there was another hijacking, another airplane was taken over, this time in Tehran, Iran. Although some 70 passengers were released, the hijackers executed two Kuwaitis and some others. An amateur radio operator in Israel said he had recorded a transmission from the hijacked airplane and heard a lot of screaming and groaning, as if someone was being tortured. As for the Iranian government, it said that it did not approve of the hijacking, all of which was probably part of the overall plan.

While the airplane sat at Tehran Airport, the stand-off was ended by a group of Iranians who came in pretending to be maintenance men and released the hostages. But the Kuwaiti government said all this was a big charade performed by the Iranians in order to kill some people, probably Kuwaitis, whom the Iranians classed as enemies.

Chapter 8

The Middle East Ferments And The USSR Declines

As the year 1985 appeared on the horizon, so also came the fifth anniversary of the Soviet invasion of Afghanistan. And this invasion promised to go on for many more years, with the US government appropriating $250,000,000 for Afghanistan's defense. On March 11th, the USSR's Konstantin Chernenko died. Only three years ago Breshnev had died and two years before that Andropov had passed away (Crozier 1999,307). President Reagan decided not to go to the latest funeral, but Vice President Bush went instead.

Nevertheless, the Soviet Union's policy of meddling all over the world went on as before. Iran was still a fermenting nation, much influenced by and often supplied with Soviet weapons and other means of support. In this way, Iran continued to be a problem to the US which strove, through Ronald Reagan, to be the peacemaker, partly because of the importance of oil. King Fahd of Saudi Arabia, knowing very well the importance of his vast oil reserves, was again trying to bring peace to the Middle East. However, Iran continued to be a problem to its neighbors and to the western powers. A report in February by the FBI warned that Iranian terrorists were "in place" in the US for attacks on public and private buildings. Yet few heeded this warning until 16 years later on 9/11/01.

The Iranians, refusing to give up their war on Iraq, bombed the suburbs of Baghdad and succeeded in killing a number of noncombatants. The Iraqis replied with an air attack on Basra as well as on five other Iranian cities. The Iranian bombing coincided with an attack by Iranian troops across the marshes just north of Basra which lies only a few miles north of the Persian gulf. But the Iraqis held them off again, took some prisoners and bombed Tehran once more, apparently aiming at the Ayatollah's own domicile. At the same time the Syrians were moving troops to invade north Lebanon. Israeli Intelligence said the Syrians were aiming to take over all of Lebanon while Syrian troops had already arrived at Tyre on the Mediterranean Sea.

With all this going on in the Middle East, Egypt's Mubarack and Jordan's King Hussein worried that Iran was winning and offered their help to the Iraqis. But as it turned out, the Iraqis told them they had things under control and in fact killed some 27,000 Iranian troops in the latest battle. Nevertheless Khoumeini claimed that Iran would continue the fight until Iraq's Hussein was overthrown (New York Times 1985, March 21).

In the spring of 1985, the spy game went on as ever in Europe. CBS mentioned that the Soviets had been bugging the communications of the French embassy in Moscow for five years. The French magazine Le Point claimed that a Soviet KGB colonel had revealed the names of KGB agents abroad and this had led to their expulsion from France. Back in 1983, as many as 148 agents had been expelled to the USSR.

Although connections between the USSR and Iran had remained somewhat of a mystery for many years, recent news claimed that Gromyko announced at a meeting in Moscow with Iran's Deputy Foreign Minister that relations would be expanded (New Haven Register 1985, April 7).

In the meantime the USSR was busy installing the new SS-25 intercontinental missiles near Yurga and Toshkar Ola, 150 miles west of Moscow. Some of the more informed people in the US may have wondered why the SALT II treaty would not have prevented this. But that treaty was never submitted to the US Senate and it had therefore no legal status.

As if this were not enough of a threat to the US, certain spies were busy at the time giving away to the USSR the most precious secrets of the U.S. Navy. In May of 1985, the FBI released the information that the U.S. Navy flier John A. Walker passed secrets to a Soviet agent via "drops" and even had held direct meetings with Soviet agents. Walker's son was also in the U.S. Navy, stationed on the carrier Nimitz and was discovered with secret material. The FBI, alerted to the case, began to investigate his father. Evidently, Walker's former wife Barbara told the

FBI in November 1984 about her husband's spying (Polmar and Allen 1997, 586). Most of what he gave away was top secret U.S. Navy tactics.

In Germany, spying of another sort went on. A plan was hatched out to steal the secret plans of the new West German Leopard tank, but in an unusual way. The entire engine of that tank was removed and put in a boat to replace its regular engine. The boat then went eastward on one of the many waterways into East Germany where the engine was removed and shipped by truck to the USSR (Time Magazine 1985, May 28).

On June 4th it was made public that a fourth man was arrested in California concerning the Walker case. Admiral Inman implied that it could have been a big loss to the US. But things did not stop there. A fifth man was soon exposed. It appeared that the Walker gang had sent the top secret Navy cipher system to the USSR. Then on top of this, nine more people were arrested concerning the Walker case. But columnist Jack Anderson was not impressed, writing that the case was only one of many. Yet the Walker ring also found out how the US was able to detect Soviet submarines at great depths, such submarines having been caused to sink to the bottom after some accident such as an explosion originating in the sub itself (Washington Week, PBS, June 7).

On June 14th, 1985, another hijacking of a passenger airplane occurred, this time during a flight from Athens to Rome, Italy. The passengers were made up mostly of Americans, adding up to a total on board of 110. The plane then went on from Beirut to Algiers. The hijackers seemed to have been Shiite Moslems. Some of the passengers were evidently released in Beirut since there were later only 30 aboard. One American had been murdered and dumped out on the airport tarmack.

On the 17th, BBC radio from London said the hostages had been moved out of the TWA aircraft. US warships were said to be headed for Lebanon. But it later came out that only three of the hostages had been released. The rest were held so demands could be made to release 700 Shiites in Israeli prisons. But Israel's Perez refused to let them go, arguing that letting them go would only encourage the Shiites further.

As for President Reagan, he was thought to have warned of international terrorists. He suggested putting sky-marshals on all commercial airplanes. He further asked for no more air service to Athens. A few days later he made an appeal via CBS radio for returning the hostages and added that it was time to stop treating the CIA as an enemy and give it more power to do its job.

Only a few days later on the 23rd, terrorists hijacked an Air India plane that was headed for Bombay, India from Montreal, Canada. It was some 182 miles southwest of Ireland and headed for London when it suddenly disappeared from the radar screen. Later reports said the aircraft had blown up and 325 people lost.

The June 14th hijacking continued until the 24th when the gang's leader, Nabi Berri, made new demands. Weinberger, in the Reagan camp, rejected these demands. The next day, Gorbachev personally spoke with Syria's Assad and told him to return the hostages. But the suspicion was that Syria, Iran, and probably Libya were in on the hijacking. Nothing happened.

But on the 26th, Nabi Berri released one hostage and said he would transfer the rest to the embassy in France or Austria. Then Syria agreed to take the hostages and they were moved to Damascus. By then, there were about 29 of them left. On the 30th, news came that the hostages were on their way to West Germany and freedom. A few days later the hostages were headed home, but still it was uncertain who had kidnapped them. According to BBC, the FBI questioned one man for seven hours to try and find out who they were.

On August 23rd A.P. wires reported that a West German counter-espionage agent had defected to East Germany, probably compromising many West German defense secrets, extremely damaging to NATO forces in Europe. As a result, a bevy of West German agents were scrambling to go east, their cover blown. By the 25th, this spy fiasco turned out to be bigger than anyone had thought. The story was that the defector had been drinking heavily and was deeply in debt. The next day, the 26th, the West German police arrested one suspected "spy" while two others escaped. A woman secretary to the West German President was strangely missing, probably gone to East Germany. But later she was arrested.

The result of all this was a national embarrassment of huge proportions. West Germany's Mr. Kohl planned a widespread shake-up of the "Dienst" (Service) actually the West German Counter Intelligence Agency. The defector, Hans J. Tiedge, was not available for interviews. Stansfield Turner was on CBS and said this was a disaster for the West, adding that the West Germans had been sloppy about handling Tiedge when he had a known record of being a heavy drinker and had lost most of his finances. Mr. Sorge, editor of Der Spiegel (the Mirror), said there was a kind of buddy-network extending from the West to the East in Germany and Hans had taken advantage of it. Turner felt that the Federal Intelligence Service had a bad record for a long time and they should have sacked him if there was any doubt about him. Kohl then fired Herr

Hellenbroich, head of the Federal Intelligence Service.

The fiasco of the Tiedge affair had bolstered the reputation of one Marcus Wolf, considered to be the world's most successful spy master. Wolf ran the Central Reconnaissance Office, the East German version of the CIA. It was evidently to Wolf that Tiedge ran in West Berlin when Tiedge decided to defect (UPI 1985, September 4).

Author Le Carré, who wrote *Tinker Taylor Soldier Spy*, used Wolf as the model for Karla, chief spy in Moscow Center. Wolf, whose nickname was Misha, was born in 1923 in West Germany at Hechingen near Stuttgart and had a long record of being anti-Hitler and pro-communist. Under Wolf, the CRO was thought to have 10 Intelligence and Counter-Intelligence departments, serving at least 3,000 agents. Wolf built a massive network of "sleeper" spies among the refugees that came into West Germany from the East. One of the most celebrated was Guenther Guillaume, unmasked as a spy in 1974 and had been chief aide to Chancellor Brandt. Another spy was Sonje Lueneburg, who mysteriously left Bonn last August. She had come from East Germany to become secretary to Economics Minister Bangemann.

Perhaps to offset the loss of Tiedge, the West German police arrested a mole named Aroski who had been operating for 13 years. Aroski probably got 5 years in prison.

The British too, had their own spy revelations. CBS radio reported on September 12th that the head of the KGB office in London had defected, thus blowing the cover of dozens of Soviet spies in Britain. Some had worked for Comsomol Pravda, or in Embassy offices in Britain. This person was Oleg Gordievsky. He had begun to spy in the USSR for the British and, unbeknownst to the Soviets, continued to spy after being placed in the Soviet Embassy in London.

By the 17th, the spy flap in West Germany continued. A secretary of Helmut Kohl, Astrid Willner, disappeared after a trip to Spain with her husband Herbert, having written a letter of resignation to Kohl. It was suspected that the US "Star Wars" and other NATO secrets might have been compromised. In fact a whole covey of women spies in West Germany had been flushed out or disappeared: Sonja Lueneburg, secretary to Minister Bangemann missing; Ursula Richter and Lorenz Betzing probably defected; Margarete Hoecke, a secretary in President Weizsaecher's office missing; Astrid Willner and husband Herbert disappeared; plus several others between August and mid-September.

In October of 1985 another spy emerged from the dark dealings between the CIA and KGB. This was Edward L. Howard, once a CIA agent, fired in June of 1983. He was said to have gone to Mexico, but wherever he went, he left a trail of double-dealing between the US and USSR (Polmar and Allen 1997, 270). Howard and another spy were identified as working for the USSR by Vitaly Yurchenko who had defected in Rome from the USSR two months ago. Howard was interviewed by US agents in late September, but then disappeared, apparently to the USSR.

Hijacking suddenly was no longer confined to airplanes. An Italian cruise ship was hijacked just after she left a port near Cairo, Egypt. A Swedish radio operator heard the ship's captain say they had been hijacked. About a dozen Americans were on board. Hearing of the news, US and Italian navy ships were sent after the liner which had headed for Beirut. On October 8th one person was said to have been "executed." Later on, news came by radio that two people had been killed.

The next day the hijacked liner was back in Port Said, Egypt, near Cairo. Rumors were that an elderly Jewish couple had been killed. But the hijackers then gave up the hostages they had taken and turned themselves over to Egyptian authorities. One of the hijackers had an Argentine passport. The Israeli government was enraged that the Egyptians had released the hijackers. One of the two murdered ones, Klinghofer by name, had been in a wheel chair and was said to have been shoved overboard. His body was later recovered from the sea. On the 11th, CBS radio in New York reported that the hijackers had been seized by US "agents" in Egypt.

On the heels of this story, another hijacking occurred, this time an airliner over the Mediterranean. But US jet aircraft forced the airplane down apparently in Sicily and was seized by Italian police who accused the gang of murder and having weapons. The ex-hostages were returned to the US in military airplanes. Then to the anguish of the Reagan government, the Italians let the kidnappers go. Italian authorities said the ringleader was Abbas, and the rest of his crew were in jail. The Italian people were outraged that Abbas had been released, but the government said they let him go because he had an Iraqi passport. Four days later the Italian government did fall while Mohammed Abbas was thought to be in Iraq.

The catalogue of spying once again got longer with exposure of Jonathon J. Pollard and his wife who were caught selling US secrets to the Israelis. These included details of the latest aircraft and various U.S. Navy information for which they were handsomely repaid. Hundreds and hundreds of publications and cables were sent. Pollard worked for the U.S. Navy and was soon up to his ears in espionage even tapping the computer files of the DIA (Defense Intelligence Agency). But by November 8th, 1985, Pollard's commanding officer got suspicious and alerted the FBI and other agencies (Polmar and Allen 1997, 442).

And hijacking continued in style. On November 24th, 1985 another airplane was hijacked over the Mediterranean. It finally landed at Malta, a small island just south of Sicily, having just departed from Athens. Seven passengers had already been killed. Then suddenly an Egyptian commando team, after blocking the airplane from taking off, broke into the plane's cabin and shot the three hijackers. It was determined that during the plane's flight, several of the passengers were killed or wounded. While the Egyptians thought the kidnappers were Palestinians, it turned out that it was Libya's Khadfi that was implicated, looking for revenge for certain dealings with the Egyptians.

In mid-December news came of the mysterious crash of a military chartered airplane off the coast near Ganda, Newfoundland. Some 280 people were killed, mostly military personnel. The only clue to what happened was the Black Box finally retrieved from the depths. The tape recorded normal events until it suddenly ended. Evidently the airplane had no warning, as from a bomb explosion.

President Reagan realized something had to be done about Libya. On January 7th, 1986, he held a press conference, called Khadafi a "barbarian and flakey." He said he was imposing a full shutdown of relations with Libya and US citizens had to leave Libya or face penalties. However, West Germany and Britain did not go along with US sanctions against Libya and the USSR's TASS wrote about "state terrorism" as if the US had invented it. By now, 26 Soviet ships were standing off the coast of Libya. Some analysts thought there could be a showdown between the Soviet and US fleets.

In response to all this, Mr. Khadafi on January 25th put on his admiral's hat, called for his sailors thousands, and sallied forth to do battle with the US fleet —or so he claimed. But nothing happened. Khadafi had drawn a line on his map at a certain latitude to include the entire Gulf of Sidra. Inside or south of the line was "death." But all this was ignored by the Americans.

Whether the space shuttle event was somehow related to all the squabble with Libya and the continued standoff with the USSR, on January 28th the latest space rocket blasted off from Cape Canaveral, Florida. All seemed to have gone well when about 1.5 minutes into liftoff, the whole thing suddenly exploded in a mass of white smoke. A big boom followed and pieces of the rocket fell variously into the ocean. The crew evidently failed to escape from the capsule. Their bodies were found later in the capsule on the bottom of the ocean.

Wails of anguish were heard across the nation. The stock of Rockwell Kent fell following news of the shuttle. There was talk of sabotage. One suggestion was that if a rifle were fired just at liftoff, no one would hear it above the roar of the rocket motors and this could start leakage of fuel which a spark outside the rocket could ignite. But the story came out later that faulty seams in the fuel tanks may have leaked and caught fire leading to the explosion. NASA (National Aeronautic and Space Administration) stated that they did not know what caused the explosion. Sabotage was not mentioned.

Rocketry had become the name of the game in international missile competition. A report in the journal Science said that the US led the USSR in almost every phase of gadgetry related to missiles, aircraft, electronics, and computers. In the meantime a new class of ICBMs (Intercontinental Ballistic Missiles) was being developed in the early 1980s by the US. By June of 1983 the Airforce had built a small single-warhead ICBM and successfully launched it, the rocket travelling 4,190 miles. Then in August Reagan and Congress agreed with the Scowcroft Commission to deploy 100 of the new ICBMs, to be called "Peacekeepers" and placed in the old Minute Man silos (AOL Internet 2001, March 23).

Peacekeeper production began February 1984 and 50 missiles were made in 1986, 10 of these deployed. Each Peacekeeper was 70 feet long, weighed 198,000 lbs., and had four booster rockets for the different elevations flown. It could carry up to 10 independently-targeted reentry vehicles. The missile was fired at first by pressurized air and the three later boosters fired in sequence to raise the missile to 700,000 feet, some 140 miles above the earth.

And the spy game went on. Just a week after the US decided to reduce the number of Soviet people in New York from 279 to 170, a Mr. Sellers was ejected from Moscow as a spy. About two days later, the CIA's Helms was asked to explain why the number of Soviets at the UN in New York City was out of all proportion with the staffs of the US or Chinese. It was calculated by the FBI that 35 to 50% of the Soviets at the UN in New York were spies.

In late March some action finally occurred off the Libyan coast. Khadafi's forces had fired missiles from warships at US airplanes in the Gulf of Sidra. According to Larry Speakes, Reagan's spokesman, a US missile ship fired two harpoon missiles at a Libyan ship to leave it a smoking, sinking wreck. Later this afternoon, the US attacked missile sites along the Libyan shore.

On April 28th, 1986, radioactivity monitors in Sweden and Finland picked up high counts of radioactivity in the atmosphere. Later today the USSR admitted that a nuclear accident had occurred at their nuclear plant near Kiev. The next day the radioactivity release was said caused by a meltdown of part of the reactor, accompanied by a fire that was then burning briskly. Swedish experts were called in to try and extinguish the fire. Actually most of the radioactivity came from radioactive iodine and cesium, these being only a little above background levels. Nevertheless the Soviet government urged Europeans to stop drinking milk for a few weeks since cows graze on contaminated grass and other plants. The Germans, not too surprised at the Soviet technology failures, could recall their belief that nothing good came from the east. Usually it was the cold weather, sometimes it was the Russians, but now it was something worse.

Evidently the first news of the Soviet reactor meltdown came from a Japanese radio operator who had talked with a Russian operator, stating that hundreds of people had been injured in the nuclear flap and that a "raging fire" was going on. In Kiev, phones were jammed with calls from Ukranian-Americans to their relatives. It came out later that two reactors had melted down during a test (which should never have been done) and presumably the uranium cylinders caught fire. Also, there was no containment dome over the plant. The Soviets, however, said that only two people had been killed.

* * * * * * * * * * * *

The question of how much the media should release about the various cases of espionage came to the fore in mid-1986. For example, an ex-spy, name of Carver, had been working for the Brookings Institute while holding an editor's job on the Washington Post newspaper. Carver claimed that the release of information about messages sent by Libya's Khadafi to Berlin, revealed which ciphers were being used (MacNeil-Lehrer Report 1986, May 13). This was thought to be a serious breach of intelligence. An editor of the Post said that Reagan himself had let the facts out, not the Post. It seems that top US government officials leak information to the media on purpose for reasons of their own. Nevertheless, DCI Casey was sufficiently upset to sue the Post and several other news services for releasing secret information. Casey even accused NBC reporter James Polk of violating a 1950 law prohibiting disclosure of any classified information about communications intelligence and referred the case to the Justice department. Polk, appearing on NBC's "Today" show had elaborated on a top-secret US program that was turned over to the USSR by a Ronald Pelton. Evidently Pelton had given away one of NSA's most sensitive secrets, called Ivy Bells. This was an eavesdropping program by submarines in the harbors of the USSR, such as in the Sea of Okhotsk. Pelton was at the time (May 20th) on trial in Baltimore, Maryland.

Pelton had been an NSA intelligence analyst, but turned coat and began feeding information to the USSR in October of 1979. The FBI got wind of his activities through taps put on several phone lines back in January, 1980. Nothing was done about it until Pelton met up with Vitaly Yurchenko, a Soviet secret agent. Pelton allegedly supplied him with reams of data about US submarines. The FBI then began to bug several of his places including his home and his car. The case finally went to court and in June, 1986, he was sentenced to life in prison.

In June of 1986, a John Walker was on trial for spying. Former CIA man George Carver testified that Walker and Jerry A. Whitworth, a Navy radio man, had run an elaborate spy ring, passing Navy secrets to the USSR via certain other people known to them (U.P.I., New Haven Register 1986, June 13). This included cryptographic data and details on coding machines. Walker paid Whitworth for the code materials. The editor of the Reader's Digest testified that Yurchenko had told him that the Walker-Whitworth case was the greatest in the history of the KGB.

Also in June a Soviet air attaché in the Soviet embassy in Washington D.C. was caught spying. A certain Mr. Ismanov was found to be picking up capsules of film that were so thin that 130 pictures could be put on a single roll. Such rolls of film were put in the ground at a drop. Ismanov was only reprimanded and sent home — but to what fate was unknown.

When Edward Lee Howard began giving away US secrets to the USSR he was still a CIA agent in Vienna. He also began pointing out Soviet citizens to Russian authorities, telling the Soviets that they were working for the CIA. As many as twelve US agents were probably killed by the Soviets as a result of his machinations. Leaving for Moscow, he was granted asylum there. An A.P. news release stated that the defection of Howard was the first to take asylum in the USSR since the 1960s when two NSA employees and several US servicemen protesting the

Vietnam war took asylum in the USSR.

The Daniloff case was an odd one since he was apparently the object of a setup. Daniloff was a newsman living in Moscow. He had been told to meet a certain "Misha" in Moscow park for some interesting news clippings. Going to the park he did accept the clippings, thinking it a gift before he left town. However, the Moscow authorities arrested him and held him for a prolonged period of time. The Soviets then offered to US State Department a swap for a detained Soviet agent in the US. But the State Department rejected the plan. Finally, Daniloff was moved into the custody of the US ambassador in Moscow.

By September 30 the Daniloff case went on. He was reported to have arrived at Frankfurt, West Germany. Meanwhile the man for whom he was to be swapped, Zakharov, pleaded no contest to spying charges and was told to leave the US along with some others from the Soviet UN mission. Daniloff finally returned to the states. It came out in October that his father had been kept in a Siberian camp for 30 years and later died in Moscow. This suggested to the Soviet authorities that D might have been working against the USSR.

Loose immigration laws continued to be a problem not only to settled inhabitants of the United States, but to the possibility of spies and saboteurs coming across the various borders to work their dirty deeds. On November 6, 1986, a new immigration law was actually passed and signed into law by Reagan. But the media had no use for it, claiming (1) that it would not work, (2) that it only gave amnesty to illegals already here, (3) that it could not be policed, and (4) that it would ruin the low-wage workers that came seasonally from Mexico and (theoretically) went back again. As it turned out, it did work to some extent and was better than the comparative free-for-all that the liberals wanted to retain.

* * * * * * * * * * * * *

The House and Senate Intelligence Committee met on November 21st 1986 apparently to put the heat on Reagan about sending arms to Iran in some kind of mysterious deal. Director of the CIA (DCI) Casey was testifying. The rumor was that it was a scheme to get hostages freed from the Middle East and this would have been successful, it was felt, if it were not for the US press. It was soon published in the news that Reagan's emissary McFarlane had made a trip to the Middle East, the purpose being somewhat mysterious, although some claimed he kept Secretary Shultz informed of it at all times. Yet NSC members were kept in the dark about the whole deal. Newsweek magazine reported in late November that Iran received $60 million worth of war matériel and spare parts for F-4 Phantom jets that they already had.

The Iran-arms deal quickly became all the talk in the media. One rumor was that Mrs. Reagan would like to see Shultz go (into obscurity), for having objected to the Reagan policy toward Iran. Then on the 25th Poindexter resigned along with one of his underlings. All this caused much cackling in the henyard and feathers flew. It seemed that arms were sold to Iran and the money received was sent to aid the Nicaraguan Contras (New Haven Register 1986, June 13). Columnist Ben Wattenberg claimed that although Reagan was indeed the teflon president (*i.e.* nothing stuck to him) the Iran affair had energized the pack, bringing back fond memories of gates past, especially Watergate. Wattenberg felt that journalists were now in the breaking-of-the-president mode and Irangate would restore past glories of other gates past.

Very soon the media trotted out Democrat McGovern who, although saying the whole thing was not that important, used that magic word: impeachment. This, of course, delighted the media. And the question arose: Did Don Regan, in the Reagan entourage, KNOW if money was sent to the Contras? Reagan called the question ridiculous. But another associate of the Reagan clan, Colonel North of the Marine Corps, was getting flak for the allegedly fouled-up scam to send money to the Contras.

In the next few days, CBS TV talked of the growing controversy while Oliver North was out looking for a good lawyer and Poindexter allegedly shredded a lot of documents. Vice President Bush, like Weinberger, said he knew nothing about it.

December came around and Reagan stated publicly that he was casting no blame on any of his cronies, or words to that effect, and said the "press" had gotten ahold of a story published in a Beirut "rag" (newspaper) that was based on a leak. But several members of Congress were not satisfied and the Democrats there wanted a "special prosecutor" appointed.

The media in its usual various forms, claimed that much of the money from the Iranian situation was not the only money banked in Switzerland, but the CIA had sent millions to Afghanistan, presumably to aid the Afghans in the war against the USSR. Colonel North, apparently entangled in the Irangate affair, refused 40 times to answer questions in a hearing, claiming the 5th amendment in facing an investigating panel, CBS TV pointed out. On the 3rd, Vice President Bush was on the

TV and said he knew of the arms sales to Iran and called it a mistaken tactic. Secretary Weinberger added to this to say that Iran was run by lunatics and until they got a better government, there was no dealing with them. Weinberger then left the country, saying he knew nothing about it. As for ex-Senator Baker of Tennessee he soft-pedaled the Irangate flap, implying that they did not need destruction of the government.

On December 8th, after Poindexter had been on the stand defending his position, Oliver North arrived, bedecked with medals, while his lawyer spoke for him. But the New York Times, CBS TV, and the Washington Post were having their field-day, mainly quoting DCI Casey and their own rhetoric. Who had initiated the deal? Some said it was an Iranian, but Casey was not talking. Then it came out that the British sent arms to Iran apparently in the deal. The RCMP in Canada then launched an investigation.

Reagan took sick, and well he might, actually with a case of prostate cancer. DCI Casey was also having health problems with a brain tumor soon to be operated on.

Evidently, Reagan could not recall giving McFarlane the go-ahead to ship arms to Iran because on July 13, 1985, Reagan was in surgery with his "colon problem" (New Haven Register 1986, December 30). Oliver North, meanwhile, claimed the Israelis had suggested a deal in which arms would be traded for money. But the Israelis heatedly denied the accusation.

In January of 1987, the media, written and electronic, figured, apparently, that the "ratings" on "Irangate" were still high enough to make them worth pursuing further. This conclusion was encouraged by news that a Federal Grand Jury would examine Irangate and probably give immunity to certain witnesses.

While a deep-freeze winter gripped Europe in which the Swedes were buried, the British frozen, the French lost in slush, and the Soviets solidified, Irangate went blithely on buoyed by the media. But Reagan said he had nothing to apologize for. Yet reports persisted that he and Casey (still in the hospital) were involved in Oliver North's deals.

In late January, Reagan was on TV, as if to prove there were more important things in the world than selling arms to some foreign country. Reagan instead attacked the aggressive activities of the USSR as it attempted to spread its hegemony to Afghanistan, Pakistan, Cambodia, Mongolia, and now Central America.

It was true anyway, that the Soviets were conducting an aggressive campaign to glean information from the US through Montreal, Canada.

The Canadians found that on the third floor of the Soviet consulate was a microwave communications center to maintain contact with agents in the Washington-New York-Boston areas. A United Press International article added that a rooftop satellite dish was concealed in a wooden shed to monitor phone calls to and from the US and British consulates and US defense contractors.

In mid-February 1987, a number of "commissions" were appointed to investigate the Iran-contra affair, but conclusions were vague. McFarlane, languishing in the hospital, said he had concocted a plan to cover up the arms deal with Iran to protect the President. And it seemed that Reagan approved of the cover-up. Later on in July, Don Regan, the President's right-hand man, claimed he tried to learn from North and Pointexter what was going on. When he found out, he told Reagan who acted as if completely astonished. Reagan then wanted to make it public, but North and Poindexter argued against doing that (Regan 1988, 42, 57). As for the Tower commission, it blamed the entire chain of command from Reagan to North and others. A German political sage opined that this is what happens when important affairs are put in the hands of amateurs.

While CBS TV claimed that Reagan's government had been severely damaged, Reagan tried to calm things down with a televised speech. He explained his transgression, admitted errors, and said he would try and improve. At about this time, William H. Webster, formerly Director of the FBI (1978-1987), was made the new Director of the CIA to serve until 1991.

In March, Oliver North decided to file his own legal suit against the various prosecutors, but Judge Barrington Parker ruled against it and threw it out of court on grounds concerning suits against prosecutors.

Next, Vice President Bush fell under fire for simply knowing about it. CBS compared the Pollard spy trial with Reagan's alleged Irangate transgressions, suggesting that the President was into Irangate up to his neck as well as in the Pollard trial. Israel was said to have paid $80,000 toward legal expenses of Pollard who allegedly had given Israel vital US secrets (New Haven Register 1987, March 16). But in the end, Pollard was sentenced to prison for five years.

* * * * * * * * * * * *

One thing certain about spying is that it never goes out of style. The British had been wondering lately why so many spies had come from

Britain's upper crust. The late master spy Maurice Oldfield, said to have been the model for John le Carré's fictional character George Smiley, had just been accused as a homosexual and a security risk. Probably, for one thing, the more educated people were more likely to be exposed to the intellectual wanderings of Marx and Lenin. Becoming sympathetic to Communist ideas, they thought of world Communism as the solution to international wars and the poverty of the masses, whatever masses could be located. If these left-wing people had been properly vetted, some said, then they might have been caught earlier. But the "good buddy" clique tended to hinder this self-examination within the British secret services.

Secrets are always hard to keep, but even the Japanese let one out they should have kept quiet. They were said to have given away the secret of silent submarine propulsion to the USSR. This silence was achieved by grinding the propellers very thin and smooth to prevent rippling and bubble-formation, which give away their presence. A Mr. Nakasone apologized for Japan and said he would come to the US and do what he could to prevent Toshiba Machinery's error from happening again.

Toward the end of November it became clear that Cuba, like a beehive that, despite various sprays to eradicate it, continued to persist as a "model" of Communist theory. A few years ago Fidel Castro sent the US a present of "detainees" which big-hearted Uncle Sam accepted. Once ensconced in the states, they were now being asked to go back to Cuba. The trouble was, they refused to go and made this clear by burning down their barracks.

One camp in Louisiana had distinguished itself by taking hostages and making demands. Then they went on a binge of rioting and proceeded to complain of the poor housing. Presumably, they never went back to Cuba.

By January of 1988, it leaked out that there was a kind of silent war over the satellites of the US and also those of the USSR. US intelligence was convinced that US satellites had been damaged by Soviet attacks with laser beams (United Press International 1988, January 10). Such satellites orbiting the earth were said to be watching missile and spacecraft launching sites and relaying this information to ground reception centers. But there was evidently no way to protect the optical sensors of the satellites from laser beams.

In mid May of 1988, the Soviets were claiming that they would soon be leaving Afghanistan. But they were leaving behind a pro-Soviet government in Kabul which might have to go on fighting to save itself from the natives. In the meantime, Iraq and Iran were still occasionally shooting missiles at each other while the Iranians were back to their old tricks of mining the Persian gulf. By this time, according to the Pentagon. the Iranians had only two operable frigates and these were said to be out of action.

In July, the Battle of the Persian Gulf went on. The US frigate Montgomery went to the aid of a Danish tanker which had been hit by rocket-grenades from an Iranian gunboat. Also, an Iranian airplane was shot down by US forces near the Hormuz straits. The Iranians were shouting to the skies that it was a passenger airplane. The US then admitted to shooting it down, killing 290 people. A Pentagon spokesman., asked about it by newsmen, could only claim that the U.S. Navy had to defend itself. Admiral Crowe responded to all the criticism suggesting that the Navy was not aware that it was a passenger airplane that their radar had detected.

In August of 1988 the spy game went on in Europe. The German "Welt am Sontag" (World on Sunday) alleged that US serviceman Conrad gave secret information on NATO's defense to two Swedes of Hungarian extraction, relaying the information through Vienna, Austria, to the USSR. He was tried in West Germany and got a life sentence, having endangered the defense capability of the West.

In the autumn of 1988, certain rumors blew across Siberia as far as Japan. This was spy information that something was going wrong in the USSR. Either Gorbachev was ill or his government was cracking up — possibly both. This, however, seemed of little importance in the West while the space shuttle "Challenger" was flying back to earth on its own to an airfield in southern California. Some 400,000 people came to see it land. This number was calculated by counting the 90,000 cars parked there, multiplying by four, then adding a few more for good measure.

That the Soviet empire was showing signs of losing some of its territory was further substantiated by news from Latvia on the Baltic Sea that was loudly complaining to the USSR for meddling in its state affairs. Estonia too, was in an upheaval, protesting Soviet rule. And even Yugoslavia, called a fragile state, was showing signs of rebellion from Soviet Communist rule. Commentator and columnist George Will in his analysis of the situation felt that ethnicity and religion could doom the USSR and claimed that 20 million had been murdered by Stalin who was now gone, along with his iron hand (ABC TV 1988, October 15).

Yet somehow, there were spies who were willing to "go over" to the

Soviet side in the autumn of 1988. Edward L. Howard, who defected from the CIA in 1985, was the first CIA agent to go over to the USSR. Admiral Turner, asked about it, said that the Soviets were paranoid over spying and even spied on themselves. Turner felt that the CIA took a beating during the Reagan years. He added that in the Howard case, the cat got out of the bag when Vitaly Yurchenko, a KGB officer, defected to the West and told of a CIA man who had gone over to the USSR. Getting wind of his danger, Howard escaped to Moscow and lived there for several more years.

On November 8th, 1988, George H. W. Bush won both the popular and electoral vote for President of the United States, defeating contender Dukakis.

As an indication of continuing problems in the USSR, Gorbachev stated that experiments in Democracy were threatening his policy of "peristroika" (reconstruction). The meaning of this word probably escaped most Americans and one talk-show host suggested Peristroika was his wife's name. But at least by now in late November the USSR radio stopped jamming US, German, and Israeli radio broadcasting. Just why this happened was not clear, but the Soviets admitted that there were big upheavals in the member state of Azarbaijan, the exact location of this state probably unknown to most all Americans, especially since there seemed to be two of them.

Only a few days before Christmas, another commercial airliner crashed killing all of its many passengers. This time it was a Boeing 747 Pan American airliner that simply exploded over Scotland. When the main body of the plane hit the ground it dug a groove that extended 1500 yards. One wing was never found, apparently blown to pieces. A "Near East looking" person had been seen leaving the airplane while at Heathrow airport in Britain, its last stop. A number of Scottish homes were wrecked and many people killed on the ground at Lockerbie. Libya was suggested as a possible source of the bomb although some "experts" thought it might have been Iran.

In May of 1989, the question of the reunification of Germany was brought up by commentator Sam Donaldson. The question had arisen as to whether there was any talk of reunifying Germany. Cheney felt that there was. In fact there seemed to be no fear in the US government about German reunification.

Bush, apparently taking his cue from Cheney, went to Europe and talked to the West Germans about the failure of Communism, then asked that the Berlin wall be pulled down. The crowd that had gathered to hear

Bush cheered mightily.

On June 4th, news came to the US that Khoumeini had died. Iran's Bani Sadr estimated that there would probably be a civil war in Iran as a result. On the 6th, Khoumeini's body was on its way to a grave yard, but was surrounded by a seething mob which, in their apparent grief, so jostled the casket that the body fell out on the street. People were trying desperately to tear off some of his clothes and keep for mementoes. He was finally rescued from the screaming mob by a helicopter, having been stuffed back into his coffin.

In July the game of spy-versus-spy went onward between the USSR and the US. Since the US headquarters in Moscow were known to be full of electronic bugs, US authorities there planned to tear down the whole building. At about this same time in the US, a Mr. Felix Bloch was video-filmed passing a briefcase to a Soviet KGB agent in the US. Bloch was seized by authorities and on questioning, was said to have been working for the CIA. The FBI, asked about the case, said that they in the FBI were not up on CIA work. In any case, Bloch, in February, 1990, was dismissed from the State Department (Polmar and Allen 1997, 75). At a press meeting Bush said the Bloch case was leaked by mistake. But a veritable crowd followed Bloch: Soviet agents, FBI men, and finally TV camera men, like a small parade wherever he went.

New signs of trouble in the USSR came to the surface in August of 1989. The Baltic states: Estonia, Latvia, and Lithuania, were in an upheaval. The latest thing there was for the inhabitants to form a human chain by holding hands one by one for miles on end. Their hope was total independence from mother Russia. At the same time the fighting in Afghanistan went on without a clear outcome. This did not bode well for the present Soviet government.

In September, the USSR's leader Mr. Yeltsin came to the US and appeared on the MacNeil Lehrer Report program (PBS TV 1989, September 10). In the midst of the discussions he made the astounding implication that the USSR was on the edge of an abyss and the nation could fall in. Yeltsin, a big man, heavy-set, made a big impression, suggesting to his audience that things better work out or there would be a revolution. Back in Moscow, it turned out that the government was not a little upset at his remarks and one government spokesman accused Yeltsin of having been drunk when he talked on the TV.

Another sign of the weakness of the Soviet empire came to light when as many as 16,000 East Germans poured through the Hungarian border into Austria, having been given passports for West Germany. A

Hungarian government representative, when asked by reporters about the situation, claimed that his people had raised the Iron Curtain some time ago and there was no real barrier now to prevent crossing the border. So they did come: some drove their cars, others came on foot with knapsacks and suitcases. As for Germany itself, one German guessed that about 200,000 East Germans might come into West Germany. A reporter, when asked why were they leaving, answered that with low wages, poor food, and many restrictions, they could not stand it any longer.

A few days later in September, Yeltsin was back in the US and on TV. He was asked if the upheaval was a failure of the Communist system. His answer was that it was only a dream. A few days later a report from Moscow to the US openly alleged that the Soviet Empire was in danger of breaking up.

In Prague, thousands of East Germans had arrived in early October with the intention of leaving for West Germany. But the Czechs soon closed their borders. One German who escaped, claimed that living in East Germany seemed to him like being born into the army. Then in Dresden, East Germany, a city still showing the brutal scars of near total devastation in WW II, there was open rioting. And on the 9th, 70,000 people marched in Leipzig's torchlight parade singing the song: "We shall overcome!"

By the middle of October, East Germany's Honecker found himself out of office and the Communist government with him. On top of this, the Politburo of the Socialist Unity Party collapsed and there were mass resignations from the SSD, the Staats Sicherheit Dienst (State Security Service).

Paul Nitze, US foreign policy expert on the MacNeil-Lehrer PBS TV program, concluded that the US had won the Cold War with the USSR, but that Gorbachev was still the leader and had to be dealt with carefully. Nitze guessed that the whole USSR might break up, a remarkably accurate prediction.

In early November, 1989, there were as many as 300 East Germans crossing the border to West Germany every hour. In a few days it was estimated that 15,000 people from East Germany had gone to the western sector. And also, all the members of the East German cabinet had resigned.

By the 9th, open travel was allowed from East to West Germany, making the Berlin wall completely obsolete. Some of the Germans could not wait to see it pulled down and set to work with sledge hammers and pick axes, saving some of the chips as souvenirs.

By mid-November, 1989, "Der Mauer" (the wall) in Berlin was broken through in several places and US Army troops were handing out rations to the arriving East Germans. In Leipzig, East Germany, 200,000 people marched demanding a free party system. Toward the end of the month, the ruling Communists in Czechoslovakia agreed to give up their power. Back in 1968, the Soviets had installed Dubchek, an "old hero" of WW II, as head of a puppet government. Although quite old, he was returning to power.

Many American troops were now headed homeward from Germany. To most Germans it was mainly a matter of indifference, since there were benefits to them on the one hand, like the money the Americans spent, and on the other hand there were clashes between the troops and the natives, as when fields were damaged by tank maneuvers.

The Russians, meanwhile, were pulling four divisions out of East Germany. But General Gavin, US Chief of Staff, on the ABC Brinkley program, said this was not a big deal since it would still leave 14 more divisions. He favored keeping NATO much alive and added that the Soviets had a mountain of ammo still there in East Germany.

Then it was Romania in mid December that was in a great upheaval with many of its citizens killed in rioting. And the rioting went on into the 20th of November. Helicopters flew over the crowds of protestors and fired into them with machine guns, thinking to disperse them, but then killed hundreds.

The Brandenburg gate in Berlin, so long surrounded with barriers since the end of WW II, was the scene of the meeting of East and West chancellors. They declared that the gate will henceforth be called the "Gateway to Freedom." A massive crowd greeted these words with wild cheering.

In Romania, Ceausescu, head of the Communist government, was on the run. Like Noriega of Panama who had become "persona non grata" in his own country, he went into hiding. On the evening of the 23rd, a German orchestra at the Brandenburg gate played Beethoven's 9th symphony along with a huge chorus of men and women, the whole crowd singing along with them to sound like the roar of the sea in a Baltic storm.

In Romania the rioting went on in the capital city. Ceausecu was captured and promptly tried by a Romanian court on December 26th where he was condemned to death for his numerous atrocities. Along with his wife, he was shot by a firing squad. Sic transit Communitas.

Chapter 9

UN Confronts Iraq, USSR Collapses, Serbia Struggles With UN

News came to America in January of 1990 that the USSR's Gorbachev had cancelled his visit to Japan. This may have seemed of little importance, but there were rumors in the US that he might have to leave office. A few days later on the 11th, when Gorbachev went to visit Lithuania, an estimated 300,000 Lithuanians demonstrated for their independence. This was the first time a Soviet leader had come there since the Stalinist era when suppression was the rule.

Germany too, still divided, vented its own frustrations when crowds of East Germans stormed the Secret Police offices in East Berlin. Their major complaint was the failure to unify Germany. Crowds shouted "Einheit" (Unity) over and over again. When Premier Modrow of East Germany tried to address tens of thousands in East Berlin, he was jeered and not allowed to speak.

The USSR's government was having its own problems, facing the growing demands of the populace. By way of concession, the government agreed to dump at once the one-party Communist monopoly of power and create a multiple party system. With the advent of the 1990s, the Soviet government made some drastic changes. Gorbachev asked for the abolition of the term "General Secretary," a post recently held by Yuri Andropov. In its place would be the term "Party Chairman." Then the question had to be debated as to what structure the rest of the government would have. Gorbachev preferred a combination of the French 5th

Republic and the US Presidency, with both a President and a Premier. The General Assembly agreed and Boris Yeltsin was elected Chairman of the Russian Supreme Soviet. In March of 1990, the Lithuanians voted to be free of the Soviet Union. But the Soviet government would have none of it, demanding that they pay 36 billion rubles before the Lithuanians could have their freedom. Lithuania's reply was to ask the USSR to pay them more than that for all the people Stalin had deported or killed (d'Encausse 1993, 240).

In May, Latvia followed Lithuania in demanding its freedom while Estonia, a third Baltic state, was making noises indicating that it would soon follow suit in seeking freedom. The Hungarians too were looking for freedom, having been occupied by Soviet troops for years. Back in 1940, Germany and Italy had given back, according to the governments of Hitler and Mussolini, much of Hungary's land lost after the Versailles treaty was signed. The German government had wanted Hungary to take over Yugoslavia, but Hungary refused to do so. Next, during 1990, the Hungarians thought the time was ripe for them to revolt.

Returning to the Lithuanian problem, the Soviets next tried force to bring the populace into line, demanding that they give up their weapons while sending aircraft to fly in low over the capitol, at the same time sending troops to approach the Lithuanian border.

By mid-May Gorbachev admitted that the USSR's economic plans had all failed. He asked for help from the West to achieve a "market (free) economy." In late May things had gotten worse in Moscow with food running out. This situation was not helped by people outside the city who came in without passes and ran off with any food they could find.

In June, Gorbachev came to Washington, D.C. for help. But his stubborn stance on Lithuania was being undermined by Yeltsin who was then busy talking with Lithuania's Landsbergis, searching for some kind of settlement agreeable to the Lithuanians.

In the meantime, a new spy case broke into the open in Germany. Former US Army sergeant Roderick James Ramsay was said to have been part of an extensive spy ring selling plans of weapons and the means of communication to agents in Czechoslovakia and Hungary. NATO plans were also given away. The FBI had been called in for a foreign intelligence investigation of a case involving another one time Army sergeant named Conrad and this led to Ramsay. Conrad acted as a kind of middle man in the sale of secrets (Polmar and Allen 1997, 461).

Back in the US in Washington D.C., it became evident that even top military brass can be subject to non-military laws. Admiral John Poindexter was handed a sentence of six months in prison for his alleged involvement in the Reagan-Iran-Contra case. However, he never served the whole six months, having been pardoned by George H.W. Bush, of course to the acute anguish of the liberal elements of the media and their adherents in Congress.

Returning to the subject of the ailing Soviet Union, after 45 years of the US trying to hold off the machinations of the USSR, it was becoming obvious that the USSR were going broke. James Baker in the Bush government on ABC TV said that if money were sent to the USSR, it would just go to Cuba. Bush, asked about it, said that he did not want to send aid money to the USSR because too many soviet missiles were pointed at the United States.

* * * * * * * * * * * *

Iraq was back in the news. It was by now mid-summer in 1990 when Iraq moved its troops up to the Kuwaiti border near the Persian Gulf. To counter this, the US moved its naval forces nearby. Kuwait was apparently important to Iraq for its oil and for its accessibility to the sea.

On August 2nd, Iraq's government decided on the invasion of Kuwait. Two possible reasons for this suggested by news services was to force a rise in the price of oil and spread Iraq's hegemony into the oil-rich Kuwaiti region. At this time Iraq had, according to secret information, an enormous Soviet-made tank force as well as missiles rumored to be able to spread poison gas – but not yet a workable atomic bomb. Yet so far, Iraq's forces were not moving.

News wires on August 6th mentioned that the Iraqis were beginning to withdraw from the Kuwaiti border. Nevertheless, Iraq's Hussein, in defiance of the UN and the US, called for a Holy War against the West. But Egypt, Turkey, and Iran declared against Iraq and put an embargo on Iraqi exports.

By mid-August Iran seemed to have had second thoughts and to have come to Iraq's rescue, suggesting they kick out the "Great Devourers" who always wanted "to fish in troubled waters." King Hussein of Jordan, on the other hand, offered to be peacemaker, while Syria supported Arabia. Egypt's Mubarak, not committing his nation, said that Iraq's Hussein had only led himself into a cul de sac. Syria wanted revenge on Iraq and promised to help the Allies of the West. It was as if the oil using nations had banded together to put down Iraq as indicated by the Germans and Japanese who were each sending aid to the Allied effort amounting to $2 billion.

In late September Iraq's government stated that if it came to war, they would attack the Middle East oil wells as well as the state of Israel. Oil was then costing $35.43 per barrel on international markets and could have gone higher if the war became bad enough, news writers claimed. But already the war was beginning when US aircraft attacked Iraq from four directions: some from Jordan, some from Turkey, some from Saudi Arabia, and apparently some from aircraft carriers in the Persian Gulf.

The end of September 1990 was marked by the astonishing news that the USSR would initiate private enterprise. Then only a few days later on October 2, Germany was officially declared "one". The old black-red-gold flag flew high again, while thousands collected at the Brandenburg gate in Berlin to celebrate the union.

Despite such fanfare in Germany, the Iraq problem went on with Hussein continuing to talk of firing missiles at Israel, where people were scrambling to obtain gas masks in case the missiles contained poison gases as some rumors had claimed.

By November, it suddenly became a "fait accompli" that Iraq had taken over Kuwait. Britain's Mrs. Thatcher was said to have told Hussein that if he did not depart Kuwait soon the Allies would go to war. Meanwhile, two tank divisions had left the US headed for the Gulf, the US demanding total Iraqi withdrawal. Iraq's answer was that there would be no withdrawal.

It was on Christmas day that Saddam Hussein promised that if war began, the first to be attacked by Iraq would be Tel Aviv, Israel. War seemed inevitable and all US nationals were already being recalled from Jordan and Sudan.

The new year of 1991 arrived, but not everyone in the US wanted to rush off to war in the Middle East. A large number of university professors demanded of President Bush that he withdraw from the Kuwait fracas and negotiate.

Despite anguished cries from various parts of America against an invasion of Iraq, Congress voted in favor of giving Bush authority to go ahead with it. On the 15th of January, British, French, and German representatives to the UN stated that they would support UN action against the Iraqis now in Kuwait. Germany pledged several Alpha fighter aircraft plus $2 billion while the French tried a last ditch peace effort but were turned down by the Iraqis. In some US cities crowds marched to protest the plans for a UN war to drive Iraq out of Kuwait.

On January 16, the Business TV news reported that bombers under UN auspices had attacked Iraqi oil installations near the Gulf. Actually, however, secret operation "Desert Storm" had already been put into motion. Fighter-bombers and Saudi Arabian F-15s had attacked targets in Kuwait along the "Wadi-el Batin" on the Kuwait-Iraq border. According to secret information available to Brzezinski in Bush's staff, the reason Hussein refused to pull out of Kuwait was that the Iraqi leader thought the US was not ready to go to war.

While Americans still debated the reasons for war against Iraq, Patriot missiles were shooting down Iraq's Scuds sent from mobile launching trucks. Yet some of the scuds managed to hit Riyad, Saudi Arabia's capital. Although UN Troops had not yet moved in late January, B-52 bombers carpet bombed Hussein's elite guards. Twelve allied aircraft were said to have been lost. Even Tel Aviv was under attack by Iraqi Scuds. Although some were shot down by Patriots, some of the Scuds escaped and caused heavy damage.

Iraq's Hussein, evidently in revenge for the threatened loss of Kuwait, gave the order to release oil from Kuwait's storage tanks into the Persian Gulf where Allied shipping had collected. This resulted in an enormous oil slick that covered the upper part of the Gulf and threatened to interrupt Saudi Arabia's water-making system.

General Schwarzkopf of the Allied Forces released the information that 39 Iraqi aircraft had been flown to Iran since the war began February 17th. This included 23 fighter aircraft. Iran was expected to confiscate such flightlings while the pilots escaped being shot down by the UN forces. Schwarzkopf stated that already two F-15s had shot down four MiG-23s near Baghdad. By now it was apparent that the war was not going in favor of Hussein. To add to his worries, Allied warships were shooting Tomahawk missiles into Baghdad while the battleship Wisconsin was firing its huge shells into Iraqi army positions, evidently preparatory to an invasion in a few weeks.

Brezhnev was said to have secretly told Iraq's Hussein to leave Kuwait in 36 hours. Bush, however, did not approve of the Soviet plan and in any case Breshnev received no reply from Hussein.

Hussein's next trick was to set fire to 120 oil wells in Kuwait, producing an enormous black smoke pall that soon lay across the Kuwait-Saudi border and drifted inexorably toward the Gulf.

The UN offensive began February 23, 1991. Although a secret at the time, the plan was for US troops to hold fast at first off the Kuwaiti east coast. Then British and French forces would move off to the west of Kuwait to form a giant enveloping action. The next day the Arabs also joined in, moving into Kuwait while US Marines were said to have gone ashore. Rumors flew that paratroopers landed on Kuwait City while about 10,000 Iraqi prisoners were taken.

On February 26th, Hussein ordered withdrawal from Kuwait, but by then as many as 20,000 iraqi prisoners had been taken. Hussein's more faithful troops, the "Republican Guards," made an advance but were shot to pieces by the Allies' superior tanks, the Iraqi tanks having been made in the USSR. By the afternoon, Kuwait was liberated by US Marines and the US embassy was taken back. Schwarzkopf said that a broad sweep had been made around the Euphrates river with British and French forces, boxing in the Iraqis.

In spite of all this, Baghdad continued to pour out anti-Allied propaganda, claiming that the Allies had lost the war. Hussein's whereabouts remained a secret while Kuwait was largely a wreck, its oil wells leaking into the Gulf and fires still burning.

* * * * * * * * * * * * * *

While the Kuwait war had raged, the Soviet monolith continued to break up. In central Asia, then part of the USSR, as early as 1988 and 1989, there had been a growing demand for change. The Soviet states of Turkestan, Uzbekistan, and Kazakhstan, which included in all some 40 million people, were in upheaval with gangs in small towns rioting. At first they armed themselves with iron bars, then later with guns, mainly picking fights with recent immigrants, their dislike of foreigners coming to the surface, this situation forced on them by the Communist plan to mix the various kinds of people in the USSR. The usual cure for such rioting had been to force them into the army while the MVD would stop their fighting by severe repression (d'Encausse 1993,211). But all this sort of thing no longer worked. The Uzbeks fought the Kirghiz, for example, taking out their latent hatreds on each other. In the Ukraine, talk of a Declaration of Independence was heard in the land.

The Soviet Union's own capital city had its problems. In Moscow, thousands jammed Manezh square, 500,000 by one estimate. For all that anyone could tell, it was a pro-democracy rally, although it was only one of about 16 others held across the Republic of Russia. In support of Boris Yeltsin, the crowd called for Gorbachev's resignation. Yeltsin wanted to replace Gorbachev with a Federation Council, which would include the presidents of 15 Republics. By this time, 10 of these Republics had proclaimed sovereignty and hoped for status like that of Russia and the Ukraine.

In March of 1991, the American Embassy in Moscow was set on fire. Strangely, the top floors of the building were most damaged where the supersecret files and espionage equipment were kept.

In the United States other sources of disruption were going on, largely ignored by the public while the government was focusing attention on the Gulf war. Asylum application by foreigners who wanted to enter the US had risen from about 20,000 in 1987 to some 100,000 in 1991. FAIR (Federation for American Immigration Reform) pointed out that a half million Guatemalans and Salvadorans had entered the US illegally and were now claiming they were seeking asylum. According to the INS (Immigration and Naturalization Service), about 50% of the claims were deemed fraudulent.

Although the USSR was also concerned with immigrants, the overpowering urge within the old USSR was for freedom for the various Republics. By April of 1991 at a meeting in Kiev, the "Big Five": Russia, Ukraine, Belorussia, Uzbekistan, and Kazakhstan, agreed to reunite nine Republics into the "Union", while Armenia, Moldavia, and Georgia decided to join three Baltic states in looking for freedom. The old Central government was not represented in this (d'Encausse 1993, 244).

On April 23rd, the so-called Novo-Ogarievo Accord was made. This reunited the nine Republics and meant that Yeltsin's plan had succeeded while Gorbachev's had failed.

William H Webster, ex-DCI, together with various FBI ex-directors, were on the MacNeil-Lehrer report (PBS), Webster concluded that with all the upheavals in the USSR, the American secret services were still very much needed even though Russia's militarist stance was fading. He claimed that Russia, now under great stress, was the only super-power capable of destroying the US. Also, since Webster had come on as a "loan" to the CIA, it was obvious that things had changed radically in the world of espionage. Evidently, in the old days, the Soviets used satellite nations and agents in those nations as spies on US technology. But all that had changed and other nations like Japan were out looking for secret intelligence to compete.

By late May, 1991, while the USSR seemed to be crumbling, Gorbachev and Yeltsin, long at odds, had finally come to terms and were asking for a loan of some $100 billion, presumably in dollars certainly not in rubles, from Uncle Sam. In June, Yeltsin was elected President of what they were calling "Russia" although the Ukraine refused to sign a treaty that joined the various Republics in the same organization as the Ukranians. By the 18th, it appeared that it was Yeltsin's job as President of much of the old USSR, to come to the US and appeal for the above-mentioned loan. But the ruin of Communism in Russia was further indicated when Moscow's statue of Lenin was pulled down to lie supinely in the street, while there were rumors that the KGB might suddenly take over the old USSR and eject Yeltsin.

In July Gorbachev was trying to reach some kind of agreement with Germany's Kohl. The Russian leader wanted $8 billion paid to the Russians for the old USSR's bases in East Germany. As for the new Germany, it was still trying to decide where to put its government. The Bundesrat had refused to move to Berlin from Bonn, although the Bundestag had already done that.

In mid-August, several thousand people turned out in Moscow to support Yeltsin's election and Gorbachev's ouster, waving their red, blue and white flags. President Bush said removal of Gorbachev was illegal. With Gorbachev out, Vice President Gdanyi Yanayev took over according to the Constitution. Demonstrations were banned by the KGB and local police in Moscow.

Overall confusion reigned as the leaders of a coup to seize the government took off for "Central Asia." Gorbachev was evidently "detained" and returned to Moscow to resume being President. Meanwhile, Lithuania was in a new turmoil, while the eight-man military coup leaders in Russia were busy trying to leave the country. One rumor was that the KGB was now supporting the parliament. On the evening of the 21st, Soviet troops were moving out of Moscow. The coup seemed to be ended and the USSR as well.

But the crowds in Moscow were milling about shouting for Yeltsin, not for Gorbachev. At 9:00 P.M. eastern US time, the chief of the KGB was said to have been arrested. Later on that day it was said that Gorbachev had been put under house arrest for several days while Mrs. Gorbachev was so frightened that she lost her voice for several hours.

On the 22nd, Yeltsin reappeared, surprisingly unruffled, saying that eight of the junta people who took part in the coup had departed. But then an hour or so later, it was reported that they were all under arrest except for one who had committed suicide (New Haven Register 1991, August 24).

The unbelievable continued to happen in what used to be the USSR.

Even the statue of Feliks E. Dzerzhinsky, appointed by Lenin to head the Cheka, was pulled down with ropes by a crowd and graffiti written all over it, none of the words very complimentary. Dzerzhinsky had often played the role of Lenin's hatchet man in the espionage business. Finally Dzerzhinsky himself died of a heart attack while arguing with Stalin in 1926.

In Lithuania's capital, Soviet troops withdrew from the broadcasting tower which they had occupied since January 13, 1991 when 14 people were killed. Lithuanian lawmakers then officially banned the Communist party and claimed ownership of its property. In Moscow, tens of thousands marched, chanting "Yeltsin!" It came out later on August 23rd that the "committee" that seized Gorbachev took the satchel containing the keys (essentially a secret code) for starting to fire the missiles, most of which were aimed at Europe and the US, presumably at military installations for the most part.

On the 24th, Moscow reported that the KGB had banned the Communist Party from its ranks and suspended the publication of PRAVDA (The Truth) newspaper. And now Gorbachev and Yeltsin teamed up to knock down the pillars of the Soviet establishment, stripping power from the Communist party and taking over the Army and KGB (New Haven Register 1991, Aug. 24). In the face of this, the Soviet Communist Party seemed helpless with six of its important members arrested after making a bid for power. Essentially, Gorbachev had been deposed and according to TASS news agency, Vice President Yanayev took over the presidential power according to the constitution (Crozier 1999, 449).

Like a sudden lightning bolt, the news came on August 25th that Gorbachev had resigned as Party Chairman of the Communist Party. He suggested that the party's vast holdings be turned over to Parliament. On top of this it was the Ukraine, the nation's second largest Republic, that declared its independence. Then also the government in Moscow approved independence for the Baltic states of Estonia, Latvia, and Lithuania (CBS radio 1991, August 22).

But Soviet Foreign Minister Shevardnadze on ABC TV's "Nightline" last week, said he was suspicious of Gorbachev's role in the coup, suggesting that he had engineered the whole thing. On top of all this, the Chief of the Military shot himself and as mentioned, the head of the KGB arrested. Later on the 28th, KGB troops were said to be going over to the Army.

By the end of August, Kazakhstan, just north of the Caspian Sea, had gone out of the old Union along with Belorussia which borders on

Poland to its west and Russia proper on its east. Then Azerbeijan, bordering on Iran to its south, was the eighth Republic declaring independence from the USSR. By now, some 10 republics had tried for their freedom. The USSR was now defunct and would have a new name: The Russian Federation.

Despite all this, the spy game went on. Some say old spies never die, but just keep on spying. Super-spy Marcus Wolf was said to have fled to Moscow. But perhaps finding only revolution and upheaval in the KGB, he returned to Germany and was apprehended by authorities there. Then the new Germany effectively gave him amnesty (CBS Radio 1991, August 25).

It was leaked out in late September that the biggest SIGINT (Signals Intelligence) station outside the Russian Federation was staffed by an estimated 2,100 technicians. Designed to monitor US traffic at Lourdes near Havana, Cuba, the station was built in the 1960s and expanded at least twice. It monitored US Naval and ground manuevers in the US as well as communications in space. The USSR used to send a billion dollars a year to Cuba, but this had been reduced lately (Washington Post 1991, September 28).

In the ex-USSR, the Ukraine had once been called the breadbasket of the nation. In early December 1991, an 85% majority of Ukraine's voters went for independence from Russia.

It was revealed about this time that very thorough surveillance of the USSR had gone on before the big break-up. Robert M. Gates, DCI, revealed that US intelligence(probably including the NSA), was engaged in unprecidented monitoring of the former USSR. This was mainly because the Russians had 30,000 nuclear missiles threatening world peace. Gates, addressing CIA employees, told them that the intelligence community was on the verge of the most sweeping changes it had undergone in more than 40 years. Evidently this was to make it more efficient in line with shrinking budgets. The present annual budget was said to be $30 billion (New Haven Register via A.P. 1991, December 5).

On December 9th, the old USSR's three Slavic Republics: Russia, Belorussia, and the Ukraine declared Gorbachev's Government: dead. Now the three were forged into a new alliance called a Commonwealth. Gorbachev then spoke of his life's work being over, while several other Republics voted to join the new Commonwealth. The Union, so long ensconced in the expression "Soviet Union" was voted out of existence. Economist Alfred Kahn felt that new separations would cause the economy to be reduced to barter, which it practically did. The Russian legislature then voted to end the Union, its end to come on December 31st 1991.

Gorbachev resigned as President on the 25th while 11 Republics would now join in the new "Commonwealth." State-owned land would be privatized. The KGB would be called the "SVR" with its enormous manpower (the SVR was for Foreign intelligence, the FSK Counter intelligence, and the SBP for watching over the President).

Oleg Kalugin, a retired general in the KGB, warned that his institution was not yet dead, although it had changed its name, but still retained the "Old Guard" and was now lying low. It had maintained all of its 188,000 officers plus hundreds of thousands of other employees. It was claimed that Kalugin had backed Yeltsin in the recent coup (New Haven Register 1992, January 14).

* * * * * * * * * * * * *

During January of 1992 in the USA, a certain unknown personality, William Clinton, had begun to run for the Presidency. But there were rumors that he had had a mistress for some 12 years while his wife was too busy running an Arkansas realty company to notice her husband's sexual wanderings. Yet what bothered some people was that the money "earned" by Mrs. Clinton went into campaign funds, or so it was alleged, when Bill Clinton had been running for Governor of Arkansas.

While the battle for the presidency went on between George Bush and William Clinton, CBS's "Inside Washington" brought up the question of bias in the media. The "experts" on the program agreed that the media (newspapers, journals, radio, and TV) were mostly left wing or at least favored the Democrats and were busy doing what they could to put Bush in a bad light.

In the meantime, the old Soviet Union's wide-spread espionage apparatus was in trouble. According to an Associated Press report from London, the Head of the Russian Intelligence Service offered to recall all spies from countries that were willing to stop spying on the Russians. Although this seemed at best naïve, Yevgeny Primakov, head of the Foreign Intelligence Service (now the SVR) was quoted in London's Sunday Times as saying that his agency faced major reductions and was shifting emphasis away from political to industrial espionage. Primakov, 62, told the newspaper that in Moscow he had closed 30 stations worldwide, ceasing operations in much of Africa and Asia and would have to cut the agencies' overseas staff by 50% by year's end. Primakov later in

December of 1992 became head of the SVR in the new Russian Federation.

As for spying in the US, it came out in October of 1992 that the CIA, back in 1962, had collected a great deal of information on the Cuban missile problem by the means of HUMINT (Human Intelligence on the ground) concerning the Cuban missiles. Coded "Ironbark" these reports were added to those from Penkovsky in Moscow. A recently released CIA study showed that the agency nearly missed knowing that the SS-4 missiles were then in Cuba (New Haven Register via A.P. 1993, January 14). This was because the Miami center's HUMINT reports were ignored in Washington D.C. Then the missile deployment in Cuba only became known from U-2 flights on October 14, about a month after the first batch of missiles had arrived on the island. Miami had the CIA's biggest station in the world and collected HUMINT from 300 people. Even on September 17, 1962, they had reports of missile–like tubes under canvas being transported on trucks in Cuba. But analysts in Washington dismissed the reports as unreliable.

As pointed out before in this chronicle, many spy cases are only revealed years after they take place. In October 1992, the Hiss case was brought up again in the news. After 44 years, a Soviet general, Dmitri A. Volkogonov claimed that the Hiss case was the result of the Cold War, as if that explained Soviet transgressions. Even Dean Rusk in the Kennedy entourage also passed off the importance of the Hiss case, suggesting that Hiss might have been a Communist, but never seemed to have passed any worth-while secrets. Most likely, Hiss was a plant and was a diligent supplier of documents to the USSR, according to Elizabeth Bentley. Hiss, by 1992 was 87 years old and still denied his guilt, only getting in a jibe at J. Edgar Hoover, picking on him for his dealings. But Chambers had given much information on Hiss and on the sending of material to the USSR.

Oleg Gordievski was a more rare case, since few Soviet spies came over to the other side. He wrote in his book with Christopher Andrew "The Inside Story" published in 1993 about the KGB controller of Alger Hiss. Gordievsky was evidently a British mole in the KGB, but was betrayed by a double agent working between the CIA and the Soviets in 1985.

* * * * * * * * * * * * *

On November 5th 1992 the exclusively American phenomenon of

the presidential election came and went. Some newspapers called it a Clinton landslide, which was a very popular Democratic thought, but inaccurate since Clinton never had a true majority in total votes. In fact generally disregarded was that 18 states, mostly in the south and west went for Bush.

One of the secrets that came out after the election was that Clinton was actually losing until the Democratic party took on Al Gore and publicized him as Clinton's running mate. Gore, resembling the suave, darkhaired movie-star-like Elliot Richardson, probably charmed a lot of the females of the species and put Clinton over the top, or so it was suggested. But a much bigger secret of the time was that heaps of illegal money were thought to have gone into the Clinton-Gore campaign. At the time, few believed it or if they did, felt it was just small potatoes. Those that knew, kept it quiet. In any case in December, Clinton make new appointments: Warren Christopher Secretary of State, Les Aspin Secretary of Defense, Ms. Albright UN Ambassador, and James Woolsey Jr., Director, CIA.

Despite all these new faces in Washington D.C., all was not serene in the Federal law department. On January 25, 1993, a direct assault was made on members of the CIA. While driving to work in the nation's capitol, two Intelligence men were shot to death and some others were wounded when they slowed down for a traffic light. It was not until the year 2002 that Aimal Khan Kasi was charged and executed for the crime. He was probably an illegal from the Middle East. The CIA had found out that the Soviets had been experimenting with germ warfare, although this was evidently not connected to the shooting and not revealed until 1989 by a Russian defector (Newsweek 1993, February 1).

A more serious problem than that, involved the loose immigration laws then current in the US. At 12:18 eastern time on February 26, 1993, an immense bomb went off in the World Trade Center in New York City. The bomb, brought in by car or truck to the underground parking garage of the building, was set off by a fuse or a remote control. It left a hole in the concrete floor 100 to 200 feet wide and wrecked six stories above it, shaking the whole structure, and filling much of it with smoke. People in the 100-story structure were trapped. Most could not escape for some eight hours. All electric power was out in the office rooms above the bomb wreckage. Five workers in the garage were killed while about 600 others were injured. A home for the commodity exchanges, about 30,000 to 100,000 people worked in the building. "Mideast" elements were suspected, according to preliminary reports.

By the 28th, ATF (Alcohol, Tobacco, and Firearms) agents were combining with FBI agents on the case. Nitrates were found in the bombed area, suggesting that a crude bomb had been made from ammonium nitrate and diesel fuel. FBI's Director Sessions released the information that 109 calls had been made to the police, claiming responsibility. One of the suspects, a Muslim, made the mistake of trying to get his money back from the car-rental agency. The FBI thought he might return and was there to greet him. The man was thought to have been involved in Sadat's assassination in Egypt in 1981.

Mohammed E. Salameh, age 25, was the man caught by the FBI at the car rental agency. He was affiliated with the Masjid Al-Salam Mosque in Jersey City where Sheik Omar Abdel Rahman preached. Rahman was acquitted 10 years ago for Sadat's assassination. But after the bombing in New York City Rahman was not to be found. Many years later in June of 2002, it came out that Rahman had bought a ticket to Aman, Jordan, then travelled to his home in Iraq.

By 1993, the CIA had developed many new methods of collecting information, including listening in on private cellular phone conversations that are relayed, but also with portable computers that can transmit digitized photographs (of people for example) that have been electronically encrypted to avoid interception. By the early 1990s, the CIA was spending about $28 billion a year. But an NSA employee said the US military almost never used CIA information, having its own intelligence organization. CIA people often used "deep cover" meaning their agents have no diplomatic immunity (Newsweek, 1993, April 12). If caught in a foreign country, they would not be bailed out by the US or the Agency (ABC radio 2002, June 3).

About this time in the spring of 1993, an event occurred that involved the ATF and FBI in something they probably wished they had never heard of. It seemed that a David Koresh, allegedly a sort of holy-roller, along with a number of adults and children, were holed up in a building at Waco, Texas. Koresh was busy defying demands of authorities to let the crowd go. The story went that after a long standoff of many days, during which Koresh continued to defy authorities, members of the ATF and FBI broke a hole in the building and threw in tear gas canisters, hoping to drive the people out. Instead of coming out, a fire began and was soon consuming the entire building and with it the people inside. Possibly, Koresh himself had set the fire while others claimed the tear gas had set it.

The media, as would be expected, made much out of the strong arm solution while no one was sure what started the blaze. Months later it was determined that the blaze began inside, possibly set by Koresh himself. But many questions remained unanswered: who, for example, had ordered the ATF-FBI attack? Eventually it was determined that the order originated allegedly with Attorney General Reno, President Clinton's appointee.

Ms. Reno, apparently adept at side-stepping accusations, was asked by Clinton to decide on whether Mr. Sessions should continue as FBI Director, as if the whole Koresh affair was the fault of the FBI. The story in the press was that Sessions' problem was that the FBI did not have enough "minorities" to please the new liberal president. So Sessions would have to go, the media opined, despite his expertise in solving the Trade Center bombing. He had been Director since 1987. Another theory of the Sessions case as to why he was asked to step down was that the Clinton-Reno duo wanted to imply that the Waco fire was the FBI's fault, a theme that the media seemed to want to believe.

In Britian too, their most secret of Secret Services, MI5, was under fire from left wing laborites because of a tabloid flap that showed pictures of royal personalities, embarrassing to those photographed. It was later determined that the pictures were faked. The war between the laborites and MI5 continued.

In July of 1993, FBI director Sessions refused to bow out, defying the Clinton ban. Sessions said he wanted to face Clinton directly and discuss any ethnic violations. Someone in the media suggested that Mrs. Clinton had influenced the President, there being some latent hostility alleged between the FBI man who had been assigned to the White House and Mrs. Clinton.

With a thoroughly liberal President in power, it was not too much of a secret that illegal immigration into the United States had become a kind of unseen creeping disaster. As an example, a ship-load of some 200 Chinese had arrived at New York City. On approaching the docks, the ship could find no place to land. The result was that many jumped in and swam for it. Some were captured, others were awaiting "hearings" but managed to melt into the asphalt jungle. Many Democrats were not averse to seeing immigration go on, legal or illegal, since the newcomers tended to vote Democrat.

As for Bill Clinton, there was even doubt that his name was really Clinton. It seems that Adele Coffelt now 75, was married at 17 to a William Blythe, the Presidents father. Yet Clinton's mother was said to be Virginia Cassidy, her lineage well-known. As for Adele, she later married a Charles Ritzenthaler. However, Virginia Cassidy married William Blythe who was then killed in a car accident. Clintons mother, Virginia Cassidy, then married a Roger Clinton from whom Bill got his name (Anderson 1990, 44; AOL Internet, Clinton, William).

One of Clinton's inner circle, Vincent Foster, was said to have committed suicide, perhaps in despondency over bringing bad publicity to President Clinton. There were other reports, unsubstantiated, that Foster felt guilty in the Whitewater affair that occurred back when Clinton was Governor of Arkansas. But, as Joe Klein of Newsweek magazine suggested, the Clinton forces were immune to embarrassment.

During August, the Foster "suicide" was much discussed in the media. A reporter from the New York Times on the MacNeil-Lehrer (CPTV) show asked: Why were there no fingerprints on the note that Foster left? Also, why was there no signature on the paper? And, it was never clear who had found the body.

Still, in the late summer of 1993, more came out on the J.F. Kennedy assassination. Ex-FBI Director Clarence M. Kelley (in office 1973-1978) told how a Soviet émigré, Golobachev, had a friend who worked with Oswald in a Soviet radio factory. Oswald was believed to have said that he would have lots of money after he killed the president. G's friend pointed out to Oswald that he would be arrested. This seemed to have no effect on Oswald and bragged that his wife would then be rich.

According to recently-released KGB files, JFK's killing was instigated by the KGB to relieve international pressures on Khrushchev. But portions of the document were blacked out and the rest of the statement withheld as classified.

Turning now to modern Russia, a revolution within a revolution was going on in late September of 1993. 20,000 people marched in Moscow to the music of Tchaikovsky's musical theme concerning the war against France's Napoleon. But Yeltsin seemed still to have the upper hand, managing to shut off the power to the parliament building. Then on October 4th, the fighting in Moscow waxed hot and heavy with hundreds killed. Finally, Yeltsin's Army people gained the upper hand, the parliament building ending up a complete wreck. The hardline Communists who made up most of the opposition were driven out.

The Soviet people in this century certainly had met a ruinous fate. Between 1934 and 1947, 15 million of them, not counting their allies, either died or languished in the Gulag according to historian Viktor Zemsov and further described by Applebaum in her book "Gulag, a History" (Applebaum, 2003). From 1935 to 1941, about 19,840,000 were deemed enemies of the people and arrested. Some 7 million of these were either shot or died in camps, according to Olga Shatanovskya, once head of Khrushchev's Rehabilitation Commission. Then Volkoganov, a Soviet official, claimed that during 1941-1954 2 million in "nationality" groups were deported, a quarter of whom soon died. Added to that, 10 million were said to have died in the 1930-1933 famine. This adds up to about 20 million that died prematurely in the early part of the 20th century. And much of this was unknown in America (Republican American 1993, December 28).

On December 13, 1993, the Russian Federation held elections. Mr. Zhirinovsky, a hard line right-winger, was automatically unpopular with US liberals. Vice President Al Gore even took the trouble to visit Russia and pour as much cold water on him as possible. Actually, Z's ambitions were intended only for Russian ears. He wanted to reunite the provinces, eject certain unwanted factions, reclaim possessions in East Asia, and generally ignore the Americans.

* * * * * * * * * * * * *

President Clinton's escapades were back in the news and were destined to go on for years to come. The conservative newspaper "American Spectator" and CBS's cable TV released the information that Clinton had been having extra-marital relations while governor of Arkansas, as told by two Arkansas State Troopers. Potential criminal violations seemed involved. Mark Shields, TV commentator, predicted that election fraud might be involved.

Clinton's doings thus became the fascination of the media. Columnist Novak (Republican American 1994, January 11) pointed to the latest revelations going back to the days when Clinton was Arkansas's governor. Following all this, only a few days later on January 9, 1994, Clinton responded to the big tabloid news by making a sudden visit to Kiev, Russia, sufficiently far to escape US reporters.

Columnist Joseph Sobran claimed that the scandal had reached the human sacrifice stage. By this time in mid-March Clinton was alleged by former Judge David Hale to have been linked to a questionable loan in the Whitewater affair. Hale then planned to enter a plea in Federal Court to avoid trial (NBC TV 1994, March 21). He claimed he was pressured eight years ago by Clinton to make a $300,000 loan to Susan McDougal, a Clinton partner. But Clinton denied pressuring Hale and

Hillary called it all hype to stop her drive for health and welfare reform. As for Bill Clinton, he evidently had no recollection of the loan.

On top of all this, Clinton's former girl-friends were coming back to haunt him. One Sally Miller started talking, but was promptly (allegedly) told to shut up and accept a Federal job. All this seemed strangely similar to the case of Jennifer Flowers, another friend of Clinton. In early May, another acquaintance of Bill Clinton arrived at the White House to claim that Clinton had made sexual advances while he was Governor in 1991. This was Paula Corbin Jones who thus joined the growing bevy of beauties that came to Washington to make their claims. She was suing for $700,000 and planned to donate the proceeds to charity. An Arkansas State trooper was said to have arranged a tryst with a "Paula" but Clinton was alleged to have told her to keep it quiet. She replied that she had several affadavits to prove his association with her.

But Jennifer Flowers had little good to say about Paula Jones. All this only added up to the symphonie pathetique that seemed to follow Clinton wherever he went, violins playing on the G-strings. None-the-less these women were making serious claims, based on what appeared to be unpardonable intrusions on innocent ladies.

By all appearances, Hillary Clinton was a partner in the Rose Law Firm and was also involved in real estate dealings near the Whitewater river. Somehow some of the money went into electing her husband Bill, but she was alleged to have shredded the documents dealing with the Whitewater real estate business. In mid-January 1994, the new Attorney General Reno began to look into the Whitewater case. But February came and not much was resolved. Hillary had denied shredding the documents, but the Washington Times newspaper stuck to its story. It seemed that the Rose Law Firm had for partners: Hillary, Associate Attorney General Hubbell, and a former White House Deputy V.W. Foster Jr., the last named found dead in a Virginia park on 7/20/93. The shredded documents were supposed to show the Clinton's involvement with J.B. McDougal and his wife Susan, both realestate dealers. McDougal was former owner of Madison Guarantee S&L Association that might have manipulated loans and diverted the money to several Arkansas politicians, perhaps including Bill Clinton.

By early March, heat was gradually being brought to bear on the White House's various shenanegans, resulting in the resignation of Bernard Nussbaum, a White House counsel. A lawyer named Fisk had been appointed by Reno to investigate the case and promptly subpoened a number of White House people, for one thing to explain how the Arkansas thrift bank had failed.

Next, President Clinton got the spotlight for sending heaps of American dollars to Georgia – not in the USA – but somewhere between the Caspian and Black Seas. Some $70 million would be sent for humanitarian purposes. The Whitewater case was momentarily forgotten.

Some newspapers, however, pointed out that a few years ago a pack of media detractors were working on Nixon in the 1970s. One of these was Mrs. Clinton and another, Bernard Nussbaum, both involved in the Nixon impeachment committee.

By the end of May 1994, Federal investigators found that Bill Clinton's Whitewater business partner had used a web of loans to divert some $12,000 in S&L (Savings and Loans) funds to Clinton's gubernatorial campaign a decade ago. About $350,000 were lost to the S&L. By this time, however, Mr. Clinton was over in Italy chatting with the Pope and perhaps talking with Italians who were referred to in Washington D.C. as "Neofascists," which must have seemed out of Clinton's usual sphere of thought.

On June 14th, William and Hillary Clinton were separately put under oath in a Federal investigation. They were asked about the Whitewater case and the Foster suicide. But the investigators only got glib explanations, the Clintons claiming their absence in most of the doings. Prosecutor Fiske asked them about the White House contacts with Treasury officials and about the failed S&L. Answers were obtuse and diffuse and the whole thing soon forgotten by the media.

****

About this same time, the media found something else to harp on. This was the mysterious case of O.J. Simpson. In basic terms it was the age-old triangle: the (ex) wife with a lover, the husband enraged to the point of allegedly killing them both. But the husband was a famous black football player which made a difference to the attitudes of certain sectors of the public.

All of America was astonished to see the suspect in his white Bronco Ford on TV tooling along the Los Angeles freeway at high speed, closely followed by 12 police cars, sirens screaming and filling up four highway lanes. Simpson finally realized that the hounds were catching up to the fox and returned to his posh spread in Los Angeles. But he was not long languishing in the slammer and soon released to stand trial in a murder case that absorbed the public and the media for months on end. In a few days the case became the love-child of the media. Reporters told of bloody gloves and digging tools found near O.J.'s house, of recordings of voices, of blood spots on the ground, of conflicting accounts of various witnesses, and of course of the dog that barked at midnight – or some other time. The trial was too hot for the media to ignore it and could only sell papers and attract more TV watchers for as long as the actors on stage could string it all out. Detective Mark Fuhrman became the hero of the prosecution and the kicking-boy of the defense. The trial went on for months and to make a long story short, the accused was excused and declared not guilty.

****

Many Americans, although suspicious of Bill Clinton's behavior, could not help admiring him for his theatrical abilities. Like a mocking bird, flitting from tree to tree while singing his song for all to hear, in mid – July he was off to Berlin, talking pre-practiced German to crowds that came to see him as much out of curiosity as to hear what policy he might be willing to reveal. In a speech to the Germans he claimed that America was on Germany's side forever. The crowd, gathered near the Brandenburg gate cheered that sortie wildly. He went on to claim that everything was possible (sounding a little like Adolf Hitler in another era) and that Berlin was now free. The crowd roared and waved. Perhaps as a barometer of the effect this speech had on America, the Dow Jones Industrial Average rose one point to 3704.

Returning in August, 1994 to the Whitewater case, Mr. Fiske, appointed by the Clinton clique, was out of office on the order of three judges. Instead, a Mr. Starr would be Whitewater prosecutor. Fiske had been Attorney General Reno's appointee, while Starr was a Republican. Democrats protested this outcome as much as they could without much of any effect.

In September of the same year, an attempt was made in the Senate to head off the Clinton-led invasion of Haiti, then in political turmoil stemming partly (although not mentioned) from overpopulation and consequent poverty. But this attempt, mainly by Republicans, was overpowered by the Democrats who wanted to see the numerous black population stop a sort of internecine war that had resulted in many people wanting to emigrate. Senator McCain (R-AZ) pointed out that Americans were against such an invasion of Haiti although already two aircraft carriers were leaving the Norfolk Virginia shipyards. These were said to be loaded with US Marines and helicopters. As might be suspected, some 2000 Haitians tried to flee their island and were picked up from the sea to be sent to Cuba at Guantanamo, this city a US possession. In any case, the carrier Wasp proceeded to Haiti with its 1800 marines, although the Defense Department, astonished at the cost of the operation, was apparently hoping that Congress would stop it.

So it was that Clinton, supported by the Black Caucus, had his way and was further supported by a UN Security Council resolution to restore Aristide to power in Haiti and eject Cedras. Moreover, the CIA had to take its lumps in the Haitian affair from the liberals in the media. The Nation magazine claimed that the CIA supported Cedras and his adherents in Haiti, although DCI Woolsey denied that "FRAPH," trying to influence Haiti's politics, had been instigated by the CIA to carry out its complex machinations.

In Congress, Republicans demanded troop withdrawals from Haiti by January. But this took time to accomplish. Meanwhile on December 28th, DCI Woolsey resigned. The media seemed to be saying that this was brought on by the Ames case and possibly also by the failure to punish certain CIA agents for the flap. Aldrich Ames had revealed over a hundred covert acts and betrayed more than 30 operatives working for the CIA (Polmar and Allen 1997, 21). Woolsey also had to face fire over CIA's huge budget. However, John Deutch was said to be in line for the DCI position.

* * * * * * * * * * * * *

For centuries, Serbia had been a turbulent state and had taken a direct role in the beginning of World War I when the Arch Duke Ferdinand and his wife Sofie had been assassinated by a Serbian revolutionist. This turbulence broke out again in May of 1992 when Serbia, still unhappy with its political status, was then part of Yugoslavia. On the 16th of that month the Serbians began the shelling of Sarajevo in southwestern Bosnia, the city where WWI had experienced its beginning in 1914. So now United Nations (UN) peace-keeping troops were sent to stop the shelling while Americans, or at least most of the media, were much more interested in the rioting in Los Angeles.

On the 27th, the UN branded the Serbs "Aggressors" and issued an ultimatum to the Serbian government to stop shelling Sarajevo. By August 1st, UN troops, now including a few from the US, moved into Sarajevo and were taking the brunt of the Serbian artillery shells and rifle fire. But the UN command post was reluctant to take action without proper clearance from the several involved nations.

Yugoslavia had long been a collection of several parts: Slovenia in the north, Croatia just south of it, and Bosnia-Herzegovina southeast of Croatia. Then Serbia to its east and south to include Kosovo. The Croats traditionally were supported by the Germans and Austrians, while Bosnia included many people of Serbian origin who were continually at odds with the Bosnians and Croats. On top of all this were the Turks, left over from a previous invasion, who supported the Muslims in Bosnia while the Catholic Russians supported the Catholic Serbs. Despite these many divisions, peace talks were beginning, sponsored by the UN and the EC (European Community).

From all of this, Americans were presented with the impression that Bosnia was now minding its own business when Serbia began shelling Bosnia's Sarajevo for no apparent reason, unless it planned to take over all of Bosnia. Actually, however, it had not been widely reported in the US, if at all, that the Serbians made up nearly half of the population of Bosnia, the rest a mixture of peoples. Also, high-level contacts between the Serbs in Belgrade and the Croats in Zagreb had fed suspicions since 1991 that the Serbs had made a secret understanding to carve up Bosnia. Whether true or not, another story was that there was an alliance between the Bosnian Croats and the Muslims in Sarajevo directed against the Serbs, which only seemed to complicate matters (Newsweek 1993, June 7).

By February of 1994, the Yugoslavian problem continued. The UN decided to present the Serbs with an ultimatum to remove their artillery around Sarajevo within seven to ten days. If they refused, the UN forces would bomb Serbian positions. But nothing came of this, at least for the moment.

In late February of 1994, a wind of another variety blew in from the east to confound the UN members. Russia's Boris Yeltsin lashed out at NATO for threatening air-strikes against Russia's traditional ally: Serbia without asking the Russian government first. Even though Russia was now the Russian Federation, not the USSR, the old cold war seemed to be reviving when 10 "Russians", probably exposed during the revelations of the Ames spy case, were found to be working for the CIA.

By March 1st, 1994, the Balkan war, now so-called, centering on Bosnia, had gone on for some 23 months. Soon afterward, several Serbian aircraft had been shot down, probably by UN forces. But the Russians said that only one Serbian airplane was shot down and added that if the airplane had violated the no-fly zone, it was Serbia's fault. The Serbian aircraft were of the C-4 Galeb type, made in Yugoslavia. Later on, the US admitted that aircraft from a US carrier in the Adriatic Sea had shot down the Serbian plane or planes.

On November 21ˢᵗ, NATO (North Atlantic Treaty Organization) members agreed that the Bosnian Serbs had to be put down and the Serbian shelling ended. The plan was to bomb the airstrips used by the Serbs in Bosnia. Such strikes had been made before, but this was the most violent attack yet. NATO claimed that their organization was trying to stop the Serbs from fighting. Willy Claes, NATO's Secretary General, as if to excuse what NATO was doing, claimed that the UN made the policy and NATO carried it out. But US Senator Lugar was not optimistic and was of the opinion that the strikes could only result in further Serbian attacks. He echoed the feelings of many Americans that they were not really interested in a Bosnian war. Very likely, few Americans knew where Bosnia was.

On the 26ᵗʰ, CBS radio reported that 2000 marines were leaving for a location in Yugoslavia. Yet two days later, Bosnian Serbs were said to have won the battle for a small but important town in northwest Bosnia. The Serbs had by then begun fighting the forces sent by the UN "Peacekeepers," but the latter were largely powerless to do much of anything. General Rose of the British maintained that his troops were not even a defensive force and added that air strikes by UN aircraft were mostly useless because of the hilly terrain. This situation had been one of the big problems for the Russians when they were fighting the Afghans in hopes of taking over Afghanistan.

* * * * * * * * * * * * *

The latest spy case was brought into the limelight by means of the David Brinkley show on ABC TV. The sum and substance of it was that Yeltsin's political plans were no different from those of the old Soviet leaders and in all likelihood this was the case.

About this same time in February of 1994, a CIA agent in Russia, James Morris, was ejected from that country. The Russians explained that it was a case of "tit for tat" since a Russian spy, name of Lysenko, had been ejected from Washington D.C. and the US.

Also in February, a new theory was produced to explain what had broken the Ames case which had come to the surface during 1994. It seemed that the East German STASI knew of Ames as an informant.

Then when the "Anschluss" (joining) of East and West Germany occurred, the name of Ames leaked out as some kind of double agent.

By the end of April, 1994, Aldrich H. Ames pleaded guilty in a plea-bargaining deal. Ames claimed that spying was only a self-serving sham. Whether just self-serving or not, others who knew the case, said he was the most damaging spy in US history. It seemed that when Vitaly Yurchenko defected in the 1980s, Ames worried that Y knew he, Ames, was a traitor (Polmar and Allen 1997, 21). A Mr. Whipple, a US ex-agent, felt that spying had changed more and more toward electronic surveillance. But without HUMINT they probably would never have caught Ames. It was obvious that George Blake in Britain and Richard Sorge in Japan, working for the USSR, were only caught after others testified. Apparently, more spying was called for, not less.

Also at this time in April, Abdel Rahman, wanted in New York City for the bombing of the World Trade Center, was sentenced in Egypt to seven years hard labor for trying to kill two policemen and for carrying a weapon. At the time, he was awaiting trial in New York City, but presently inconvenienced in Egypt.

As 1994 came to its troubled end, CIA Director Woolsey resigned. The media suspected that it was the result of the Ames case and possibly also of the failure to punish certain CIA agents for the intelligence flap. Ames had revealed over a hundred covert acts and betrayed more than 30 operatives working for the CIA. For details see Polmar and Allen's "Spy Book," (1997, 21-22).

Chapter 10

Bombings And Bosnians, The Clinton Follies, And The Kosovo War

A sudden disaster on the 19th of April 1995 befell an otherwise peaceful America. The Federal Building in Oklahoma City was practically demolished by a bomb. It had been brought up in the street next to the building's front in a rental truck and parked there. The whole truck quickly exploded, causing the front facade of the building to collapse. At least 19 were known dead and about 300 missing. Many more in adjacent buildings were wounded, so powerful was the bomb. The modern steel and concrete structure had housed the offices of the Secret Service, Alcohol, Tobacco, and Firearms (ATF), the Department of Defense, and a big daycare center on the second floor for Federal workers' children. Windows a mile away were broken.

Two men, apparently whites, had been seen in jogging suits just before the explosion. Perhaps by design, this was the date —April 19th — when the Waco Branch Davidians in Texas were burned up in their stronghold. It was also the date of the beginning of the American Revolution in 1775. Not until the year 2003 was it suspected that Muslim extremists were involved in the bombing.

On the 21st, two suspects were sought. One of these was a Tim McVeigh, the other named Nichols. This Nichols had a brother, suspected of being involved. As for the building itself, more bodies were found each day as the wreckage was pulled apart. Some people were found still alive in the rubble. McVeigh was apprehended some several months later, but he had little to say and the case seemed to be stalled at that point. In 1997, McVeigh was condemned to death by a jury. His motives and connections remained largely a mystery.

* * * * * * * * * * * *

Americans had cause for worrying about another part of the world, thanks as much to modern communications as to any deep interest in the eternal problems of the Balkans, an often mountainous region east of the Adriatic Sea.

Supposedly, the United Nations had solved the latest upheaval, this time in Bosnia, a part of Yugoslavia, by bringing in a mélange of foreign troops of different nations. But once arrived, they found themselves inadequate to the task and not much of anything was accomplished (ABC TV 1995, April 24). General Rose of the NATO troops was criticized for doing nothing but just what he could have done remained unclear. As a result, Britain's Lord David Owen talked of a possible withdrawal from Bosnia.

The Bosnian situation was basically this: there was a large portion of land in the eastern part of it taken over by Serbian armed forces. And there was an even larger area in west-central Bosnia occupied also by Serbian troops. Then on the northwest side of Bosnia, the Serbs had driven some 50 miles in to land held by the Croats, but containing Serbian civilians. The Croats, in a strong drive, managed to pinch off the Serbian salient and by May 5, 1995, most of the Serbian troops managed to escape. UN forces called for peace.

By the end of May, Britain decided to send 6,000 troops to Bosnia to stiffen the UN and therefore NATO resistance, then try and retrieve hostages held by the Serbs. But there was a missing piece in the jig-saw puzzle of the Bosnians and Serbs as exhibited by the Western press. This was that nearly half of the Bosnian population was made up of Serbs while the rest were a collection of Bosnians and other peoples (Purkovic 1973, 983). The Serbian connection with the Russians was largely founded on similar languages using the same Cyrillic alphabet, having an often Catholic religion, and having a history of being on Russia's side in the WW I struggle against Austria-Hungary.

Although four senators, McCain a Republican, Lieberman a Democrat, Smith a Republican, and Hamilton a Democrat, agreed not to send US troops to the Bosnians, Senator McCain felt there was a need to send arms and equipment that the Bosnians had requested. It was therefore a surprise to the US public that US aircraft were actually taking part in the fighting in northern Bosnia. This came out because a US F-16 jet aircraft had been shot down in northern Bosnia on June 2nd. The airplane had been part of a NATO attempt to guard the no-fly zone. At the same time, about June 4th, there had been an arms embargo put on sending arms from the US to Bosnia. Senator Lugar, concerning the embargo, decided it was not wise to give it up.

On June 8th, Captain Scott O'Grady, the pilot of the US jet aircraft that had been shot down on June 2, was able to send an SOS message. He had managed to hide in a stand of pine trees for six days, living on insects and such as he might find. His SOS resulted in the dispatch of a rescue team of two Marine helicopters that hied him away to safety. Thus began the American involvement. Curiously, it was a Sam missile that had shot him down. This was of Russian design, brought from Iran.

In regard to the shoot-down of a US airplane, this was blamed on a snafu in UN air Intelligence that had caused the US aircraft to fly over a place where there were SAM missiles, (CBS TV 1995, June 10). Meanwhile. the inhabitants of Sarajevo were said to be not only starving but running out of water. Russia's Yeltsin at the time admitted that the Serbs were now their allies and claimed that a deal had been made to return hostages taken by the Serbs in exchange for no new air strikes on the Serbian forces.

While all this was going on, the new Soviet "MIR" space station was united with the US shuttle. If it proved nothing else, the Russians and Americans had come a long way from the bitter, lengthy Cold War. Nevertheless, President Clinton officially approved of a "Rapid Strike Force" to be used in Bosnia, although most Americans had only a vague idea where Bosnia was. Naturally, Senators Dole and Gingrich wanted to know why Congress had not been told of the President's decision. The answer implied that they did not need to know.

In early July the Serbian shelling of Sarajevo continued, this time to rain shrapnel on the UN headquarters. Several people were wounded including an A.P. reporter. In the final two days, 13 civilians were killed and 88 wounded. Bosnian President Izetbegovic claimed 10,500 civilians had died in 1,154 days of Serbian attacks on Sarajevo.

One UN peace-keeping force was overrun by Bosnian Serbs and the next day the Serbs had captured 15 Dutch peace-keepers. The UN then threatened new air strikes. One Dutch group fought off the Serbs for hours as the Serbs invaded what was supposed to be a "Safe Haven," declared by the UN.

While 40,000 refugees fled north in Bosnia, some of them in trucks or buses, the French government in Paris under Jacques Chirac stated that all French troops would be withdrawn from Bosnia. Various horror stories were spread around, many of them of questionable accuracy. But whether true or not, the British public took them at face value and asked for their troops to be brought home.

From Russia came the news that Yeltsin apparently had had a heart attack. If his health were really failing, the Duma could remove him from power by a one-third vote or even impeach him. Otherwise the Parliament could remove the President by a two-thirds vote in both houses. If Yeltsin died, the Prime Minister would step in as temporary President. But Yeltsin soon recovered.

By July, 1995, Britain, France, and the US agreed on massive bombing of the Serbs to keep them from taking Sarajevo and Grozni. Already, the French were moving their "Rapid Reaction Force" to Sarajevo while the Croats were offering to support the Bosnian Muslims. This was a slap at the Serbs since the Serbs were usually Roman Catholics.

By the first of August, the British had 4,500 troops in Bosnia, the French 4,700, and the US 1,200. At about this time the US House passed an arms embargo lifting bill and they were even considering sending 20,000 US troops to Bosnia, while actually, few in Congress knew the true background of the Serbian struggle. The Europeans, better acquainted with the Balkan nations, saw the possibility of plunging all of Europe into a Balkan war.

Croatia's President Tudjman announced that he would demobilize the Croatian army and declare the three-day offensive a success. But tens of thousands of Serbs who had been living in Croatia were now fleeing east, perhaps 200,000 of them, and there were few among the Allies who cared. One column of cars was said to have been 30 miles long. As the Serbs left Croatia, the Croats threw manure and bricks at them in their cars.

Al Haig, meeting with the US ambassador to Russia, Mr. Pickering, concluded that the UN was incapable of running military operations and that NATO had straight-armed the UN in undertaking the bombings. Although NATO aircraft severely bombed the area around Sarajevo, the Rapid-Reaction forces shelled a location where the Serbs had fired at a NATO reco-airplane. Undeterred by all this, Serbian General Mladic predicted that he would take all the UN Safe Areas and that he could finish the war in a few months. Participating nations in the air strikes were

US, France, Britain, Italy, Germany, and the Netherlands. It was interesting to observe in a photograph of a German airplane that the old Maltese cross had been painted on the plane's side, this symbol used by Germany in WW I.

By mid-September, the Bosnian Croats were rapidly taking over the Serb-held territory of western Bosnia. Very little about this was mentioned in the US news. A week later, NATO bombings were stopped while the Serbs withdrew more of their big guns from around Sarajevo. Finally, in October, the Bosnian government agreed to make peace with the Bosnian Serbs. The Croats were not directly involved, but would be present at a peace conference to be held in France. Although the Bosnians were then shooting artillery shells at the Serbs, the cease-fire for the most part still held elsewhere. After this, things quieted down.

* * * * * * * * * * * * * * *

The various and sundry dealings of William Clinton, now ensconsed in the office of the Presidency of the United States, were beginning to catch up with him by late October, 1995. A Congressional Oversight Committee, headed by D'Amato (R-NY), planned to subpoena certain of the Clinton people. Of course they might have failed to come, but were invited anyway. One thing that had come up lately was that a handwriting expert had concluded that Vincent Foster's suicide note was not written by Foster. While Mr. D'Amato tried to continue the Whitewater case the media tended to downgrade the effort, finding certain things about D'Amato that would put him in a bad light, although the worst they could find was that he stayed out late playing poker with his friends. People came, people talked, but not much of anything came out of it.

At the same time, the CIA was taking its lumps from the liberal side of the media. Although having gotten used to such treatment, they felt somewhat wounded when Director Deutch admitted that the CIA knew that information from Russia came from double agents pretending to be loyal to the US. Apparently, the successor to the KGB, the SVR or the Russian FSK (Counter Intelligence) controlled the double agents. Allegedly, as many as 12 CIA agents passed on tainted information without informing the recipients of the taint. Senator Specter (R-PA), then head of the Senate Intelligence Committee, was indignant, concluding that things were worse than previously believed. Be that as it might, nothing much came of it.

The Whitewater case was of greater interest to the public. On November 2nd, the Whitewater Committee called two White House aides before it: Susan Thomases and "Maggie" Williams. Their mission was allegedly to keep law enforcement officials out of the Foster affair and they were said to have signalled Mrs. Clinton at the end of their efforts that their mission was accomplished. The committee intended to call Mrs. Clinton herself, but she was evidently busy claiming that Republicans were turning old people and little children out into the streets as a result of their mistaken policies.

While a peace accord concerning Bosnia was signed in Paris on December 15th by Izetbegovic for Bosnia, Milosevic for Serbia, and Tudjman for Croatia, the media were still trying to put down Richard Nixon's image. This came out, for example, in the latest Oliver Stone film. George Will said that the film was an "extended lie" while Alexander Haig agreed that the film was simply "not true" (Brinkley TV show 1995, December 24).

By mid-January, 1996, two governmental investigations were going on: one into the question of Hillary Clinton's law firm billing records, the other into the Whitewater case. Not a great deal came of these, but in April another of the numerous mysteries that seemed to follow the Clintons wherever they went came out when Ron Brown, Secretary of Commerce under Clinton, disappeared in an airplane crash off Croatia's coast in the Adriatic Sea, according to the news. Later it came out that the aircraft had hit a mountain, killing all aboard. Assistant Secretary of Commerce Meissner was also in the airplane.

By the end of April Hillary Clinton was claiming that she had nothing to do with moving White House documents to other locations. However, documents were examined for fingerprints and the results allegedly showed that they matched those of Hillary. Meanwhile her husband was testifying to the Whitewater Committee via an electronic gadget over a period of four and a half hours. Little of this was leaked out.

Finally, in late May three Clinton associates were found guilty in the Whitewater case. Ken Starr, the prosecutor, was obviously pleased while Bill Clinton was said to have looked somewhat haggard.

In mid-June it was alleged by several Republicans that Mrs. Clinton hid law firm records from investigators and that, among other things, White House officials showed improper conduct in handling documents in Foster's office after his so-called suicide.

About this same time, FBI man Aldrich, once assigned to the Clinton White House, appeared on the Brinkley ABC TV show to defend himself against the slings and arrows of critic Sam Donaldson. Aldrich did well in answer to questions about the behavior of various White House inhabitants, but then Clinton's spokesman George Stephanopoulos, came on to pronounce Aldrich's claims as a pack of lies. Aldrich's book, published later, made it clear what sort of things transpired in the White House. Generally, Aldrich was snubbed by those inhabitants and made to feel the unwanted man. He had evidently met Clinton only once and although the President was polite enough, he never saw him again.

During July, practically nothing was said of Aldrich's book, nothing about Clinton's land deals, nothing about Hillary shifting the files around, and nothing about a lot of other strange things. Instead, reports mentioned Clinton raising up the indigent, Clinton lowering the jobless rate, Clinton saying all the right things to salve the common public woes.

* * * * * * * * * * * *

On a pleasant summer evening, July 17, 1996, one more Boeing 747 passenger airplane was flying out of New York for Europe to add to the hundreds of such flights across the Atlantic. When just south of Long Island, it simply blew up, débris scattered in the ocean near Long Island. By-standers on the shore said they saw a rocket-like flame rise up at the airplane just before it exploded. But other theories as to the cause of the disaster were abundant. One was that a spark in one of the gas tanks had ignited the hi-test gasoline. Another theory was that a suitcase bomb in the baggage compartment, the contents of which were rarely inspected, had exploded and set off the gasoline. Just before the event, there had been a threat by Arab extremists that there would be a surprise for Americans soon to come. In the months that followed, these various theories were kicked all around, but years later the theory of the rocket, probably a missile, was most supported by the evidence. One report claimed that about 100 people had seen a flare rise up to the plane, followed by a big flash of light.

Clinton himself was often in danger in various aircraft that were at his disposal. One of these aircraft, loaned by the military, carrying a Secret Service man and several Clinton staffers, developed engine problems and crashed into a mountain. All on board were killed, but little was said about it except that Clinton had not been on board. The White House refused comment.

Still another bombing occurred at the Olympic Games in Atlanta, Georgia. Two people were killed and 110 wounded. Very little was released on the origin of the bomb. This occurred on July 27, only about a week after the Boeing passenger plane went down on July 17th. Then the Clinton aircraft went down on August 15th.

On September 3rd, Clinton felt like doing some bombing of his own. This was to blast Iraq with missiles, apparently because of Iraq's behavior in invading its own territory in northern Iraq although the people there had been treated harshly for seeking their freedom. Russia and France, however, wanted nothing to do with joining the US in punishing Saddam Hussein, Iraq's dictator.

By September 5, 1996, three different presidential airplanes or helicopters had recently been wrecked in accidents. Clinton seemed to lead a charmed life, but all this paled before the rising suspicions about campaign contributions.

* * * * * * * * * * * * *

There was a story going around Washington D.C. that during the Democratic campaign, the Democrats had received some half million dollars from an Indonesian company called Lippo. The Democrats claimed that the donation was legal. But this was only the beginning of an ever-growing flood concerning fund-raising that in time became a nationally-known ocean of scandal.

The national elections in early November gave the Republicans a majority in both Houses of Congress. As for Clinton himself, although he failed to receive 50% of the popular vote, he won enough electoral votes so the Democrats could shout that it was a huge lead. Actually he received only 49% of the votes, Dole 41%, and Perot 8%. Yet Dole got almost all the southeastern states and most western ones as well. This resembled the case of Woodrow Wilson who, back in pre-WW I times, failed to gain a majority for both his terms in office, yet was elected.

And it did not say much for Clinton that almost all his cabinet resigned: Christopher (State), Perry (Defense), Kantor (Commerce), O'Leary (Energy), Pena (Transportation), Riley (Education), Reich (Labor), and Cisneros (Housing).

By January of 1997, many people in the US were becoming suspicious as to where the Clinton camp was getting all its money. This was a secret worth exploring, many Republicans were thinking. One thing discovered was that Democratic fund-raising in the months before the election included the wining and dining of Taiwanese people whose money, after suitable "laundering," somehow found its way into the Clinton campaign.

The liberals in the US tended to favor Communist rule in China, but this rule was based on quicksand. The death of China's Deng Xiao Ping was reported February 20, 1997. He had actually mainly ruled by simply killing off his opposition. Liberals in the US had favored him until the fiasco at Tiananmen Square when tanks and troops crushed the rioters. After that, US Liberals changed their tune about the previously pristine appearance of China's government. But the soft-on-China attitude of the American government may have contributed to much of the flood of money from China and vicinity into the Democratic coffers.

Back in the US at the White House, stories were released to the media that anyone could buy a night in the Lincoln bedroom for a certain fee measured in thousands of dollars. It came out (Republican American 1997, February 26) that a certain Johnny Chung donated $391,000 to the DNC (Democratic National Committee) whether for sleeping in the famous bed or not.

Another case of illegal donations came out soon afterward, alleging that Vice President Al Gore had been caught soliciting contributions from a telephone in the White House. This activity was specifically forbidden by law. Gore apologized and claimed that he was not aware of the ruling.

One way the Clintonites garnered votes was to admit some 1.2 million aliens into the US so they would allegedly vote for Clinton. This was brought up by Congressman Rohrabacher, but was heatedly put down by the pro-Democrats. Statistics showed that there had been a 25% increase in "legal" immigration in 1996 over that of 1995. Of the majority of 1.2 million coming in last year, about a million people were approved without checks on criminal backgrounds.

The question of unfettered immigration came up again when Mr. Livingston (R-LA) and Mr. Rogers (R-KY) went after FBI Director Freeh for allowing 180,000 Africans to become US citizens without any criminal checks on their backgrounds (C-SPAN TV 1997, March 7). Besides this, 1,200,000 aliens were said to have been granted citizenship in exchange for votes. Freeh replied that the FBI had no time frame for acting on these problems. However, the FBI did inform the INS that they could get clearance for the immigrants and did check their criminal records. But Rogers blamed Clinton and the system for the mess, not Freeh.

There was soon a move in Congress to take action against the "Chi-Coms" (Chinese Communist people), but no action could be taken without the appointment of an independent counsel and Attorney General Reno did not want any such independent counsel.

Rogers then brought Reno herself before the subcommittee (C-SPAN TV 1997, March 7). He asked her directly about her responsibility in alleged lying to Congress about the entry of legal and illegal immigrants. Ms. Reno answered that it was her responsibility and that she did know of inaccurate arrest records and had asked for an investigation of the affair. Rogers then asked about the rumor about the Border Patrol and its faked reports. Reno could only claim that she had tried to keep Congress informed through the Inspector General.

As for Ms. Meissner who seemed to have headed the INS, she claimed that pressuring from the Vice President and President was present in February and March. She added that the goal of Citizenship USA was to speed up hiring procedures. But Freeh maintained that the FBI did pass along the information to the White House about the Chinese campaign contributions. Clinton claimed that he was never informed about it. Reno explained all this away as a communications foul-up.

The Scripps-Howard newspapers in April 1997 told how the White House memoranda revealed that Clinton had personally orchestrated the fund-raising of the DNC (Democratic National Committee) for the prior year's election despite Clinton's denials that fund-raising had anything to do with his campaign. Nevertheless breakfasts, kaffee-klatsches, and dinners were expected to raise $50 million, then Lincoln bedroom visits were expected to raise $100,000 per visit. Old Abe's ghost must have looked on in disgust.

The burning question of illegal and legal immigration continued in the US, especially in California, despite Washington's attempts to sweep the problem under the rug. Governor Pete Wilson tried, back in the early months of 1997, to sue the US government for $2.5 billion to repay the state for taking 1.7 million illegal immigrants. But a Federal Appeals Court threw out the suit.

Toward the end of April, the Whitewater case went on. Prosecutors, headed by Kenneth Starr, concluded that they had found extensive evidence of possible obstruction of justice, including witness-tampering, perjury, and document destruction. However, some of the people involved refused to come before the committee, challenging Grand Jury subpoenas. Furthermore, some others refused to turn over documents.

Then also, the media's news-handling came under fire from a group of anti-Clintonites. Commentators Ted Koppel and Vince Foster of TV fame were criticized for ignoring news adverse to the Clintons. They, of course, denied such doings and were on the air to say so.

In May, the FBI alleged that the Chinese government had plotted to donate illegally $2 million to US Democratic campaigns, while various US blue-chip companies had evidently given millions more (Knight-Ridder newspapers 1997, May 19). Most of this money went to Democrats, some of it to Republicans.

While Clinton seemed to be saying how wonderfully well his NAFTA (North American Free Trade Agreement) had worked, columnist Sam Francis averred that this had only increased immigration to the US from Mexico and created a $16 billion trade deficit in the US. Evidently, as many as 3 million Mexican trucks crossed the border each year into the US, 8,000 a day. Also, generally going unnoticed, drugs were commonly smuggled over the border each day (Republican American 1997, May 19). The DEA (Drug Enforcement Agency) had objected to the NAFTA agreement with Mexico, but found a deaf ear in the Clintonites. To the American people, the whole affair was in the realm of secrecy based on their own ignorance of the facts.

Although Bill Clinton continued to show his deftness in jumping over the various accusations like an adept hurdles runner, his lady friends, more numerous than anyone knew, still came back to dog his footsteps. Paula Jones was only one of many going to court, charging sexual harassment by the President. Then on May 27, 1997, the Supreme Court ruled that Clinton was not above the law in such matters. It also upheld a Circuit Court ruling in Saint Louis that Paula could go to court with her suit against Clinton.

More important complaints against Clinton were overshadowing his various amours. Fred Thompson, chairman of an investigation into illegal contributions to the DNC, concluded that Communist China had schemed in secret to influence the US elections in 1996. He claimed that high-level Chinese government officials crafted a plan to increase China's influence over the US political process. He added that the investigation resulted in the conclusion that the plan continued.

On July 17th, a CIA operative came in to testify while sitting behind a screen. He verified connections between the US and Chinese Intelligence. Later, Arlen Specter (R-PA) asked John Huang (mentioned above) some pointed questions. Huang then admitted that he was in the Chinese Air Force and had joined the so-called Lippo group.

On the 24th, the Thompson committee tried to persuade the Justice Department to grant immunity to the nuns who had acted as go-betweens for the allegedly huge donations through Al Gore to the Clinton campaign but Reno refused to do so. Achieving immunity would have allowed the nuns to talk without fear of reprisal. Clinton persisted in claiming that he could not remember the incident. Gore, meanwhile, who allegedly engineered the $80,000 donation, was keeping quiet at the time about the affair. Thompson was not in a legal position to do anything further on the case.

In late July, 1997, the mysterious Charlie Trie, who had been suspected of making huge donations from some part of Asia, finally surfaced. According to Rush Limbaugh, talk-show host (ABC radio 1997, May 19), Trie received from Asia by wire $910,000 in cooperation with a certain Ing Lap Sing. Trie had been in the US for some 20 years as a restaurant owner in Arkansas, known to Clinton. The money was sent by a Mr. Wu via Mr. Sing. But Charlie Trie refused to talk, evidently because he wanted to stay alive.

According to the FBI, Charlie Trie was known as Yah Lin Trie and the DNC fund raisers tried to make money off Trie's friendship with Clinton while laundering Asian funds in six-figured donations to the Democratic party (Republican American 1997, July 30). FBI agent Campane said it was certain that Trie used foreign money in wire transfers to pay donations amounting to about $200,000. Evidently, using foreign money to make political donations is illegal. Where did Trie actually get the money? According to the FBI agent, it came from a foreign source, but he was not saying which.

Next discovered was a Mr. Wu, apparently linked with a Wan Jun. But since Wu could not speak a word of English, he escaped talking to the committee. Perhaps they never found a translator.

By the end of July, Clinton was finally sufficiently annoyed (so he made out) to complain that the system needed correction. But Thompson felt laws had been broken and the President was obstructing and confusing the investigation.

Now in early August Bill Clinton's various lady friends appeared again to chase him down. This time it was Paula Jones who felt that she had been mistreated by Clinton. Also a Kathleen Willey appeared on the scene, claiming that she had been groped by the President. Then there was Linda Tripp, an ex-official in the White House who claimed that Kathleen was not really upset after the alleged groping and therefore it was only a consensual agreement. Strangely, Kathleen Willey's husband died, said to have been a suicide.

In September, the nuns mentioned above were alleged to have given money to the Democratic campaign and then admitted that they altered the temple's books and destroyed documents to hide illegal contributions made after Al Gore had visited them. As a result, the Republicans on the House committee sent a 24 page letter to Reno demanding a special prosecutor be appointed to investigate Gore, Clinton, and Hazel O'Leary. But of all this, nothing came of it.

Late in that month, several Clintonites were under fire. Hazel O'Leary of the White House was being investigated for an improper donation to a charity, supposedly in return for meeting a Chinese official. Also, Mr. Espy was indicted on 39 counts of giving out improper gifts. Commerce Secretary Brown was next suspected of fraudulent doings and Housing Secretary Cisneros was charged with misleading the FBI concerning $200,000 he had allegedly given to a mistress.

When October came, Thompson brought out the names of Gene and Nora Lum who had been given immunity and had pleaded guilty to fund-raising wrong-doing. Mr. Burton (R-IN) on the panel made out that the seeds of this scandal were probably planted as early as 1991. The Lums admitted that the Clinton campaign produced a letter endorsing the candidacy of the leader of an Asian country in 1992 for a $50,000 contribution to a Democrat-affiliated group the Lums had formed (Republican American 1997, October 9).

By mid-October, 1997, the case of the Lums remained mysterious. Columnist Novak suggested that one of the money-donors could bave been the President of South Korea and the Democrats were scared that this would promptly leak out to the media (Republican American 1997, October 14).

Whether all these revelations had anything to do with it or not, the bottom seemed to have dropped out of the Hong Kong stock market, while the Dow Industrial Average in New York City fell 350 and trading had to be momentarily stopped. It closed down 554, the greatest numerical drop in the Dow's history with *700,000,000* shares traded. The London exchange also took the biggest one-day loss in its history.

On November 1st, Thompson decided not to pursue the committee's case against the White House beyond the end of the year. Some elements of the press called it capitulation, but Thompson felt the committee had done what it was supposed to do and was not supposed to prosecute anyone.

* * * * * * * * * * * * *

Iraq's Hussein decided in early November to defy the Americans and not allow inspection of his so-called storage sites. Bombing by the US was predicted by certain US news sources. Why was the US so concerned about Iraq? Some people in the media said it was the oil, plus the possibility that Saudi Arabia would shut off its oil pipes as well as Iraq's. Furthermore, Israel continued as the ally of the US and had been threatened at one time with bombing by rockets sent from Iraq. In fact, several Scuds had been fired at Israel, most of these shot down, some however, escaping and causing havoc.

By mid-November, Iraq's Hussein announced that he would allow inspectors back into Baghdad. This seemed to follow a deal made with the Russians, possibly through Yevgeny Primakov, originally of the KGB, later in 1991 head of the SVR, then nominated for Prime Minister in 1996. In any case, US U-2 flights were continued over Iraq for the time being.

Another point of view concerning Iraq was provided by a Mr. Farrakhan, a black who was head of the "Nation of Islam" in the US. He claimed, with some justification, that the US was starving little children in Iraq, as reported in various US newspapers with accompanying photographs thereof. Farrakhan blamed it on the UN blockade and then personally visited Iraq, at least to find someone who would agree with him.

By the middle of January 1998, Iraq's government went on stonewalling US inspectors from entering that country. Iraq had objected to "too many Americans" in the inspection team. Clinton, meanwhile, was asked what he thought of the Iraq situation. He stepped around the question by claiming that he was watching it.

But the parade of feminine pulchritude continued to bedevil him. Allegedly, Clinton advised Monica Lewinsky to lie about their relationship, according to lawyers for the prosecution. Who was Lewinsky? She had been classified as a "White House Intern," but actually had no particular title. Hillary Clinton, asked about it, was not impressed by what Lewinsky said and opined that her husband had been dabbling in this situation for six years.

In late January, Lewinsky talked with Linda Tripp, mentioned above. Tripp was wearing a wire recorder provided by the FBI. Not aware of the recorder, Lewinsky then told Tripp that Clinton and Vernon Jordan (a Clinton front-man alleged to be a procurer of the fair sex) had told her to lie about the deposition. The tape recording was then put in the hands of the Starr committee investigating the President's activities.

Shortly after all this rhubarb over lady friends, which gave great copy to the nation's newspapers, Clinton's benefactor Charlie Trie reappeared at Dulles airport only to be nabbed by an alerted FBI. Some columnists have suggested that Clinton brought him back to take the heat off the sex scandal, but more likely Clinton followed his old pattern of simply ignoring the storm.

About this same time, Iraq was the subject of much commentary by such programs as CNN's Crossfire. Congressman Ron Paul was on as guest. Paul's reasoning was that if Clinton was going to talk of war on Iraq, then why not on some other country like China? He went on to argue that the US was mistaken in fighting the Spanish-American War and World War I. At least it was a different point of view from the current one bandied about by most of the media.

Next to appear on TV (ABC 1998, March 2) was former FBI agent Gary Aldrich who had written a book on his stay in the White House. He defended himself very well from a barrage of left-wing, pro-Clinton questions by trial lawyer Lionel. He tried to explain how difficult it was to keep track of the President who often slipped out for some kind of meeting in a nearby hotel, with whom was not specified.

Despite all this, the case of the election-influencing came back again that March (Middle American News, Raleigh, NC 1995, March 7). The story went that James and Mochtar Riady, friends of the Clintons, had a long-term relationship with a Chinese Intelligence Agency, according to a Senate committee that was formed to investigate illegal foreign influence in recent US elections. Evidently, NSA and FBI were able to intercept phone conversations from the Lippo group based in Jakarta, Indonesia (Washington Post 1998, March 7). Jon Juang ran the Lippo's US operations and was later appointed by Clinton to a post in the Department of Commerce. Juang was alleged to have been a tool in the Riady group for the US government.

Turning back to Iraq, ex-CIA Director R. James Woolsey (DCI 1993-1994) was on TV's C-SPAN to support the anti-Saddam Hussein "Nationalist" party in Iraq as well as the US's Radio Free Europe for broadcasting into Iraq. He warned that anthrax bacteria could be used by the Iraqis on Iraq's enemies and added that US troops had begun the procedure of inoculating themselves against anthrax. These bacteria can be identified by culturing them on agar and observing them under a light microscope, while viruses can be seen with an electron microscope.

By mid-March the US Senate was trying to claim that Iraq's

Saddam Hussein was a war criminal. But certain Republicans would not go along with the idea. The Iraqi government, hearing about this, replied that Bush and Clinton were the war criminals and wondered how, in defending their country, the Iraqis could be war criminals.

Russia, in these days, was also a problem to certain other nations, despite its apparent collapse. The GRU still functioned and had a station in Havana, Cuba that monitored all US military movements in the Atlantic. They were said to be listening in on all telephone calls and radio signals that could be picked up from the US, according to Diaz-Ballart, a Republican Representative. Furthermore, Soviet reactors were still being built in Cuba. These observations were supported by Knight-Ridder news that had found out that the Cubans had their own listening device called the Electronic Warfare Battalion. Also, near the Russian base just north of Havana, was a Cuban-run signals intelligence operation as revealed by a defector to the US. The Russians often gave summaries of Russian intelligence while the Cubans jammed Radio Marti in the US by means of a network of transmitters around Cuba's coasts, called "Triton."

* * * * * * * * * * * * *

In April of 1998, a Federal Grand Jury investigated a release of rocket technology to the Chinese government. This technology could guide missiles to their targets. Allegedly, it was Clinton who permitted the export of guidance systems to China. All this involved the Loral company, guided by a certain Mr. Schwarz, a big contributor to Clinton's election. Evidently, the Defense Department balked at giving away the guidance systems' plans, but Clinton had promptly overridden Defense six months previous.

On April 20th, 1998, the New York Times called the transfer of missile technology to China treason. Don Feder in his column (Republican American 1998, March 7), pinned the blame for the deal on the Loral Space and Communications Company and Hughes Electronics for giving away technical secrets to the Chinese. When the rockets were tested by the Chinese using the Loral plans, they often crashed, but Loral and Hughes showed the Chinese how to solve their problem.

As for Charlie Trie, he was said to have had connections with certain casino owners in Macau (Macao in southeastern China on the coast), reputedly an absolute den of thieves, spies, and murderers as well as agents working for the Chinese People's Liberation Army.

In mid-May of 1998, the Justice Department began an inquiry into Clinton's deal with Loral Space & Communications Ltd. that involved a $600,000 donation to the Democratic Party. Johnny Chung, now called a cooperating prosecutor's witness, told the Justice Department that he received $300,000 from Chinese military officials, $110,000 of it going for political contributions. Chung evidently kept the rest.

Another Chinese character, Wang Jun, came to the US associated with the well-known Johnny Chung. Jun's China-State-Controlled enterprise was said to have had a multibillion interest in Hong Kong's biggest satellite company. Meanwhile Wang Jun evidently met secretly with Clinton's appointee Ron Brown at the White House. Clinton had given Brown authority to approve future satellite hi-tech transfers to China (Republican American 1998, May 12).

The question then arose as to how much material had been sent to China as a technology transfer. DCI James Woolsey (in office 1993-1994) concluded that the loss had been substantial. It was later found out that Commerce had sent China 50 supercomputers for decrypting secret messages, all this going on since 1993. Woolsey called for an investigation of the US government. On top of all this, Richard Allen, National Security Advisor, claimed that China had missiles aimed at the US. These were evidently 13 CSS-4 missiles (C-SPAN TV 1998, June 19).

Late in July, Clinton was finally subpoenaed to appear before a Grand Jury investigating the Lewinsky case, but was allowed to answer questions by videotape from the White House and the tape played before the jury. As for Ms. Lewinsky, she was given "transactional immunity" (the broadest form of immunity). As time went on, it appeared that it would boil down to her word against his. But they had to wait until mid-August to hear Clinton's claim that he had not had sex with that woman, although sex was not clearly defined.

Whether connected to Clinton's travails or not, the news suddenly came that US missiles were being fired at certain nations overseas. One of these nations was Afghanistan, hit by missiles fired from the Arabian Sea and the Persian Gulf. As many as 75 missiles were fired at Afghan targets, while in the Sudan, that vast country south of Egypt, missiles hit a pharmaceutical manufacturing plant at Khartoum, mostly making aspirin. Columnist Novak pointed to the remarkable coincidence between the President's personal problems and the sudden bombing of nations with which we were not at war (Republican American 1998, September 24).

On September 8th, prosecutor Starr sent his massive report to Congress. Escorted by FBI agents and uniformed guards, the many boxes of Starr's notes were headed for Capitol Hill and the Judiciary committee, then were to go to the House and Senate. Could the President be legally indicted? Starr's answer was in the affirmative.

In December, the Committee dedicated to impeaching the President voted "for" impeachment on the first three articles of four, alleging perjury and obstruction of justice. But it still had to pass a two-thirds vote in the Senate, which might not happen.

By late 1998 a new book (Timperlake and Triplett 1998, 129) told how Riady and the Lippo group funnelled millions into various Clinton campaigns. Clinton was supposed to have been closely linked with Hong Kong billionaire Nina Wong. Officers of the Peoples Liberation Army (of China) got millions from Wong to be sent to the US in support of Clinton's campaign. All this went back to the 1992 Clinton campaign when the Riadys gave millions to it. Also, Chinese criminal gangs called the Triads then global, were sending money to the White House in exchange for various favors.

By mid-December, 1998, a fourth resolution to impeach Clinton was passed. This was supposed to go next to the full House of Representatives, but Iraq's problems came to take up the media's attention. Both Clinton and Britain's Tony Blair then approved of a missile strike on Iraq's capital city, causing the impeachment debate to be postponed. Although several nations protested this move, including Russia and various African nations, it came out that the bombing had already occurred. Actually, the only damage admitted by Iraq was to Saddam's military center where 62 troops were said to have been killed. The Russians were said to be livid with rage about it and recalled their ambassador while many African nations protested in the UN. China called it a "vicious bombing."

On January 7, 1999, Clinton's trial began. Although the US public may have thought they would find the "smoking gun," the prosecution tried to show that Clinton had lied and committed perjury besides suborning witnesses (trying to influence witnesses criminally). By February 12th, the votes on Clinton's alleged perjury were split about 50-50. As a result, it was not a two-thirds majority required to impeach. Why did so many Republicans let Clinton go? It was likely, as suggested by Rush Limbaugh on ABC radio, that it was because of their constituents (those voting as Republicans). Even censure failed to receive the necessary votes. Clinton was off the hook.

* * * * * * * * * * * *

Back in May of 1998, the problem of Israel versus the Palestinians went its violent way. In the West Bank, generally-speaking east of Israel up to the Jordan river, there were scattered pockets of Israeli settlements amid Palestinian controlled land.

The Palestinians claimed that the Israelis were always increasing such settlements, then maintaining that they had "security control." Mrs. Clinton, visiting that tortured land, put in her oar and stated that Israel should help create a new Palestinian state. Israel's Netanyahu was clearly horrified by this statement while the Palestinians went on bargaining for 13% more land.

On May 9th, the Palestinians rioted in Ramallah, West Bank, just north of Jerusalem. As had happened over and over, the Israelis tried to quell the riots, killed five Palestinians and injured about 200 more while 22 Israeli soldiers were wounded. Although the Palestinians claimed it was the 50th anniversary of their dispossession, it was also Israel's 50th for its independence. Palestinian leader Arafat called for an independent Palestinian state and to celebrate it in what they called their eternal capital, which is Jerusalem. But the Israelis were acquiring new weapons such as the Arrow missile which was successful in shooting down Scuds (New York Times, Sunday, 2002, October 6), sometimes sent at them by the Iraqis.

* * * * * * * * * * * *

It can be safely said that spying will never go out of style. In 1995 NSA (National Security Agency) decided to tell all, or at least something (C-SPAN TV 1995, July 14). It was already known that NSA had grown out of Army Intelligence when there were only some 200 employed. By the time Venona was begun during World War II, thousands had been hired while ciphers were at least partially broken. This continued for about 20 years. Beginning about 1944, NSA worked mainly on breaking Soviet codes and ciphers while the Soviets were avidly seeking to obtain details of the US atomic bomb program.

One NSA representative, William Crowell, revealed that the Soviets at first had used a number-encryption system in making up a message to send, then used the "One Time Pad" for further encryption (see Chapter 2). He claimed that this was finally broken by an army of about 5,000 workers, no doubt making use of the newly-developed computers, their size greatly reduced in later years by the invention of tiny transistors to replace the much larger glass vacuum tubes, well-known in old-fashioned radios.

In 1997, a seemingly harmless sort of man, Theodore Hall, admitted to having spied for the USSR in the 1940s, giving them important atomic bomb information. He had entered Harvard College in 1942 and by 1944 had contacted a Soviet agent while Hall was working in Los Alamos, New Mexico. He was alleged to have sold information on the bomb to two other spies: Joseph Albright and Marcia Kunstel. But Hall was finally exposed by the work of Venona and this was only made public much later in 1996 to preserve sources of information (Polmar and Allen 1997, 251).

Another spy case involved David S. Boone, an agent operating from 1988 to 1991. He was claimed to have failed to keep his cover. The FBI evidently lured him back from Germany where he had been residing in comparative comfort. Later in London he was contacted by a so-called Russian spy, actually an FBI agent, and questioned. Boone's name had come up when the Ames case broke and East Germany had collapsed. Boone allegedly sold the Russians top secret material on where US missiles were aimed.

In mid-January of 1999, Jonathan Jay Pollard, a US Naval Intelligence analyst who had been spying for Israel, was denied his freedom when National Security people united in opposing his release. Even Albright, Secretary of State, supposedly told Clinton that there were no compelling foreign policy considerations to let him go. Also, the Defense Department strongly opposed his release. Although all this annoyed the Israelis deeply, Pollard stayed in prison.

* * * * * * * * * * * * *

The problem of Serbia reared its head once again, but in an entirely different part of it. In February of 1999 the Serbs were refusing to allow NATO troops into what they considered to be their Kosovo. This province of Serbia had been joined to that country since 1912, before World War I had begun, but over the years, Albanians had been drifting into Kosovo, many lured by good wages in the silver mines there. As a result, Serbian police were trying to force more Albanians back to Albania.

For some reason not clearly stated, NATO, made up largely of European nations, decided to try to force Serbia into stopping the ejection of

Albanians from Kosovo. But Serbia's leader, Milosevic, said he would not allow foreign peacekeepers into Kosovo province, thus defying Clinton's decision to not back down from stopping the Serbs from ejecting Albanians. Albright admitted that any bombing of Serbia would be futile. The French offered a compromise, but the Kosovo Albanians did not like it and the Serbs ignored the French offer.

In March of 1999, the US House of Representatives easily passed a bill not to prevent US forces from going into Kosovo as "peacekeepers." This word was really a euphemism for kicking the Serbs out of Kosovo. The Serbians, in hopes of encouraging the Albanians to leave Kosovo, began shelling part of that province. This only irritated the NATO powers further.

Not everyone in the US Congress wanted to rush into a foreign country without knowing much about the situation. Trent Lott came out of a Senate closed-door session on Kosovo to express his negative feelings about putting US troops at risk in a foreign land. Anyway, Milosevic was still ignoring NATO's threats and warnings. However, the Serbians were determined to cut a swath through what some called the Ethnic Albanians to split them in two, while the Russian government was sending MiG aircraft to the Serbians. On the Albanian side, the British were planning to assist the US effort, whatever that might be.

Although it was not quite clear what they would bomb, the US Senate voted on March 23, 1999 to favor the bombing of Serbian forces trying to take back Kosovo. Even the usually critical media in the US had become feverish in wanting to force the Serbians out of their province of Kosovo.

Columnist Don Feder came up with 18 reasons NOT to bomb Kosovo and send troops (Republican American 1999, March 24). He pointed out at length among other things that there was no peace to keep and Kosovo had been Serbian since 1912. He also said what others were saying, such as that fighting by other nations in Kosovo violated international law. He offered many more reasons to stay out of the squabble.

On this same date, bombs were heard in Belgrade, Serbia's capital city. Other news said that NATO was beginning to bomb Kosovo, while NATO aircraft claimed to have shot down three Serbian MiG jets. So it was that a war was on, undeclared. Serb TV, repeated in the US, showed wounded people in hospitals in Belgrade while in Montenegro, crowds threw rocks and bottles at US newsmen and their cars. Refugees from Kosovo were flooding into Montenegro.

About this same time the Serbian ambassador to the US was on

CNN TV to defend Milosevic as a hero and claim that Serbia would fight to retain that province of Kosovo. Then also, Yugoslavia's Foreign Minister Jovanovic brought out his point that whatever NATO claimed, it was not true.

Clinton, for his part, sent 100 combat-ready US Marines to protect the US embassy in Macedonia, just south of Kosovo, and invoked the so-called War Powers Act. This meant he was notifying Congress that he was going off to war.

This evening, a report in the US was that a US "Stealth" bomber had been shot down. It was thought to be invisible to radar, but this was not quite so.

It had remained more or less a secret that NATO's actions were not at all approved by Serbia's neighbor, Greece. The Greek government, in fact, had nothing good to say about NATO's actions and, like the Macedonians, Greeks were now rioting against the bombings. As for Americans, about 50% were found to be against involvement in the Balkans and the rest either undecided or for it.

Russia's disapproval appeared in the form of several warships that came into the Adriatic Sea where US destroyers had been shooting missiles into Serbia. Clinton then authorized $50 million to aid the presumably ethnic Albanians in Kosovo. In the meantime the US naval forces were running out of missiles and back in the States there were no production lines to replace them. Then all the upheaval in Kosovo spawned some 55,000 refugees fleeing Kosovo into Montenegro, 15,000 into Bosnia, 118,500 into Albania, and 47,500 into Macedonia according to reports from Serbia. Many Kosovars (probably originally Albanians) were being accepted in the US. In fact some had already arrived in Waterbury, CT, where there was an "American Culture and Islamic Center." There were, however, a few dissenting voices concerning US involvement. General Shelton of the US Army was against sending troops to Serbia at all, but the US government paid little attention to that.

Almost all of the refugees seemed to be Albanians, perhaps 361,000 of them, leaving Kosovo for somewhere. By now the CIA's Tenet, although a voice in the wilderness, tried to talk the US government out of bombing Kosovo, arguing that it would cure nothing.

But the bombing of Pristina, the capital of Kosovo, went on. C-SPAN TV showed films taken in Pristina and other Serbian-ruled towns while the female announcer, then in Pristina, told all about the barbaric American criminals. Then the films showed utter chaos: flames, twisted girders, ruined buildings, bodies, and so on, reminiscent of WW II.

While the Russians were sending tons of supplies in secret to the Serbians, NATO bombers hit a transmitter tower in Serbia perhaps to prevent sending of news favoring Serbia. Some of the more aggressive Senators in Washington, like Chris Dodd (D-CT), urged the sending of ground troops to Serbia, while others like Dan Quayle expressed the opinion that the war could not be won and would have no end.

As for the Russians, some 56,000 were said to have offered to fight for Serbia, while in the US, many people wondered if it could lead to a new World War. Unconnected to this and somewhat of a secret, $4.8 billion had been sent to Russia and Belorusskaja to bolster their economies courtesy of Uncle Sam.

In mid-April the bombing went on. Serbian official Mr. Zabronovitch said that the Serbs were being killed by NATO, forcing them over the border and challenged NATO to justify the bombing. According to him, 75 Serbians had been killed, including little kids, women, and old people.

And now, to add to the danse macabre, Clinton and Gore urged the acceptance of 20,000 Kosovars (possibly Albanians originally) to come and live in the US and stay with any relatives and friends that happened to be around. But Mr. Husseini of Yugoslavia maintained that NATO had violated its own charter given them by the UN in using troops against another nation. Costs, he claimed, were astronomical. At the same time the Russians expressed the idea that NATO's only purpose was to provoke them (the Russians). Lek Walesa in Poland warned that the bombings could lead to WW III.

On April 28th, the House of Representatives voted on whether to declare war on Yugoslavia. Practically every member, Democrat or Republican, was against it for a variety of reasons. In fact protests against the war in Serbia reached outlandish proportions when a group of women, stark naked, ran all around certain government buildings in Washington D.C. Whether their nakedness helped to determine the outcome of voting in the House and Senate or not, voting was clearly against Clinton's request to call it a war in Yugoslavia.

On top of all this, NATO bombers managed to blow up the Chinese embassy in Yugoslavia. NATO representatives claimed it was all a mistake and apologized to the Red Chinese, stating that their aim was bad. This did not at all satisfy the Chinese ambassador who faced American TV to proclaim that bombing innocent Chinese was not good. He then argued that the bombing was a violation of the UN charter. It came out during the same day that three Chinese had been killed. Rioting around the US embassy in Beijing then became violent.

Some eleven days later the Chinese were still complaining about the bombing of their embassy, as reported in the Chicago Tribune. The Chinese predicted that this was all a scheme to stop the emergence of a powerful China.

The Germans had their own reasons to dislike the bombing. Their Foreign Minister Fischer came to the US to try to persuade Madam Albright to ease the bombing. The Germans were evidently worrying that the NATO alliance was coming apart.

On May 28th, Slobodan Milosevic was pompously indicted by the International Criminal Court at the Hague. A few days later, he accepted a peace plan for Kosovo in which it was agreed there would be no mass expulsions and NATO strikes would be ended, now having gone on for 11 weeks.

Russia, however, did not intend to let all this go by without some positive objections in the form of armed forces. On June 11, Russian troops along with armored vehicles, moved into what they called Yugoslavia (CNN TV 1999, June 11). Secretly, they had come into Bosnia, then to Belgrade in Serbia, and finally arrived in Pristina, South Serbia, Kosovo province. All this made a big problem since France, Germany, Britain, and the US had decided they were going to carve up Kosovo to suit themselves, each country with its own area of control. Crowds in Pristina cheered on the arrival of Russian troops and vehicles. NATO had been caught flat-footed.

US newspapers called the Russian invasion a mistake while Ms. Albright was busy shouting victory from the roof-tops, yet some Americans wondered if all this Clinton-Albright enthusiasm to bomb the Serbs, so unpopular in the US, was to get the minds of Americans off the Clinton follies.

* * * * * * * * * * * *

By August of 1999, problems of spying became more evident at the Los Alamos Laboratories in New Mexico. Evidently, three officials at those laboratories had been disciplined for mishandling an investigation into alleged Chinese spying. All this seemed to involve a three-year FBI investigation of a Mr. Lee. Not much more was said of the whole thing at the time. It was later to become an embarrassing revelation.

As for spying in Great Britain, the names of former KGB spies were smuggled out of the ex-USSR in mid-September. These included a number of Britishers, one an 86-year-old female who had been spying for the KGB. This stimulated a British newspaper to come out with a statement to the effect that the British were getting upset by "spies that came in from the mold."

Returning to the US, the war-fever generated betwen the FBI and the Justice Department waxed hotter each day. FBI agent Daniel Wehr told a Senate Government Affairs Committee, led by Senator Thompson, that a Justice Department attorney said things so couched in legalese that it was boiled down to something like "the solicitation of funds (as Clinton had done) was taboo to investigation." All this sounded much like the tune so often played by Attorney General Reno.

Shortly after this, Agent Wehr and agents Roberta Parker and Kevin Sheridan were still assigned to the investigation (of the Presidency) apparently in connection with the Charlie Trie case. Parker testified that the Justice Department agent refused to take into consideration evidence involving Clinton's legal defense. Then mysteriously, Parker's notes disappeared. Thompson, not a little upset at this, wanted to know where they went, knowing they contained material on the Trie case. Later on, Trie himself was said to have destroyed certain documents, yet the Justice Department did nothing about it.

By December 28th, most Republicans were willing to wait until Janet Reno left office in 2001. In this connection Novak's column (Republican American 1999, December 12) reported that Dan Burton, Chairman of the House Reform Committee, was not waiting. Allegedly, Burton accused the Justice Department of obstructing the exposure of certain Puerto Rican criminals whom Clinton had pardoned, but Reno went on refusing to name independent counsels.

While all this investigation faltered, the struggle between the Russian secret services and those of the US continued unabated. According to Curt Weldon (R-PA) in the House of Representatives, parts of the secret files of the KGB had been copied by hand and smuggled out of Russia in 1993 by a defector. He had brought them to Britain where they were translated and a book published called "The Sword and the Shield." The files revealed that caches of weapons had been distributed in various states in the US, some said to be small nuclear bombs. Two such caches were found in Switzerland and one in Belgium. Mr. Lebed, governor of a Russian province, verified that such caches might contain nuclear bombs. But by this time research carried on at the Lawrence Livermore Laboratories in California had produced a detector for the presence of nuclear bombs. The so-called "Cryo 3" could detect X-rays and gamma radiation from a hidden atomic bomb (Hoffman 2002, August 16), in such situations as airports where baggage was inspected.

Terrorism was by this time more commonplace. On October 30th, another airliner, having left New York City headed for Egypt, crashed in the Atlantic near Nantucket Island. Only a little débris and an oil slick were found. The FBI stated that terrorism was not the cause, yet the radar had shown the aircraft nose-diving into the ocean. Cockpit conversations were later retrieved from the Black Box and showed that the pilot and co-pilot had fought with each other. One tried to crash the airplane while the other tried to prevent it. This was the third airliner to crash near US shores in recent years: one off Nova Scotia and another near Long Island. The pilot of the latest crash was found later on to have been from the Middle East.

By the end of the century, enciphering and deciphering of important secret messages sent by radio, telegraph, or satellite had reached new levels of complexity. Instead of using Arabic numbers 1 to 9 and 0 in various combinations, much code in the 21st century was using only the zero and number 1 in varying combinations, for example: 0001100111100000100 and so on. To break such a code, computers of an advanced type had to be employed and even these might fail. In fact, a recent article in Science (Science 2002, September 27) mentioned that even the latest ciphers might have a hole that could be attacked by the code-breakers. Such a cipher might have an unpredictablility of the algorithms used (combinations of zeros and ones) that would require 2 to the 128th power and even 2 to the 256th power operations, trying each possible combination to come up with a readable message.

The year and the entire century ended with Russia's Yeltsin announcing his resignation on December 31st, 1999. Vladimir Putin was expected to take over his position. There was speculation that the drive to oust Yeltsin might have originated from Yeltsin's family or even Mr. Putin, at one time head of the KGB, and from Yeltsin's advisors who felt he had no hope of winning the next election. Yeltsin had stood out as as leader in holding together the new Russian Commonwealth.

* * * * * * * * * * * *

Looking back at the 20th century with its hopes and fears, storms and blasts, loves and hatreds, wars and peace, ruins and successes, one is inclined to conclude that this is how people are and most likely they will never change.

After the great monarchies of Europe had fallen, the populace only found itself with new leaders bearing different titles. The Czar was replaced by a dictator, the Kaiser replaced by a Socialist fanatic who also failed. Although Roosevelt and Stalin had won over the forces of German and Japanese expansionism, there were certain basic flaws in the thinking of both of these people, perhaps by a process of thinking guided by expediency. Roosevelt seemed to have made the fundamental mistake of looking on Stalin as a great hero, calling him "Good Old Uncle Joe." Yet once the brutal force of Stalinism was gone, many Russians realized that the Utopian dream of Communism was at best just another form of government forced to use repression to keep its power. Roosevelt evidently could not see that Stalin sought world domination and in all of that, Communism was only the fellow traveller in the grand scheme for domination of other nations.

The creation of the United Nations and its Security Council was to many a step in the right direction, but the one-vote-one-nation concept assumed that all nations, large or small, should have an equal say. Also, a single vote could cancel an accepted conclusion.

The age-old rule known to ecologists who study relationships among animals, plants, mankind, and the environment was expressed by what one economist called the "Territorial Imperative," namely the need to expand a species' territory at the expense of its neighbor. Almost all species tend to over-produce and must therefore expand, often only bringing about their own ruin, otherwise conquering a neighbor. It would seem that one nation should be the strongest, but follow the principles of democratic representation for all.

Bibliography

ABC TV, American Broadcasting Company, 1982, 1987, 1998.

Anderson, Christopher. *Bill and Hillary.* New York: William Morrow, 1990.

Anonymous. *Jutland, Battle of.* London: Encyclopaedia Britannica, Supplementary Volume 31, with 7 maps, 1922.

AOL Time Warner Internet. Google Search, *Clinton, William.* 1995.

Applebaum, Anne. *Gulag, A History.* New York: Doubleday, division of Random House, 2003.

Bodiansky, Stephen. *Battle of Wits.* New York: Free Press, 2000.

Brinkley, David. ABC TV, American Broacasting Company, 1988, 1995.

Bullock, Alan. *Hitler, A Study in Tyranny.* New York: Harper and Brothers, 1952.

C-SPAN cable TV. Prime Time Public Affairs, 1998.

Cate, Curtis. *The Ides of August.* New York: Evans and Company, 1978.

Caudry, Charles. PBS, Public Broadcasting System, Washington Week in Review, 1985.

CBS, Columbia Broadcasting System. New York: 1969, 1973, 1979, 1995.

Colodny, Len, and Robert Getlin. *Silent Coup: The Removal of a President.* New York: Saint Martin's Press, 1991.

Cooney, David M. *A Chronology of the U.S. Navy.* New York: Franklin Watts, 1965.

Crozier, Brian. *The Rise and Fall of the Soviet Empire.* Rocklin, California: Prima Publishing, Forum, 1999.

De Castaing, Jacques Chastenet. *Mata Hari.* Encyclopaedia Britannica, Volume 14, 1973.

D'Encausse, Hélène C. *The End of the Soviet Empire.* New York: Basic Books, Harper Collins, 1993.

De Mirjian, Arto Jr. and Eve Nelson,Editors. New York: *Front Page History of the World Wars.* New York: Arno Press, 1976.

Depuy, Trevor N. *Korean War.* Chicago: Encyclopaedia Britannica. Volume 13, 1973.

De Weerd, Harvey A. *World Wars.* Chicago: Encyclopaedia Britannica. Volume 23, 1973.

Embleton, Clifford. *Falkland Islands.* Chicago: Encyclopaedia Britannica, Volume 13, 1973.

Evans and Novak's column (in) New Haven Register, Connecticut, 1977.

Fay, Sidney B. *Origins of the World War.* New York: MacMillan, 1930. A mine of information on the secret plans of European nations before World War I.

Flynn, John T. *The Roosevelt Myth.* San Francisco, California: Fox and Wilkes, 1984.

Gelb, Norman. *The Berlin Wall.* New York: Random House, 1986.

Grant, R.G. *MI5/MI6; Britain's Security and Secret Intelligence Services.* New York: Gallery Books, 1989.

Haig, Alexander M. Jr. *Inner Circles.* New York: Warner Brothers, 1992.

——, *Caveat; Realism, Reagan, and Foreign Policy.* New York: MacMillan, 1984.

Hamm, William A., Henry Eldridge Bourne, and Elbert Jay Benton. *A Unit History of the United States.* Boston: D.C. Heath and Company, 1935.

Hart, Liddell. *World Wars: The End of the German War.* Chicago: Encyclopaedia Britannica. Volume 23, 1973.

Hartford Courant, Connecticut, 1982.

Hayes, Grace P. *World War I.* New York: Hawthorne Books, 1972.

Hayward, Steven F. *The Age of Reagan; The Fall of the Liberal Order, 1964-1980.* Roseville, California: Forum Prima, 2001.

Herman, Arthur. *Joseph McCarthy; Reexamining the Life and Legacy of America's Most Hated Senator.* New York: Simon and Schuster, 2000.

Herzfeld, Hans. *William II. German Emperor.* Chicago: Encyclopaedia Britannica. Volume 23, 1973.

Hillgruber, Andreas,and Jost Dülffer, Editors. *Geschichte der*

Weltkriege; Mächte, Ereignisse, Entwicklungen, 1900-1945. Ploetz im Verlag Herder, Freiburg im Breisgau, 2003. Gives detailed dates of events in WW I and II.

Hoffman, Ian. *Lab Helps in Bomb Detection.* Oakland, California: Tri-Valley Herald, 2002.

Kanitz, F.P. *Das Königreich Serbien und das Serben Volk,* 1904-1914, Volume 3. Cited in Encyclopaedia Britannica, Volume 20, 1973.

Karnov, Stanley. *Vietnam; A History.* New York: Viking, 1983.

Knight-Ridder Newspapers, 1997.

Kohn, Hans B. *Origins. World War I,* Chicago: Encyclopaedia Britannica, Volume 23, 1973.

Layton, Edwin T. *And I was There.* New York: William Morrow and Company, 1985.

MacNeil-Lehrer Report. New York: PBS Public Broadcasting System, 1986.

McCulloch, David. *Eight Days with Harry.* American Heritage Magazine. Article on H.S. Truman, 1992.

Middle American News, monthly newspaper by Middle American Institute, North Carolina, 1997.

Morison, Samuel Eliot. *The Oxford History of the American People.* New York: Oxford University Press, 1965.

Natkiel, Richard. *Atlas of American Military History,* Greenwich, CT: Dorset Press, 1986; reprinted 1990.

NBC, National Broadcasting Company, 1994.

New Haven Register, Connecticut, 1974, 1978, 1981.

New York Times, from Interavia Ltd., London, 1973; Missile Technology to China, 1998; Arrow missile, 2002.

Newsweek magazine, 1975, 1978, 1993.

Norman, Bruce. *Secret Warfare; The Battle of Codes and Ciphers.* New York: Dorset Press, 1973

NSA, National Security Agency, under Department of Defense, organized in 1952.

Page, Bruce, David Leitch, and Philip Knightley. *The Philby Conspiracy.* Garden City, New York: Doubleday, 1968.

Parade Magazine (in) New Haven Register, 1977.

Parrish, Thomas. *The Ultra Americans. The U.S. Role in Breaking the Nazi codes.* New York: Stein and Day, 1986.

Pavlowitch, Kosta S. *Serbia.* Chicago: Encyclopaedia Britannica, Volume 20, 1973.

PBS, Public Broadcasting System, 1989.

Pitt, Barrie William Edward. *World Wars.* Chicago: Encyclopaedia Britannica, Volume 23, 1973.

Ploetz, Karl. *Auszug aus der Geschichte. Der Erste Weltkrieg. Der Kreig zur See.* Würzburg: A.G. Ploetz Verlag, 1956, (Ploetz Verlag now in Freiburg im Breisgau, Germany).

Polmar, Norman, and Thomas Allen. *Spy Book; The Encyclopedia of Espionage.* New York: Random House, 1997.

Posner, Gerald. *Case Closed; Lee Harvey Oswald and the Assassination of JFK.* New York: Random House, 1993.

Prittie, Terrence, C. *Berlin.* Chicago: Encyclopaedia Britannica, Volume 3, 1973.

Purkovic, Miotrag, A. *Bosnia Hercegovina.* Chicago: Encyclopaedia Britannica, Volume 3, 1973.

Rather, Dan, and Gary P. Gates. *The Palace Guard.* New York: Harper & Row, 1974.

Regan, Donald. *For the Record; From Wall Street to Washington.* New York: Harcourt and Brace Javanovitch, 1988.

Republican American, Waterbury, Connecticut, 1991, 1997, 1999, 2001.

Romerstein, Herbert, and Eric Breindel. *The Venona Secrets.* Washington D.C.: Regnery Publishing, 2000.

Rubin, Trudy. column in New Haven Register, Connecticut, 1992.

Schirmann, Leon. *France Might Reopen Case of Mata Hari.* Waterbury, Connecticut: Republican American, 2001.

Science, publication of American Association for the Advancement of Science, 1975, 1977, 1978, 1979.

Scott's Personality Parade, (in) New Haven Register, 1977.

Sontag, Sherry, and Christopher Drew, with Annette Laurence Drew. *Blind Man's Buff. The Untold Story of American Submarine Espionage.* New York: Harper-Collins, 1998.

Sorensen, Theodore C. *Kennedy.* New York: Harper and Row, 1965, Time magazine, 1985.

Timperlake, Edward, and William C. Triplett II. *Year of the Rat. How Bill Clinton Compromised U.S. Security for Chinese Cash.* Washington D.C.: Regnery, 1998.

UPI, United Press International, 1976, 1985, 1986.

U.S. News and World Report, 1978, 1979.

Vance, Cyrus. Washington Week in Review, PBS, Public Broadcasting System, 1978.

Wall Street Journal, 1967.

Warlimont, Walter. *Inside Hitler's Headquarters 1939-1945.* New York:

Weidenfeld & Nicolson Ltd., 1964.

Warner, Oliver. *Great Battle Fleets.* London: Hamlyn Publishing, 1973.

Washington Post, Washington D.C., 1991, 1998.

Washington Week in Review. PBS Public Broadcasting System. 1979.

Weinstein, Allen, and Alexander Vassiliev. *The Haunted Wood.* New York: Random House, 1999.

West, Nigel. *Mole Hunt.* London: Weidenfeld and Nicolson, 1987.

Winterbotham, F.W. *The Nazi Connection. The Revealing True Account of the Master Spy Inside Hitler's Reich.* New York: Dell, 1978.

Index